CW00545077

Scent Magic

Notes from a Gardener

Scent Magic

Notes from a Gardener
Isabel Bannerman

PIMPERNEL
PRESS LTD
www.pimpernelpress.com

For Chrissie and Lucy

There Dawn comes, the wind falls, from yesterday's
rain, in the shade, a new perfume is born; or is it
I who am once again going to discover the world
and apply new sense to it? ... In future I shall gather
nothing except by armfuls, great armfuls of wind,
of coloured atoms, of generous emptiness that I shall
dump down proudly ...

Colette BREAK OF DAY

Pimpernel Press Limited
www.pimpernelpress.com

Scent Magic
© Pimpernel Press Limited 2019
Text and photographs © Isabel Bannerman 2019

All rights reserved. No part of this publication
may be reproduced, stored in a retrieval system or
transmitted, in any form, or by any means, electronic,
mechanical, photocopying, recording or otherwise,
without prior permission in writing from the
publisher or a licence permitting restricted copying.
In the United Kingdom such licences are issued by
the Copyright Licensing Agency, Barnard's Inn,
86 Fetter Lane, London EC4A 1EN

Any copyright holders we have been unable to reach
are invited to contact the publishers so that full
acknowledgment may be given in subsequent editions.

A catalogue record for this book is available from
the British Library.

Designed by Dunstan Baker
www.greygray.co.uk

Cover: *Lathyrus odoratus* 'Matucana'
Page 2: *Dianthus* 'Mrs Sinkins'

ISBN 978-1-910258-49-1
Printed and bound in China
by C&C Offset Printing Company Limited

9 8 7 6 5 4 3 2 1

Contents

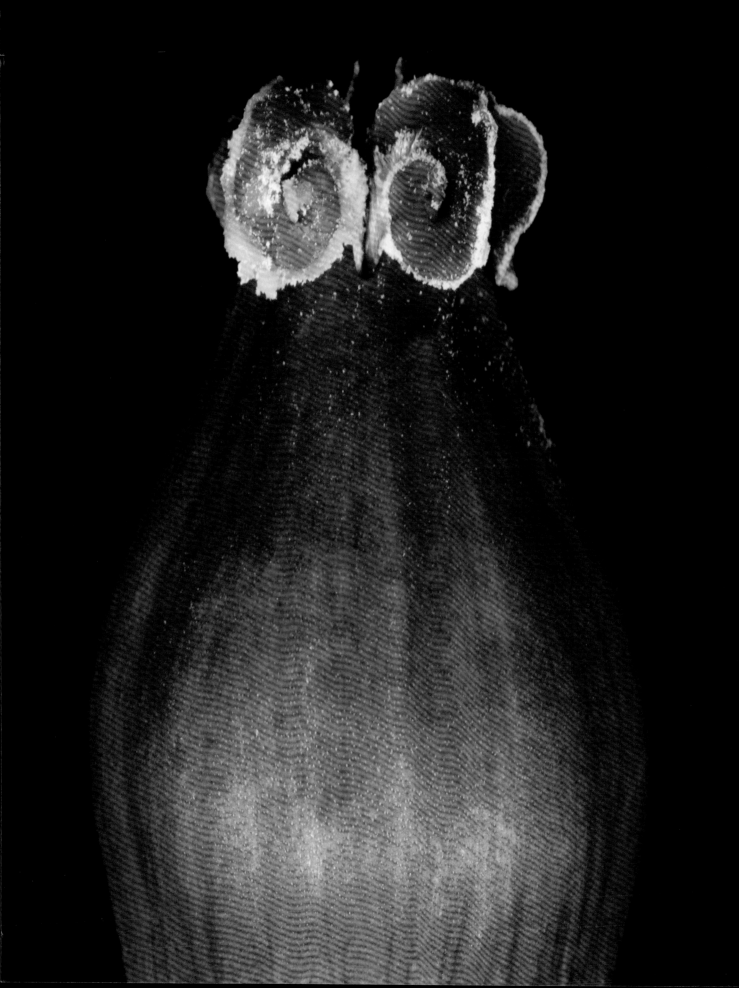

Foreword

I have been led by my nose all my life and have compulsively missiled my nose at everything in sight from flowers to fabric, car bonnets to curtains, food to flesh and everything in between. It's an utter mystery to me why all humans don't do so, as every animal I've ever met does. I tried to make scent for an American girl I had a mad crush on when I was 12 years old in 1969, boiling up gardenia and rose petals in sugar water, sealing the concoction in jam jars and burying them in the garden, hoping that by some magical osmosis they would transform into perfume. It took me another few decades to finally produce a professional unisex scent range, called *Jack*.

The first time I ever visited Isabel and Julian's extraordinary garden it was the scent that overwhelmed and impressed me, almost more than the visual splendours they'd conjured up out of the earth. As I blindly made my way into perfumery without any formal training, Isabel has likewise forged her way, motivated by her singular passion and vision, to become one of the world's foremost garden designers. Whilst obeying the classical rules of structure and symmetry, her designs are infused with a unique individuality and romantic sensibility which are her signature style.

It's no surprise that her writing is so sensual and irresistible. Not since reading Peter Susskind's novel *Perfume* have I been so gripped as I have by Isabel's scented garden journey.

Richard E. Grant

Pregnant peony ovary

Preface

The airing cupboard at Trematon smells comfortable this early winter morning. I write in here, a bit like a loft for silkworms to spin cocoons in, because it is the only place that is warm at dawn. Silkworms are unbelievably sensitive to smell; a strong smell such as frying onions will make them curl up and die. But the cupboard is a safe room, with only an internal window looking on to the stairs. A place of constancy, where everything is clean. In spring I will move back to the room with the view of the estuaries, the Lynher and the Tamar, over the garden.

Trematon was a total seduction: we fell in love with its serenity and the way it has sat for a thousand years as a look-out over the estuaries. It was headquarters for the Black Prince in the summers of 1355 and 1363. In 1549 the people of Cornwall, many of whom only spoke their own Celtic language, rebelled against being forced to use the new *English* Prayer Book in their churches '…we the Cornishmen, whereof certain of us understand no Englyshe, utterly refuse thys newe serveses.' Sir Richard Grenville the elder, grandfather of the Elizabethan naval hero, his wife and other gentlemen, all protestants, had taken refuge inside Trematon and were besieged by the rebels. Grenville opened the sally port to parley with the rebels but was seized and threatened with death unless those inside the castle surrendered. In *Sir Richard Grenville of the Revenge* A.L. Rowse writes that it was 'a humiliating experience for an old warrior'. In 1587 the treasure taken on Drake's Cadiz raid was brought up from the San Felipe, moored in Forder water, and stored in the keep for a few days. It continued to be used as a prison and the interior of the bailey was used as a market garden. In 1807 the house within the castle was built by a canny man named Benjamin Tucker who rose from humble Plymouth origins through his work for the Navy to become Surveyor of the Duchy of Cornwall. Having wangled a hundred-year lease out of his master 'Prinny', the Prince Regent, he collaborated with a naval architect and pupil of Sir John Soane called Daniel Asher Alexander – they had worked together building Dartmoor prison – to build a minimalist house which must have been the height of modernity in 1807. This butter-pat edifice is oblong, rendered and creamy, with huge windows, filled with light. A most rational and rewarding house. At the end of the nineteenth century, Katherine Parnell, the mistress formerly known as Kitty O'Shea, came here only two years after her marriage to and the sudden death of Charles Parnell, the great Irish Home Ruler. And the Foot family, Liberals of Plymouth who distinguished themselves in left-wing politics, lived here insulated by even more books than we have now.

We came above all to make a garden here. As if it wasn't romantic enough, soaking in silence, girdled by ancient tooth-like walls, we fell to imagining the battlements smothered in downy pillows of rambling roses and saturated in the scent, instead of the usual numbness of the scheduled monument. We moved in in January; the central heating didn't work and winters in Cornwall are not so much cold as dim, like a Rembrandt. In a Cornish winter electric algae and cushions of bromeliads spread incrementally, velveting tools and twigs while you sit by the fire eating crumpets. The first summer it rained, as if for Noah's pleasure, day after day. The slugs were the size of sea cucumbers and our task was negative: to eradicate weeds – petasites, the winter heliotrope introduced in

Honesty in the border

9

the nineteenth century and now curse of the lanes everywhere mild, and ground elder and bindweed – whilst we dreamt of colour and scent.

While gardening – making this garden and designing other gardens – my good fortune is to be the accomplice of the most observant, sensual, kind, comprehending, communicative, funny, original thinking co-conspirator that anyone could have the luck to encounter. Mr B, as he is styled in these notes, has taught me about observation, to take notice, and to relish. He is addicted to many things, gardening and scent among them. The business of smell is so deeply subjective that we have many differences. Mr B often did not agree, and the reader will often not agree, with my verbal interpretation of smells. Mr B comes at things from a different flight path to mine, never ceasing to astonish, even puzzle me. But we almost always end up in the same place. This garden has been a playground for our daydreams and a larder of smelly things. But gardens are full of contradictions too. Nothing is ever quite right, or if it is, it is because you never meant it so, it just happened. But the witchcraft of scent somehow acts as an emulsion, fusing all, it is tranquillising for the gardener. Despite its capriciousness it goes on giving a thousand things back. To appreciate it I try sometimes to be as aimless as a child, to be a trespasser on my own patch, as if I'd never been in this place before. It is the same when photographing: divining the moment when there is something I have never seen before in the viewfinder, my resolutely familiar world has dissolved.

The presumption tends to be, when I have mentioned this project over the past decade, that I am writing a book about 'perfume' – a word that implies much, loaded with a baggage train of implication stretching back along the Silk Road and into the ancient world. Marvellous to speak of, and very much part of what I wanted to explore, but not central. This is a book about what I smell in my garden, notes I have made about the smell of plants and, as I became more enmeshed, the business of smell in general – though this last would take another book to explore properly. Smell is all about instantaneous judgements deep in the ancient bit of our brains. Judgements about our connection with the outside world, with the dead meat smell of *Eucomis* and what dead meat means to us. Smells have a life force that speaks to us in an old language, and what I am interested in was expressed by Antonin Artaud: 'where there is the stink of shit there is a smell of being.'

Smell is our constant unacknowledged companion. Smell is everywhere yet unseen. We breathe, we smell; that which we breathe in is full of smell, and that which we breathe out is usually smell-less. It is a chemical and constant exchange. Perception of smell, however, is intermittent, somewhere on the edge, happening but not really registering. Smells tend to slip away, even when we focus on them. This is core to their elusive, ungraspable quality. But it is also core to our being able to deal with so much bizarre disordered information. Evolution has arranged things so that when we are stable and cognisant, we need to rationalise our perceptions and not be overwhelmed by them. Sight, sound and touch are physical senses but smell and taste are chemical; in the exchange in some extraordinary way what we smell becomes part of us. This makes smell such an intimate sense and such a vulnerable one too, because it is a direct molecular combination with bits of the outside world, the substance of our *Umwelt* – the world as it is experienced by any organism. All sensory perception is making sense of the world about us, but the olfactory membrane is the only place in the human body where the central nervous system comes into direct contact with the outside world.

Briefly, what we smell are light organic molecules, tiny clusters of atoms bonded together. They are all organic compounds, compounds usually built around carbon, the 'Lego' of life: hydrogen, oxygen, nitrogen, sulphur and, to a lesser extent, phosphorous and bromine. The clusters of these atoms are tiny (only a small molecular structure can 'float' in a gaseous way) but highly complex. We breathe in and the contents of the air washes over two postage stamp sized patches of receptors at the top of the nose connected to several slender waxy rods protruding through the through holes in the skull. This physical chemistry is processed in the limbic lobe, one of the oldest parts of the brain and the seat of sexual and emotional impulses, which seems to govern much behaviour and motivation and memory. The patterns of molecules are decoded by the sensory neurones here and electrical impulses are sent to the 'nose-brain' of the cerebral cortex to be re-coded, turning patterns into sensory experience, rather as pixels make a picture on our screens. The patterns are myriad and the differences minute – operating on an atomic level, the position of single electron can totally alter the smell of something.

It is memory that everyone mentions when they talk about smell. Research on smell memory has now confirmed the everyday impression that these memories are laid down by experience right from the beginning, like a reference library, and that there are what are called 'memory bumps' – like bumper crops – in childhood and adolescence which remain stable over very long periods; the curve for forgetting them seemingly different from memories laid down by other senses. They lie in the limbic system which has nothing to do with conscious thought, and the sense of smell has the power to suppress the rational, critical left brain and to stimulate the creative, dreamy right brain. When we hallucinate, we temporarily lose the balance of sensory suppression between the two but interestingly we rarely dream about smell. In trials just over 20 per cent of women recorded smelling their dreams and this pleasure was accorded to only 2 per cent of men. When we sleep, we seem to dampen down all the senses. The necessity for smoke alarms is based on research that proved that 80 per cent of people will not smell the smoke while they are asleep; they will wake up only once they cannot breathe. The exaggerated perception of smell, hyperosmia, is very rare, and very disturbing. Dr Oliver Sacks related a case study where a patient found for some few days that his smell perception became inexplicably uninhibited; the raised intensity and dominance of his smell perception created turmoil, his understanding of the world was seriously compromised, and he found it almost impossible to reflect or reason in the abstract. Sacks concludes that some inhibitor, designed to keep the perception of smell in its place, must be part of the olfactory system. This profound, learnt, recall makes sense when one considers that evaluation of smell is one of the most important evaluations an organism can make. From the cognitive point of view the hedonic information, the perception of pleasantness and unpleasantness, is the most salient part of olfaction. Two perceptual pathways are used through the brain, one for processing averse responses and one for appetitive, and our responses are infinitesimally fast. The question of survival is at the root of everything.

Of all our five senses the sense of smell is the first to develop. Even before we are born, *in utero*, our sense of smell is already fully formed and functioning. At birth we appear to have almost no inborn preferences as regards smell, apart from an immediate draw to breast milk. The world of the newborn is like swimming in a multisensory soup; it is a synesthetic world distinguishing much less clearly between the senses. But in time, and of necessity, an infant learns to sort and tame sensory impressions.

The sense of smell supplies us unobtrusively, very strongly in the subconscious, with a constant stream of information about our surroundings, homely and unhomely, about family, siblings, mothers. Smell tells us much more about the people around us than we generally appreciate; it is designed to tell us about our kin, our genetic relation to others for the avoidance of inbreeding, which is linked with the quality of our immune systems. Grown women can recognise their offspring by smell, and pre-adolescent children can recognise full siblings but not half- or step-siblings. We are social beings and our sense of smell informs us continuously with useful social as well as environmental information. Among carnivores it is as important to be aware of each other as of prey. There is a smell clinic in Dresden where Dr Thomas Hummel's researches show that women are typically better at discerning and then recognising olfactory signals. Hummel's conclusion is that women continue to be more aware of smells as social signals because they tend to be more socially aware, and he observes that women come to his clinic for help because they are upset by the social effects of losing their sense of smell, and men come because they are missing the hedonic effects.

Plants and insects
The great evolutionary scheme of things seems to have created invertebrates as the servants of plant propagation. They developed to do the bidding of plants. Evolutionarily plants are clever, and imitative. Wind-pollinated plants came first and have little colour, little scent and huge amounts of pollen – think grasses. Plants pollinated by insects are entomophilous; they produce less pollen, but it is sticky and protein laden and such plants must expend energy on nectar production and must also communicate with their pollinators somehow; they must advertise through colour, pattern and smell. The real relationship between plants and insects began with beetle-pollinated plants in the early Cretaceous, around 120 million years ago, when a new pollination strategy developed, and flowering plants first appeared. It seems likely that beetles led the way in insect pollination, followed by flies. Beetle-pollinated plants tend to be dull in colour, rich, foxy, fruity, even stale in scent, and have prominent anthers heavy with pollen like *Magnolia grandiflora*. Fly-pollinated plants have little or no colour and little or no scent, although carrion-fly-pollinated plants come in flesh colours and have strong rotting-meat smells, like eucomis does. Bee-pollinated plants tend to have yellow and blue flowers and a fresh mild smell. In wasp-pollinated plants, colour is not important and usually dark, the scent is sickly sweet like that of *Angelica gigas*. Butterfly-pollinated plants must have a landing pad – this is more important than the colour – and the smell is generally fresh, sweet and light such as that of buddleia. Moth-pollinated plants have light-coloured flowers which are more visible in the dark, and a strong sweet smell – perhaps the best of smells – for example, nicotiana.

Pollution is a huge factor in inhibiting pollination. A study done by the University of Virginia concludes that air pollution is definitely destroying plant fragrance and thereby inhibiting insect pollination. The difference in distance that scent molecules can travel in unpolluted air is between a thousand and two thousand metres as compared with less than a couple of hundred metres in modern major cities. This is because the volatiles emitted by plants in their daily converse

Oxeye daisies everywhere

with insects react chemically with ozone, hydroxyl and nitrate radicals in polluted air, and this reaction destroys smell – as we and, more importantly, the insects know by experience. The study estimates that air pollution is effectively destroying the smell molecules emitted by plants all the time by as much as 90 per cent. This suggests strongly, as does literature and nature writing from the past, that before the Industrial Revolution things smelled almost ten times more noticeably. Scent loss must be a huge factor in the catastrophic invertebrate collapse we are witnessing. What we also need to fully grasp about the knock-on effects of the dissipation of scent molecules for invertebrates and vertebrates is that it is in their *grub* stage, when they eat and are eaten in vast numbers, that invertebrates play a huge role in the lower food chain. Caterpillars are one of the most important things that moths and butterflies offer the ecosystem – their grubs are food for almost everything else, and an estimated 95 per cent of nesting birds rear their young on insects and caterpillars. There is a chain of which we are barely aware, simple enough, everything working together. Scent in plants, moths, birds all intimately entangled in a reproductive cycle which we are blithely destroying. The intricate sophistication of moths' co-dependence with night-scented plants, for example, is difficult to comprehend. Smell volatiles are particularly important in pollination by moths; expert sniffers, although they lack noses, they detect molecules of smell through antennae whilst foraging for nectar. Female moths pick up pollen grains all over their hairy heads and fertilise plants, whilst male giant silkworm moths search for virgins and have huge antennae that are feather-shaped, bristling with hairs that are so sensitive that they can smell a single molecule of bombykol, an ingredient of the female pheromone, as much as seven miles away and are seemingly able to estimate distance by its dilution. The phenomenal evolutionary achievement that this represents is dependent on an infinitesimally delicate balance between each moth and the world about it, its *Umwelt*. A balance which is being toppled and tampered with by mankind.

The scented part of the plant

Most insects, when not in search of a mate, are in search of nectar, carbohydrates which can be found aplenty, and readily absorbable, through the sugars in solution that go to make up nectar in a flower. As it contains sugar, nectar naturally smells sweet, but it is not *the* scented part of the flower. Pollen is not the scented part of the flower either, although like nectar it does have a smell, a good smell. It adds to the overwhelming complexity of the scent, as in the case of roses where that waxy smell we recognise is pollen. Pollen is also rich in proteins and this has come to offer another reward to the pollinator. An extraordinary thing about the genius of pollen is that it enables the genetic material to travel safely without water to the female stigma, which may be a very large distance away. All this required co-evolution of insects and flowering plants. Plants have evolved different lures to encourage specific pollinators and to keep their fidelity. Orchids have the most complex and profound co-evolutionary history with their pollinators. Our native pyramidal orchid, *Anacamptis pyramidalis*, for instance, has a carnation scent by day but a very foxy smell at night – spread-betting the odds of pollination.

Scented substances have almost certainly developed out of the waste products of plants' and animals' biochemistry. They are the by-products of metabolism. Waste products are not only useless in the living cell, they are positively poisonous.

Curiously these poisonous qualities may also give them antiseptic and anti-bacterial properties. Scent molecules occurred first among those products that living organisms expel as excreta. Natural selection seems to have ensured, little by little, the retention of the scented molecules among these products and control of their distribution around the organism and their specific functions. Whether flower or leaf scent came first is difficult to ascertain. But, leaf scents being less refined and less varied than flower scents, it is thought that those plants where leaves, petals, seeds, wood and roots are all scented, such as *Magnolia kobus* and *Chimonanthus praecox* (syn. *C. fragrans*), are at some intermediary stage of evolutionary development. In these examples the flower scent can be recognised as the elaboration of the leaf scent, more sophisticated and more delicious. Protection against predatory insects and grazing animals is key to most leaf smells. Aromatic plants wear their essential oil in a layer of glands, on their outer surfaces generally. What Richard Mabey describes as an oil skin in reverse. In extreme dry heat the plant must preserve water to maintain turgidity and carry on photosynthesising. Some *Cistus* species secrete a resin, labdanum, on to the surface of the leaf whose stickyness reduces the speed of its evaporation into the air and acts as a browsing deterrent. In thyme, sage and many other labiates – which give off their smell at a touch or in bright sunshine – the oil is stored on the surface. Aromatic and repellent-functioning leaves provide us with a bounty of flavours for cooking: bay, sage, rosemary, thyme and hundreds more.

Many marigolds are used in companion planting as their scent wards off whitefly in the air, but the pong in their roots will kill eelworms in the soil up to a metre away and discourage the growth of expansive weeds like ground elder and bindweed (don't rely on it though). Underground there is so much more to discover to do with scent. The secretions from the roots of potatoes can induce hatching in eelworm eggs, and so it may be that many underground creatures are as specific in their reactions and as sensitive as moths. Immense, complex and barely understood is the network of chemical activity that goes on underground, much of it scent based in the darkness, and unwittingly disturbed by our reckless use of synthetic pesticides and fertilisers.

The essential oil of flowers is invariably more complex than that of scented leaves – compare rose-leaf geranium with the flower smell of a rose. The rounding and shading of floral scents are due to many closely related chemical compounds being present; this provides 'colour'. The essential oil exists ready formed in the mature flower bud. But if you have ever opened a bud before it is ready, the alchemy of scent has not yet happened. It is thought, therefore, to be the case that the essential oil is stored along with a glucoside, the combination of sugar and oil unlocked by the action of a ferment, which is produced at exactly the right moment within the living cells of the plant. The action of glucosides must be reversible or at least switchable on and off with the opening and closing of flowers. This is most probably regulated by temperature.

A synchronicity must exist between the quarry and the forager, plant and animal, between the activity, the likely presence, the abundance, the desire of the pollinator and the secretion of the nectar, the reward. Scent molecules can travel further in relatively high humidity and warmth. The production of fragrance is costly to the plant, it does not waste it. Warm, humid and still are the optimum conditions for smell to evanesce, and in the landscape these conditions may be found more readily in woodland and protected valleys. In the permanent twilight of woodland white smelly flowers like lily of the valley and woodbine have a distinct advantage with pollinators. Conversely the eddies and coolth of high mountains mean that 'alpines' – as they are known to gardeners – are not generally scented. However, in the heather and grasslands of the British Isles other terrifically smelling things abound such as the bog myrtle and the common fragrant orchid.

Undoubtedly white flowers are the most highly scented. The reason that white and light flowers are often highly scented is that they are pollinated by night-flying insects. About 15 per cent of all white-flowered species are scented but only about 9 per cent of red flowers. Red flowers are almost invisible in dim light and tend to close early of an evening. The link between scent and colour in flowers is their function, but it is not all that close. It is accepted that scented flowers, such as night jasmine (*Cestrum nocturnum*), are often highly inconspicuous, but it is worth remembering that to the small short-sighted insects who pollinate them they are perfectly conspicuous as well as scented.

Smell is the sense for which we struggle to find the right words. We all have difficulty even perceiving the detail in a smell, but the problem is not so much the words; the problem is the fleeting nature of the perception. Perhaps this has led to the side-stepping of the importance of smell: it is so disorderly and, for all its unfathomable complexity, too primitive for words. There are great books on scented planting. Stephen Lacey has published two and my copies are always to hand and well thumbed. There is Roy Genders, a prolific and rather forgotten post-war garden writer whom I often return to, particularly good on scented wild flowers and hedgerow plants, along with long-time hero Richard Mabey. But, good as all these books are, none of them told me how it 'feels' to smell *Matthiola incana* after a shower in April. They don't attempt, and maybe for good reason, to transduce much beyond 'sweet', 'aromatic' and 'spicy'. They don't leap from the page and exhort one to go out and smell as Thomas Treherne (1636–1674) does, writing on the smell of lilac: 'It made my heart to leap, almost mad with ecstasy, so strange and wonderful.' There is something so ardently childlike here, and also in the writings of William Blake, Walt Whitman and Gerard Manley Hopkins and Colette, which encompasses these almost unspeakable emotions.

Latin is a succinct and graphic language, perfect as the universal language of science. I relish the smell words that do get used in botany; they start with the obvious: *fragrans, odorata*. Sometimes compounded as in *odorus mellitus* (honey scented) – also *melliodorus*. Less recognisable are *graveolens* (strong-smelling) and a favourite of mine, *suaveolens* (sweet-scented); *suavis* – sweet; *dulcis* (sweet also) – as in *dulce et decorum est pro patria mori*. *Thuri* is incense – as in thurifer if you were ever a Catholic altar boy; *thymi* is thyme, and of the teas, but not tea scented. Turpentine or terebinth, coming from the terebinth tree, is *terebinthae* or, equally, *resinae*. While *velutinus* is velvety and *fulgens* is glittery, *fumosus* is smoke-grey and not smoky-smelling for which there is no word, but *formosus* means beautiful. *Foetidus, foetens* and *foetulentus* all refer to stinkyness; *putidus* is putrid and *stercoreus* is smelling of shit. *Pungens* in Latin means stinging in all senses but became a smell description for botanists. *Saccharatus, saccharifera* and *saccharinus* all mean sugary. *Nauseosus* is a good word. *Pudicus* means bashful and shrinking and *impudicus* means shameless and immodest – not 'stinking' as I had always assumed, since it is the descriptive part of the name of the common stinkhorn or

Phallus impudicus; but it is significant to me that the botanists noted the shame rather than the smell.

Carl Linnaeus, the father of taxonomy, attempted the first classification of smell in his *Dissertatio Medica Odores Medicamentorum Exhibens* of 1752, the first of many such attempts, all of which are useful in their way, but serve mostly to enforce Linnaeus's view that scent defies us and is disorderly. Linneaus's life and work sit right in the middle of the sort of Bayeaux tapestry way we envisage western civilisation, from Plato to Nato. And looking very broadly across that time our attitudes to smell, as recorded in words, have seesawed quite a bit. In his treatise *Philosophia Botanica* (1751) Linnaeus introduced a radical new system for classifying botanical material which involved surveying a plant's reproductive organs and categorising them through binomial nomenclature; the inclusion of the secondary 'diagnostic' term enabled botany to unfold, in his terms, 'like the territories on a geographical map'. In such a system smell is almost absent, inconsequential, yet he did offer a brief theorisation of olfaction in plant reproductive organs before dismissing its importance in scientific study. Scent and taste should be included in descriptions, he says, but he then reminds his readers that 'scent never clearly distinguishes a species' and since the sense of smell is 'the most obscure of the senses' and because the 'scent of all things very easily varies … scents do not allow for fixed boundaries and cannot be defined.' Taxonomy is therefore predicated on observable characteristics, the blueness, the hairlessness, the toothyness, the lippiness, but not so often the stinkiness. Of the smell words in botany I have counted thirty out of roughly two and a half thousand generally used Latin descriptive epithets. Thirty smell words among the fabulously obscure visual descriptive references that sound as if they might come in handy when describing one's foes. Words for hatchet-shaped, emetic, blushing (*erubescens*), thick-skinned (*callosus*), bald (*calvus*); scurfy is *furfuraceus*; brown and dusky is *fuscus*; dangerous is *infestus*; and dirty, that terribly dangerous word, spoken in my primary school with consummate awe and reverential fascination, so useful in plant description and so intelligible in Latin, is *sordidus*. The Linnaean binomial descriptive system revolutionised botany, but smell got left on the sidelines.

This book then is about what *I* smell in *this* garden – terroire is intimately connected with smell as with taste. I started making notes over ten years ago in the artist's notebooks in which I daily rewrite the list of unaccomplished things from yesterday. In 2003 I had begun to experiment with making images of plants on my flatbed scanner, a strangely intense process which I tend to indulge in late at night. In the morning I often find my office, a narrow file-filled submarine, filled with scent. Many flowers emit more scent when stressed or dying in a last gasp for paternity. The images I was making were uncanny and seemed to connect with the smell thing. The germ of the idea of a book was born: the magic of scent, in notes and images from the garden. Information is everywhere, information is cheap, so this book is not really about information, it is about the uncanny feeling, the unsettling disorder, the subjective, the inadequacies of the intellect, the obscurity of intuition. The intention is simply to encourage curiosity. An experience in which we engage our sense of smell is a bigger experience. All the senses are brighter if we use them, and thereby we live more in the present.

Overleaf: Wooden cannons
in the mist

17

Winter is Sweet

Busy old fool, unruly sun,
Why dost thou thus,
Through windows, and through curtains call on us?
Must to thy motions lovers' seasons run?
Saucy pedantic wretch, go chide
Late school boys and sour prentices,
Go tell court huntsmen that the king will ride,
Call country ants to harvest offices,
Love, all alike, no season knows nor clime,
Nor hours, days, months, which are the rags of time.

John Donne THE SUN RISING

New Year's Day and 'the busy old fool' has been poking fingers of light through gaps in the shutters, laser sharp, swimming with motes, since official sunrise at sixteen minutes past eight. Today the sun rose in the south-east 127 degrees from north, so far round as to be behind the curtain wall and hidden for hours by the copse on the other side of the road. It will set at twenty-three minutes past four this afternoon, 234 degrees south-west round by the front gate. The day length is one minute and one second longer than yesterday, and the length of possible daylight has increased by only just over five minutes since the solstice, and throughout those ten days the sun has risen at almost the same point. All the balmy feasting of Christmas and New Year occurs at this ebbtide of the year, the ten darkest days before the whole thing swings back in the right direction and the daylight increases. All this I learn with a child's delight from timeanddate.com. 'Dates are based on the Gregorian Calendar' the website tells me. In the old Julian calendar, everything is thirteen days behind, and for this reason the October Revolution – in a Russia that still lived by the old calendar – happened in November. I live by a Julian calendar, Mr B's calendar, which is not so much thirteen days behind as the calendar of a peasant, ruled by the seasons to reap and to sow. He was once writing a cheque in The Fine Cheese Co. in Bath, one of his favourite haunts, and he had to ask them what year it was. The nice girl behind the counter looked bewildered but proffered him the news that it was 2009, and he had the quick-wittedness to inform her that, being a Time Lord, it was difficult to be sure.

There is a strange phenomenon evident at Trematon: I found it hard to believe when our neighbour along the river first made the claim. It is, more often than not, sunny at daybreak here. However drizzly the day, shrouded the moor, blanketing the sea har, somehow the sun rises gloriously over Devonport as if on a stage. Like a Court Masque, cloud curtains part for twenty minutes to an hour, and in bars, like soap, sunlight floods across the water. In winter, it floods horizontally into every room in the house, because the house in the castle was so designed.

Wintersweet
Chimonanthus praecox

New Year's Day

Today I am John Aubrey's 'shiftless person, roving and magotie-headed', feeling querulous. Best then to disappear down a virtual rabbit hole, learning about incomprehensible but romantic-sounding things such as Nautical and Astronomical Twilight. I watch from the extreme comfort of my bed the Navy Larks across the estuarine stretch of water below the castle which is called the Hamoaze, part of the River Tamar.

The hyacinths that we grew for Christmas are out now, late arrivals, and all the more welcome. After the partying everywhere, indoors is a mess and smelly. It is time to throw out stinky vases and face up to the Christmas tree, the dusty festoons of fir and ivy branches desiccated, scentless. What a blessing, amidst the chaos, that the hyacinths are sturdy and proud, glowing with colour and such a funny adolescent smell that delights at a distance, draws you in and can then repulse and send you reeling. Hyacinth smell is bluebell on steroids, gives one a lift, that acid drop scent indoors in January. Such a lift has always been a tonic: over the winter of 1688 and 1689 an astonishing 26,290 hyacinths were purchased for the Sun King Louis XIV's private garden, the most exclusive space at Versailles, the Jardin du Roi, accessible only though the apartments of his mistress Madame de Maintenon.

HYACINTHS

Wild flowers imported from the eastern Mediterranean and Asia Minor until, in the mid-sixteenth century, they began to be grown and bred commercially in Holland. By the late eighteenth century in Britain they were grown by 'Florist' enthusiasts and were more popular than tulips. It is from the nineteenth-century craze for forcing them indoors that we get the overblown *haute couture* versions, which are industrially produced in Holland these days. The wildlings were more like pale blue sea creatures. *Hyacinthus orientalis* var. *albulus*, the Roman hyacinth, native to Provence, has much bigger gaps between the 'nails' as the botanists call the flowers; these are thick with scent, the cushioned, narcotic, indole-rich scent we look for in hyacinths but purer. They crop up in Ovid and Virgil in connection with feasts and festivals. In 1759 Madame de Pompadour had 200 hyacinths grown 'on glasses' during the winter, and these were golden days for the florists of Haarlem. The history of the hyacinth is the history of Europe. All parts are highly toxic.

I pottered out with Popeye the pug early this morning, just as the light began to glimmer. The winter box smell was warmly washing the still air about my feet, even though the wind high in the holm oaks made them quaver blackly against the dawn. Barely a bird's eye open this dawning, yet yesterday evening, in the same kind of light on the back of the hill, it seemed that every garden bird was posting a last urgent twitter.

Bulb planting. Late as usual. Nose down into the cool. Opening the boxes, the smell of bulbs is a head burst, as immediate as a drenching. There are a lot to plant. I'm quavering at the reality of planting as I do every year, anxious recipient of my own mad ordering. We are also moving aconites, spreading them about by the tiny thousand. Bees are out and about, earth is smelling rooty, rotted, safe.

The Hamoaze through a window

22

Now is the end of the paperwhite narcissus, some of the simplest and best things to grow if you want scent or if, like me, you are not very good at growing stuff indoors. They are fast, fragrant and beautiful. They smell rounded and lemony; some describe it as a bit 'horsey', but my nose reads mammalian and warm. Scent often degenerates, and theirs, like hyacinths when they go over, can become faecal. This is a manifestation of the chemistry of the plant following pollination, designed to deter further pollinators. Mr B will diligently shuffle them out of the house. But in my experience entropy can be forestalled by keeping bulbs in a less lived-in room – even just a 'night nursery' – that is not blazed in central heating. In the sitting room at Christmas, paperwhites are a transient joy and, like the rest of us, fall over as soon as they have done their star turn.

Scented pelargoniums are overwintering in the gloom of the back passage. Caught a whiff of them whilst digging out my coat today, which in a synesthetic way struck me like a shaft of sunlight and made me think of September when they will be at their fullest and smelliest.

EARLY NARCISSUS

Narcissus 'February Gold' is one of the earliest to flower and *N. poeticus* var. *recurvus* one of the latest; this can be as late as June in the wild in the high Pyrenees, Maine or Canada. But in February and March the strongest-scented daffodils are the jonquils. They differ quite a lot from most daffs in having rushy dark green leaves less than knee height. The small, yellow groups of flowers have been famous since the sixteenth century for their intense, tingly, roundly warm scent. Slightly less powerfully scented are the Tazetta types, of which the paperwhites, *N. papyraceus* and the cultivar 'Grand Soleil d'Or', can be forced for Christmas and winter flowering indoors. A hybrid, 'Trevithian', is good and reliable to grow outdoors.

If you're just beginning to garden, in a flat with no outside space or starting out somewhere new in September, they are an excellent project. Prepared bulbs will shoot up and fall over before you know it. But you can then cut them and put them in a vase. Plant them in anything with gravel or compost – just add water.

Twelfth Night

Epiphany, and a lucky day of sunshine. The first gift of the year, like incense brought to the manger, snowdrops wafted a mellifluous veil across the garden. Watery, balmy, syrupy, but with a correcting sharpness in it, like lemon with the sugar, a bit like paperwhites, though the scent of snowdrops is finer: it has a far-away quality and, for all its honeyed tones, remains aloof. Snowdrops never smell rank, they just stop smelling once pollinated. The pleasure that they bring is not just the smell, but the combination of bees drowsing amongst them, and by February, with the willow leaves just 'peeping' as John Evelyn puts it, they dance in the watery sunlight of discernibly longer afternoons.

My nose is twitching like Samantha from *Bewitched*, prickling with anticipation. As a child, I was convinced I was a witch. Witch hazel, I love. *Hamamelis mollis* is special. Out there in the garden (where I hate to go in this weather until I have to do it) *H.* × *intermedia* 'Pallida' is un-crinkling in

Scaffolding on house and fleece on *Echium pininana*

25

its reluctant way. What a treat. When I see an old one, bigger than two people standing arms outstretched, blanketed in lichen, I think of impossibly slow growth and 'had we but world enough and time' we would all grow witch hazel. As I write I am preparing to abandon another dozen I have planted in the last seven years and start anew somewhere. Yet someone else will enjoy them as I know they are enjoyed at the last garden we made and had to leave at Hanham Court. I love that smell, a clean sanatorium smell of pure alcohol and Elastoplast. Mr B says it smells of swimming pools – which takes one by surprise on a winter's day. I get something hinting at clean straw, echoing the sensational hot straw colours of *H. × i.* 'Jelena' and 'Diane'. I think that the heat in the colour somehow reduces their pungency, but Mr B says the rusty red ones smell good, of cigar boxes and cinnamon. Vita Sackville-West wrote:

> … the Witch-hazel, *Hamamelis mollis,*
> That comes before its leaf on naked bough,
> Torn ribbons frayed, of yellow and maroon,
> And sharp of scent in frosty English air …

WITCH HAZEL

Hamamelis × intermedia 'Pallida' is the one with the most scented and most luminous pale sulphur flowers, shining out on the dullest day. Glacial in their growth, witch hazels are grafted, hence expensive, and they look like a flattened hazelnut bush the rest of the year. For me this is a bonus: they fall into the category of plants that have great qualities but are self-effacing. Those with hotter colours such as the ember-bright *Hamamelis × intermedia* named 'Jelena' are gorgeous but have slightly less scent. They are all easier to grow in leafy woodland and shade. On very cold days you need to breathe on the flowers to warm them up before they will release their scent. 'Advent' is one of the earliest and strongly scented, which E.A. Bowles, the renowned early-twentieth-century gardener, called the Epiphany tree because it opens around the 6th of January and because it smells of frankincense. It flowers in stalkless crowded clusters of gold. It is worth knowing that large plants establish better than small ones for some inexplicable reason. This is off-putting because a 10-litre plant is best, but at a price which is hard to justify for something that looks like a nut bush and takes forever to get going. However, for luminosity and scent when there is almost nothing else in the garden, they come second only to the fabled wintersweet.

Glasshouse goodies. Now is the time when I wish for more glass and better husbandry skills. Lemons and mimosa could be sniffed, a minuscule holiday in the mind. If only I were better at it. None of these are flowering just now, but I can visit the VMH down the road for a long draught of her lemon blossom (such a light word for such a waxy thing) and dream of Cordoba or the orange groves around Catania. A very naughty Sicilian Count once told me he could smell his orange groves from inside the de-pressurising cabin when landing at Catania Airport. Lemons are much easier to grow than oranges, but the older I get the more attempts at citrus growing I have abandoned.

Hamamelis x intermedia 'Jelena'

Mimosa *Acacia pravissima*

I think of having a greenhouse with mimosa flowering now. Celia Lyttelton in her book *The Scent Trail* likens the scent of mimosa to a dessert wine; golden, summery, dry, earthy all at once with a 'buttery pulverulence'. It seems to me that those fluffy heads smell of pollen.

MIMOSA

The mimosa *Acacia dealbata*, the silver wattle, is a half-hardy, evergreen, large upright shrub, growing up to the size of a small tree, with ferny leaves that invite stroking. In late winter it breaks out in racemes of small, singing yellow powder-puff balls. Differing clones exist of milder yellows to off-white flowers; 'Exeter Hybrid' is a pale-flowered version that can be enjoyed at the Temperate House at Kew. Mimosas come from Australia but are naturalised in the Mediterranean, where they were originally grown for the perfume industry. As they are tender, they should be given the shelter of a garden wall and if one has the opportunity it is great to grow them under glass as well. Easier to grow, although much less refined and beautiful, is *Acacia pravissima,* whose leaves and habit are coarse and whose flowers are a fuzzy mass compared to the passementerie bobbles of the silver wattles, but they flower generously and smell delicious.

The treasured wintersweet is out. Our first wintersweet, planted in hope seven years before, finally flowered the day our son Ismay came into the world. It was the beginning of 1989, which proved to be a momentous year. I remember the following December jiggling him my arms and wondering if it was feasible to take the fat buddha baby to Berlin to see the wall being picked to pieces by happy Germans. I still regret not going. But on the day of the boy's arrival Mr B came home alone, mid-morning, put diesel in the petrol-drinking car and drank the only thing in the house – a bottle of whisky – whilst ringing everybody in the phone book. He then tottered into the garden and found the first flower ever on the wintersweet. Some flower it was; new-born, naked and tallowy, its yellow plum translucence was stained dark sloe purple by a row of short inner tepals. This solitary anemone thing had opened mysteriously from nowhere, from bare twigs. In truth the globular buds can be seen in summer in leaf axils all over the mature shrub. They swell and yellow, like drops of honey, throughout December, when the days are dim and empty of prospect, everything sluggish and drained. How curious and affirming to find, then, strange grey pearls opening into starry, shaggy sea anemones that hang down shamefaced in the low winter sunlight. The scent is sort of radioactive, incandescent on the impoverished winter air. Brought indoors, the essence of sweetness will irradiate a room so long as it is kept cool enough. It has a smell like jasmine, but much more luminous, tenuous and sublimated. As with any truly magnificent perfume it is both ultimately refined yet undeniably powerful, charismatic. Despite being enslaved to this plant for twenty years, only this spring did it become evident to me, while photographing different stages of the life cycle, that the leaves, twigs and seedpods smell, also. Perhaps they have set more seed in recent hot summers. The gourd-shaped pods of seed, if crushed, smell of dusty cloves, spiced wines and the depths of unused drawers.

WINTERSWEET

Chimonanthus praecox flowers in December and January. It is possibly Mr B's desert-island plant, understated yet devastating in looks and scent. It easy to grow: plant it well (guinea plant, guinea hole, as the saying goes) and leave alone in a corner to enjoy at the dead of winter. It flowers at the joints of the previous summer's shoots. It is important not to hack them back in a frenzy of autumnal tidiness because you will cut off the flowering wood. It should, if necessary, be pruned straight after flowering, but we prune by picking as much flower as we dare. The flower is a unique transparent yellowish ivory. In his *Trees and Shrubs Hardy in the British Isles,* W.J. Bean is unusually lyrical about this plant, going out on a limb to recommend that one 'associate them with sprays of *Mahonia aquifolium*' in 'a charming way'. Introduced from China as early as 1766 they must have been available enough generally by the early nineteenth century to be worth John Claudius Loudon's describing the garden variety 'Luteus' in his *Hortus Britannicus.* It has no merit in shape or look in summer, but it is this unassuming quality which I like. Please don't breed a variegated one to give it more 'interest'.

Mahonia japonica smells of spring in winter. Passing it on our way in through the garden it is redolent of comfort and homecoming, a feeling that is laid down in the cellars of my brain. I would always think that I wanted to plant it each time I came across it in my mother-in-law's garden in Wells in winter. But I never did. The primrose sprays of lily-of-the-valley-scented flowers are spriggy and full of charm in a jug. You would never guess that it comes from a gawky, hopeless, prickly bush that always feels plonked like it doesn't belong.

January 20th

This was my mum's birthday. Everyone dreaded it. How she hated being born in the dark month after Christmas. Nothing my father could do would make it better. Not bunches of flowers, not a bottle of Hammam Bouquet from Penhaligon's, not National Theatre tickets, and certainly not when he bought her a Hoover. She inculcated the dread of January in me – just as I now realise, she inculcated a fear of the telephone. It was always the wrong time to ring my mother, and as a result, I grew up thinking it was always the wrong time to ring anybody. My mother loved flowers although she saw no fun in gardening, and loathed games at school (perfectly understandable), loathed outdoors, loathed the country, loathed anything that required physical effort apart from re-arranging furniture, re-hanging pictures and painting around them when she wanted a new look. This was her therapy. I too find being busy helps. I redecorate in my head in the small hours, and I also try to revisit gone places in detail, to remember smells especially; I find it calming. The garden, though, is the greatest defence against dark emotions, and so also is Mr B, my guardian archangel.

Nearing the end of the grim month, and writing this my head is filled with the idea of snowdrops. Mr B adores them. I am a bit more like plant collector Reginald Farrer who wrote: 'the Snowdrop gives me chilblains, only to look at it – and the very sight of a Snowdrop will always make me hurry to the fireside. Was there ever such an icy, inhuman bloodless flower, crystallised winter in three gleaming petals and green-flecked cup?' Out there the buds are piercing the earth like so many infant finger nails. They do mean hard wintry work as well as hope. Every winter we weed through the steep-sided dell; lying on our bellies we do it, like a couple of seals. We split bunches of the beauties and spread them round, greeting the first big pearl drops of *Galanthus* 'S. Arnott'. Rank upon rank the simple *G. nivalis*, the milk flower of the snow, stand to attention, Iced-Gem white and fragile. The faint flame-like spathes bend and bow, their fattening dewdrops, spring open in display and are then magnetised towards the earth. The smell of newly extracted honey, with bees dozing about among them is to be savoured best in this way, lying on one's side in combat with hard earth, in feeble sunlight. The Turkish plants such as *Galanthus elwesii* are said to have more almond in their scent. No one really bothers to write about the smell of snowdrops. There is, though, an elusive, stopping moment, when the snowdrops smell in wafts and it is almost possible to sense spring stepping up from the Scilly Isles at 2 miles per hour.

SNOWDROP

I like the romance of their names: the French call them *perce neige* and *galantine d'hiver*, while the British have names like Candlemas bells and bells of hope. Native to the Balkans and Caucasus, their specific names are a novella of their extraordinary breeding history. Many were brought back from the Crimean War. Mr B is an enthusiast in a way that I shall never be (I have always found obsession in others strangely attractive). He is fascinated by the details and markings and he is not mad about doubles. For love of all things *Galanthus* we have endured years of purgatory, dividing and planting them out in the depths of winter. Never buy dried-up old bulbs in autumn – they may work if you soak them immediately and thoroughly, but it is better to buy them 'in the green', and not so much more expensive because there are no failures, and no heartbreak for

Three galant *Galanthus*

30

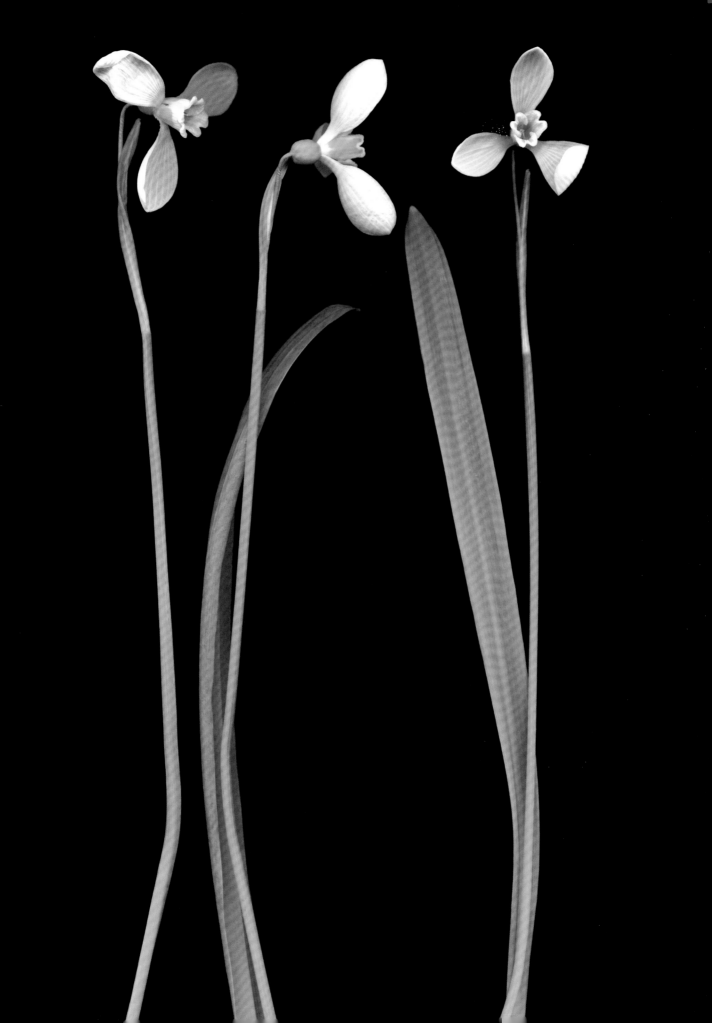

lost labours. For snowdrops, as for many things, Mr B's recipe for planting particular favourites is based on a set of criteria that include above all fast reproduction, reliability and a good pong. He plants for largesse and beauty 'S. Arnott' and 'Magnet'; *G. elwesii* and 'Atkinsii' for their ability to multiply incrementally; 'Daglingworth' and 'Wasp' for refinement. Dancing lightly in the slightest breeze is a quality which I have learned to love. For scent on the breeze from the more recherché varieties I would plant 'Babraham Scented', 'Mark's Tall', 'Arthur's Germolene' (don't you love the names?), 'Peardrop'– said by aficionados to be the best scented – and also *G. woronowii*. Canon Ellacombe noted 'their thorough hardiness' and their 'patience' in the face of winter.

Getting through January is a trial. Year after year I struggle through and celebrate its end with a big booze up. February is even worse. But daylight is growing and with it much else. I feel like a bulb buried in sleep rather than earth, not unhappy down among the worms … but luckily something urgent stirs somewhere. Were one to examine it in cross-section, it would be an embryonic tail, a bud, a hardened apex in the very vulnerable soft centre of being. Somehow it is pressing out, smelling of curiosity.

February

January is done with, thank god. I woke late, nearly eight, and felt the sun in that crack in the sky over Devonport fingering the shutters. Waking in the dark as a child, I liked to know the time. When we were children, we lived in a country village by the church, and the church clock struck the quarters all night, which was very comforting. I did have my Timex watch from my sixth birthday, but it was not luminous, unlike my father's. That was given to him as an early birthday present in May 1944, to carry him into battle in Normandy. Nobody knew when or where the invasion of Europe was to be, but they knew the time was coming. He gave it to me to wear in the 1980s and it was stolen about five years ago to my bitter regret. We children went to bed extremely early, even though my sister Fans was six years older than me, and were not allowed out of bed until late in the morning on pain of the ire of our mother. As soon as the clock struck eight, I would pad into Fans's bed. She called me the amphibian because I was always so cold and drew heat from her, but eventually she would play. The wallpaper was pink carnations on green stripes, very strong and engraved in the memory. Fans was known as Miss Information, for she was very sure of her facts, and I was known as Bella-the-Smeller, more because it rhymed than because I hated to wash, put on clean clothes or brush my teeth. She added the couplet 'Bella the smeller, the dirty, dirty stinker' in an affectionate singsong voice. I always was a smeller.

The earth smell is awakening. Wintersweet lingered while I raked the delphinium walk buffeted by a hectic storm. Sarcococca was smelling rather curiously of fennel, of liquorice, and was sweetly comforting. Mr B picked a big bunch for the kitchen table where it smelled much more sophisticated, like narcissi. But by supper time it had stopped smelling, being too warm we thought. We used not to grow it much, but we found a great mound of it surviving in an old bed when we moved to Cornwall, and discovered its considerable charms. Now we use it a lot professionally. It can be clipped into neat evergreen mounds or edgings, and flowers at a most unlikely time. You can plant a lot together and quickly attain a big dome like an ancient bush. Now, when things are at their most drear, it offers a great hug of warmth, a buttery, spicy smell. It is such a well-mannered, unassuming evergreen, great for shady corners, but not just as a stop-gap, half forgotten. Plant it in a spot where you will pass frequently during its four-week flowering and you will be showered with the scent of consolation and joy.

SWEET BOX

Sarcococca is a cousin of box and known as winter box, sweet box and sometimes Christmas box; it's just as evergreen and just as tameable. I think it clips well, but at the expense of the flowers. The leaves are rather confusingly described by Bean as 'elliptic or elliptic-lanceolate, long-acute to acuminate, obtuse to cuneate' – which might be a description of me by my husband, but taken altogether means small, shiny and pointed. They are slow-growing, and hermaphrodite in that they have male and female reproductive organs on the same plant. These are highly scented, crowded in short clusters of males with clusters of females. In the male there are filaments that extend way beyond the tiny white sepals, while the even smaller sepals of the female flowers hide their super-shy stigmas – the whole thing sounds like a hideous party. I think both emit the scent, the white filaments waving about to entrap insects into picking up pollen and then accidentally lodge it on the waiting stigmas just below. Their job done, the masses of filaments fall like frosted sticks to the ground. This biology results in black berries or red berries, shiny as porcelain. The smallest sweet box is *Sarcococca humilis*, which is a good choice as a replacement for box edging. It makes plump bushes because, unlike box, it suckers freely. Perhaps the most desirable of all the sarcococcas for both scent and shape is *S. hookeriana* var. *digyna*, whose narrow, pointed leaves make it graceful. If you like a touch of purple, there is a similar form called 'Purple Stem'.

Something is surfacing that is a smell you cannot exactly smell. It reaches a deep gallery in the primal mind, sets me twitching, alert, adrenalin rising, time to get going. Felt it first today. Smelt it first today. I know it is a smell because, although the light is changing, and the earth-plant engine is fuelling up on each additional lumen of light per day, to my dim perceptions nothing *looks* different. But something smells different.

A smell that everybody notices is the *Daphne odora* 'Aureomarginata'. Mr B says it smells of honeysuckle in a Devon lane, all heart and hope: it brings you summer.

Sweet pea seedlings that I just managed to sow last week are doing well. I find sowing my sweet peas now saves my sanity, filling my head with the smell of warm propagators and new shoots. I garner what sun there is on mornings in the greenhouse. I rescue *Dianthus* Spooky Group seedlings from neglect. These are my pet plant. Easy to grow from seed, so frayed and fragile in flower that a shower can demolish them. They are weird, wonderful and smell of old ladies, though not everybody gets it. I grow *D. superbus* as an annual, although some have lived on, but what a discovery. The grey-leaved tufts produce long stems topped by strange bedraggled, fringed petalled flowers in pink and picotee. Rainbow Loveliness Group is a favourite, white with a green eye. To me they smell a lot of cottages and cottage gardens, very light and limpid, sugary, violets and soap, as delicate as they look.

Mr B brings me a sprig of *Prunus mume* 'Beni-chidori', the Chinese plum or Japanese apricot. I am a sucker for shocking pink, I insisted on planting it. Now it is huge and strapped to the wall. The straddling branches are set round with single, shrieking, cerise flowers. It needed to be cut back and so wands of it were brought into the house (although technically this is the wrong time to prune a plum). It does smell, of apricot and almond, the 'blossom' smell that blossoms smell of. And, curiously, the sap smells too. The cherry growers of Kent have told me that the sap of prunus is colossally sugary, and they thrilled me explaining how it rises through the trunk and branches in a rush just before they pick. We put *Prunus mume* with some branches of *Daphne bholua* 'Jacqueline Postill' in a glass vase – too pretty. Mr B says the name 'Jacqueline Postill' puts him in mind of a lady in charge of a coachful of WI members. I think it sounds like an American saying 'hostile'; but she isn't, she's a real charmer.

It would be extraordinary if it snowed.

DAPHNE

Daphnes are sparsely branched, evergreen or deciduous, and can grow to be tall shrubs. In Britain the native daphnes come from dry woodland and well-drained limestone or chalky soils generally; they have small flowers, white through shades of pink, tubular and with four petals opening to form a star, in terminal clusters in spring. Our native *Daphne mezereum* was known as 'paradise plant' on account of its scent, described by Richard Mabey as 'Windolene', a great smell. Also native in Britain, *D. laureola* has acid-green flowers, very smart for small flower arrangements, emitting a musky call at twilight to moths and night insects. *D. mezereum* var. *rubra* has flowers on the ends of naked stems – a small and short-lived plant in my experience. *D.* × *burkwoodii* 'Somerset' and 'Somerset Variegated' are crosses with loads of pink flowers with stronger pink reverse of the petals in spring.

Some think the finest daphne is *Daphne bholua*; the mature shrub, tall as a garden door, covered in flower in late February, is a joy to behold, and to smell, pick and bring indoors. 'Jacqueline Postill' and 'Gurkha' are the top varieties but have recently been difficult to get hold of; native of the Himalayas and first introduced in the 1930s, these are often regarded as the all-round best, though most plants sold today are micro-propagated and seem to produce fewer flowers. *D. bholua* 'Garden House Enchantress' is a particularly floriferous form also, selected from many seed-raised plants down the road at The Garden House in Devon, and bearing a multitude of heavenly scented white and purple-pink tinged flowers in the depths of winter. It looks wonderful underplanted with a carpet of magenta or white *Cyclamen coum*.

D. acutiloba 'Fragrant Cloud' is a selection from plants introduced by Compton, D'Arcy and Rix from south-west China. The long, narrow, dark-green leathery leaves provide a fine backdrop to the deliciously and spicily scented creamy-white flowers, borne over a long period in spring apparently, although I have not been able to get one even from Pan-Global Plants.

My favourite though is a native of China, brought back here just at the end of the nineteenth century although long cultivated by the Japanese. I came across it first when visiting Mr B's mother's garden in Wells in Somerset, where it filled the mediaeval long garden behind the house with its magic perfume; it is *Daphne odora*. This low mounding evergreen can get to be as big as me, but that happens rarely. Recently a lot of our

Rare snowfall on the pots
of pelargoniums

new plantings have not been long lived, and we guess that this has to do with micro-propagation. We have a long running battle about whether they like shade or sun. Mr B says rightly that they were originally woodlanders and struggle in full sun, and yet there was one in the corner of a front garden in Bath, against the hot limestone, facing south, which was the biggest and smelliest I have ever seen – and it was there for years. *D. odora* 'Aureomarginata' is the commonest and most hardy form available and remains for me the star of the spring garden. In February the tight pink pips of the daphne buds begin to swell, promising better days. Middle winter drags on until, on a brisk bright morning, tempted out, you recognise a presence in the garden, like a friend entering the room, unseen but palpable. Daphne is one of the most deliciously perfumed of evergreens and will swash its corner of the garden with smell for some weeks to come. The scent is almost edible, candied but packing a sharp, sherbet punch, warmed by a whisper of clove. It clouds the air but is a pleasure to drink deeply.

Ash Wednesday
Lent begins. I no longer believe in any of it, not since I was a teenager, but the whole thing remains a very potent part of my being: the ritual, the rhythm and also the contemplation. If I were to be anything now, I would be a Buddhist, but Catholicism provided a strong code, and an abiding appreciation of nature – not, as it turns out, the work of Christ Pantocrator, but of something infinitely more magnificent: chemistry, biology and physics. And yet, fasting and abstinence are rather good things, rather lost things, and they remind one how fortunate it is to be born middle class and here and now, rather than a nineteenth-century peasant

and almost starving by the end of winter. Looking up from reading T.S. Eliot's 'Ash Wednesday', through the darkling old glass, the light was imperceptibly inking out of the sky. I thought again on the lines I'd just read:

Lady, three white leopards sat under a juniper tree

Juniper is high, wild and pungent, a plangent smell and a bitter one, windswept with resilience. These trees are disappearing fast all over the world, and sadly even from the last great forests in high Pakistan. Elijah, the Lord's prophet, fleeing for his life and pursued by Jezebel, shelters in the desert, wracked with anxiety, under a juniper tree. The juniper, we learn, is an evergreen that is able to survive in the Sinai desert and thus represents a constant source of nurture and nourishment in the harsh waste land. Eliot, the poetical prophet from Missouri, wrote poetry that works on subconscious effects perhaps, poetry that was to 'to depict not the thing but the effect it produces'. The words themselves point to meanings and moods beyond explanation, which are, like smell, both above and below explicit articulation. Thus, like music, and smell, the poetry of words takes the reader beyond words to the wordless. When asked for the meaning of 'Lady, three white leopards sat under a juniper tree', Eliot is said to have replied that it meant: three white leopards sat under a juniper tree.

In the garden, juniper trees are, for me at least, perpetually married to island beds and miniature rockeries. But, as fashion has swept away these low-maintenance archipelagos of my childhood, I find myself looking more fondly upon the few survivors. Miniature conifers were funny enough to begin with – small and podgy like garden gnomes – but how many times have I laughed aloud to see them grown to giant monsters a million miles from the cutesy snow scene envisaged when they were brought home proudly from the garden centre. Yet whenever we come to a new garden project and pronounce the death sentence upon a couple, I sidle up and smell their luxuriant, mind-tingling, gin smell, releasing images of my small self on hot days squirrelling inside a thuja hedge, scraping knee skin on flaky bark.

Outside the greenhouse I stop to pick some sweet violets in the shade. Inside, the sweet pea seedlings are coming on; opening the propagator lids lets out a temperate blast of green growth and all the energy of cell division, which I sniff along with the violets. Violets have to be sniffed. But, much more extraordinary, the mignonette has flowered in the greenhouse. I have been trying to grow it for years in order to experience the smell. Last summer I finally got some plants going which I have overwintered in pots, as precious as Dumas' 'Black Tulip'. 'Sprays cut in the autumn will keep indoors all winter in a cool room and retain their fragrance,' says the Chilterns seed catalogue. The Edwardians grew Tree Mignonettes for the table. Such patience, such endless time there was. There was a relish of small things, like violets. You rarely see a violet. They were still grown in Devon and Cornwall when my mother died in 1995. Mr B was deputed to do the flowers that grim week before Christmas. He went to his mates at Bristol market and they got boxes of violets sent up from the west, six or ten deep, mourning purple, wrapped and cushioned in a couple of their own leaves to make a sweet-smelling posy. Old growers say they used to pick fifteen hundred bunches a day, or was it an hour?

SWEET VIOLETS

Violets are cosmopolitan, inhabiting cooler regions of the earth. Native to Europe and our chalky or clay soils, they like their feet cool and damp. The only scented British species of violet is *Viola odorata*; they are hardy low-growing perennials, with lusty heart-shaped leaves in bunches. Purple or white flowers, sometimes tooth yellow which I particularly like, are held aloft, tiny and butterfly-like, but visited by sawflies, wasps and bees and ants. They were indelibly part of the sensory Paradise garden of literature until the last century when they became part of the diminishing wild-wood world, little more than an ecological statistic, but to Milton they were part of the normal tapestry:

> ... underfoot the violet,
> crocus, and hyacinth with rich inlay
> broidered the ground, more colourful than with stone
> of costliest emblem

It is funny how we value Chinese marble floors and not our own beauteous pasture. Not funny but frightening how the depleted world becomes the 'norm'. Violets are very shade tolerant but flower better in the spring sun in deciduous woodland, needing shade in summer. They spread by runners or seedlings and can be used in all the dusky corners of the garden.

I caught a foxy whiff from the euphorbias just now, or was it just the first hint of crown imperials? This, the feral smell of spring, of chicory coffee and fox dens, is disconcerting.

Some of my auriculas have grown beards like Mr B, who says he is anxious about looking old and grey like Jeremy Corbyn. I reassure him he is more Captain Haddock and occasionally *Father Ted*'s Father Jack Hackett. I whopped off the mouldy leaves, but it was a bad sign. Everything is so saturated, the pond so high the air about smells of water, yet it's too cold to smell snowdrops *en masse*. The dell should be full of their smell, like honey frames raided from the hives by moonlight as we did one July the night before our holiday in North Cornwall.

PRIMULAS & AURICULAS

Primulas have five species native to the British Isles. Primrose, *Primula vulgaris*, is the one we all know, with hardy ground-hugging rosettes of puckered leaves and a mass of luminous lobed flowers. It is most characteristic of British woodland and verges, especially, I would like to claim, here in the South West. Perhaps it is just that in our 'plashy places' it fills the lanes with an air that breathes oncoming spring. The blessing of an un-cloying scent extends to the four wildlings: *P. farinosa*, the bird's-eye primrose; *P. scotica,* the Scottish primrose; *P. elatior*, the 'true' oxlip; and *P. veris*, the cowslip – always associated with nightingales, I think on account of being the last primrose to flower and not until May when the male nightingales arrive. *P. auricula*, bear's ear (or, as I like to think of it, 'pug's ear' auricula) is an alpine and also scented; it is usually yellow but can be found in stormy violet shades. Leaves and stalks are glaucous, glabrous and utterly different in feel from the common primrose. Mr B and I had a 'Show Auricula' moment when we lived at Hanham Court, partly because the annual West of England

show of the National Auricula and Primula Society was held down the road at Saltford on the Avon. I defy anyone to go to one of these shows and not be engorged with heinous avarice. Covetous urges aside, it is also a great adventure, and a wonderful way to tap into the quietly beating heart of horticultural folk. The 'show bench' has always crossed boundaries, always been an urban as much as a rural preoccupation, most famously illustrated by the weavers' societies of the Industrial Revolution, such as the weavers of Paisley. But, show auriculas are recalcitrant. You can tell from their groupings – self, fancy, green edged, grey edged and white edged – that they are going to be tricky. I started out with border auriculas, whose stormy colours are bizarre enough and whose scent is better than their show-girl cousins.

For scent in summer the Himalayan cowslip, *Primula florindae*, is the most rewarding surprise, which should be much more widely grown. Found in Tibet by Frank Kingdon Ward in 1924, it has brilliant yellow trusses waist high in July. It loves moving water and shady cool. You need to get your nose right up to it to get the big primrose pepper and powdery cowslip smell. If happy, it will spread like a weed, as it does at the Castle of Mey in Scotland, where there grows a true carpet of late-flowering giant primulas even in the impoverished soil and shade of canopy of sycamore trees.

I smelled wallflowers, jasmine and skimmias in B&Q. *Skimmia japonica*, the Japanese skimmia, is famous for its great orangey neroli smell – a 'granny' smell with a touch of Italian *pensione*. It is not something Mr B and I seem to grow much; I love to smell it at the garden centre, but I can't think how to use it. It ticks all the boxes for some people though: evergreen, compact, mound-forming, and with scented flowers. But for me and Mr B it is slightly soulless, as if formulated by a committee.

The corylopsis is out, a very heartening sign. It is great to pick for the kitchen table and mix in milk jugs with primroses and snowdrops, to cool down an aconite and cyclamen posy. *Cyclamen coum* are out now and do smell in a similar and dainty way to all the above. Which makes me think perhaps there is a smell of winter. Yesterday I was hit by a burst of angelica when weeding midget plantlings. They smelled crunchy through the earth. Startling and zingy, this is a leaf smell, almost certainly designed to ward off browsing by ruminants and rabbits who presumably, unlike us, don't take to star anise and aniseed balls.

CORYLOPSIS

A small genus of deciduous shrubs and small trees from North East Asia with bristle-toothed leaves resembling hazel. *Corylopsis sinensis* is from central and western China and was brought to these isles by Veitch Nurseries of Exeter in about 1901; Veitch also introduced *C. spicata* from Japan in about 1863. The flowers come in early spring, a pale subaqueous yellow in pendant inflorescences, usually scented, and Bean, who thinks it not among the very first rank of garden plants, admits that they have a soft beauty of their own, special for being among the very early flowerers, and with a friendly cowslip smell. *C. sinensis* var. *sinensis* 'Spring Purple' (syn. *C. sinensis* var. *willmottiae*) has what we are after: primrose flowers out of a greenish calyx in dangling clusters during February. It is easy to grow in a moist leafy soil and with sun. I would not call it a top scented shrub, unnoticeable were it flowering at any other time, but it is the colour and dangling quality that makes it really pretty. Leaves can be slightly silky when young as in *C. platypetala* –

Euphorbia characias subsp. *wulfenii*

worth seeking out in the gardens of Trewithen in Cornwall and Furzey near Lyndhurst in the New Forest, where it is nearly the size of a large shed, so it seems to be quite hardy.

ANGELICA

Angelica archangelica. I like the name as much as I like this architectural, super-green, fennel-scented thug of a plant. Save seed or see it self-sow madly and then one year it disappears. The sweetly scented and edible stems are majestic looking with handsome foliage out now, but in early summer it explodes with bursting umbels of small green flowers. It is good at partial to full shade and this, and its architectural presence, means that it looks wonderful at the back of the border.

ALEXANDERS, FENNEL AND DILL

Smyrnium olusatrum, alexanders, is a scented biennial with shining bright green leaves early in the year, sometimes flowering as early as February in Cornwall, and growing wild throughout Europe, Turkey and Algeria. It has stems up to my waist, and umbels of green yellow flowers about a hand's width across. Usually found near towns that were important in Roman or Mediaeval times, it loves the coast here and in Norfolk.

Like alexanders, wild fennel, *Foeniculum vulgare,* is indigenous to the shores of the Mediterranean and probably came here with the Romans. I love its flower, which can come early from last year's plants; the new seedlings get everywhere but I love them for their flavour, featheriness, flowers and seed heads.

Giant fennel, *Ferula communis*, is such a good plant to grow, but it slips away and vanishes although perhaps not if it has a goodly supply of water. It is of less interest as a smelling thing, but it is statuesque and bold, with toxic yellow flowers way up high. It seems to like standing in water, where, like zantedeschias, it can survive a good deal of frost and throws out a froth of marine-looking leaves at the base from which the towering inferno grows.

Dill, *Anethum graveolens*, is an annual with acid green umbels in June and July. The delicious scent of the feathery leaves is well known, but it was Sarah Raven who awoke the nation to their beauty and ease for picking and planting

The flowers of winter, waving for pollinators on their wintery reef, all have a similar smell, sweet like honey, offering sustenance and energy in these spare days for weakened wild and solitary bees and also hoverflies who are particular good at operating in low temperatures. Certain hoverflies, such as *Lampetia equestris* or *Eumerus tuberculatus*, are responsible for pollination and at this time of year it seems that they favour white and yellow flowers. Just possibly for this reason – and very little research has been done on hoverflies compared with that done on bees – white and yellow is the palette of winter flowers (if you exclude the exceptions which prove the rule, *Cyclamen coum, Prunus mume* and camellias, very few of which are scented).

I like to see Dartmoor lowering on the northern horizon, like a land belonging to different tribesmen. Sometimes I think I can smell the sea to the east; maybe it's a fantasy, a thought, provoking a sense of iodine and salt. Gulls hardly ever cry here, perhaps the jackdaws see to that, but if you hear them it's a sign that the wind has changed, backing easterly, storm laden and brisk.

February suddenly smells of tomorrow.

Snowdrops, aconites and
Cyclamen coum

Equinox

The wind, one brilliant day, called
To my soul with a smell of jasmine.

'In return for the scent of my jasmine,
I'd like all the scent of your roses.'

'I have no roses; all the flowers
In my garden are dead.'

'Well then, I'll take the waters of the fountains
And the withered petals and the yellow leaves.'

The wind left. My heart was bleeding. And I said to myself:
'What have you done with the garden that was entrusted to you?'

Antonio Machado THE WIND, ONE BRILLIANT DAY

I didn't know anything about the author or his work until I happened upon this poem, and now I know only a little more. Antonio Machado (1875–1939) is one of Spain's greatest twentieth-century poets, a man who, in the words of a fellow poet, 'spoke in verse and lived in poetry'. It seems to me to get to the heart of that deep regret so many of us feel about our paltry endeavours.

But in March it is my birthday, and then St Patrick's Day, and then the spring equinox. Daylight is lengthening by a solid three and a half minutes every twenty-four hours. The sun will rise on the most equal day for night at six twenty-five in the morning and set after twelve hours and one minute. It might snow now it's March, but Cornish snow is like slush-puppies.

Everything will come right. In the stretching days we will have a whole new go at the garden.

Meanwhile Mr B has been emptying bags of composted bark mulch all smelling of foul tannin; it is the only smell in a cold that pinches at fingers and nose. There is a not-forgetting sky, borage blue, accompanied by the black bruised clouds of an iron March day. Smelling jasmine in the greenhouse is like clambering into laundered sheets.

Yesterday the scent of mimosa arrested us in the sunshine, alongside an arsenic-almond smell. I'm still not sure what it was. Arsenic is usually some kind of cherry and being so early in the year it must be wild cherries or blackthorn.

Arrival of bulbs bought in the green. Crocuses come in clear plastic bags smelling of melon and cucumber and woodland floor. Other bags contain reticulate irises – a great treat. I put my nose among the inky spears and smell iron and earth, elemental smells that are prized in claret and truffles, and harbour echoes of childhood when one was closer to the ground. Childhood was inky and earthy. Imagining the apple trees were rain forest and the paths the Orinoco, I used to 'swim' through the orchard naked on my belly feeling the cool grass and inhaling the sod below.

Prunus mume 'Beni-chidori'

BULBOUS WINTER IRISES

The reticulate iris comes as a bulb in its own net bag made of fibres, like a reticule, from the Latin for small net. They are hardy jewels, early flowering and native of Asia Minor. Most often they are the colour of the sky in those places, profound shades of azure. Plant in autumn in a pot of sandy soil and leave outside, bringing them in as they begin to flower, and afterwards you can plant them out and they may establish. They are drought tolerant but seem to thrive here in the soggy South West. In this garden 'Katharine Hodgkin' (usually sold as *Iris reticulata*), planted by our predecessors, flourishes in the long, wet grass of the orchard, their success an incomprehensible mystery. But for scent in winter, pots for the bench and tablescapes, the most obvious and obtainable is called 'Harmony' – visually an electric charge at the fluorescent end of the spectrum, violet flashed with Hi-Viz yellow – and the sniff of cooling violets. Sarah Raven sells a lovely scented one as *Iris histrioides* 'George'. They are part of a subgenus of iris called *Hermodactyloides* which have square-section rushy leaves. The hugely desirable widow iris, so called because it is almost black, scented and super-chic, is often sold now as *Hermodactylus tuberosus* after a period of being called simply *Iris tuberosa* (although many nurseries are going back to this, preferred, name). The scent and habit of these gems seems to me endlessly mysterious. Like lily of the valley they either love you or leave you. At our house called The Ivy, our first garden, there was an ancient patch of them in a cool corner of the walled garden we did not own but battled against the developers over. I expect they are still there. Yet Mr B and I have never managed to establish such a patch ourselves from seed or bulb. All these snow-melt plants of the high mountains have a fragile strength, which suits the mind mid-winter, and deer don't like eating them, which is a plus.

Yellow is the colour of spring and spring smells yellow to me. *Iris danfordiae* is a shining yellow bulbous perennial from the meadows of Turkey. I fancy a flush of them coming after the aconites, in time with the *Cyclamen coum*, their honey scent intermingling.

The real winter iris is the Algerian one called *Iris unguicularis*, which means 'with a small claw'; this is difficult to say or remember, particularly as when I first started gardening it was called *I. stylosa*. It comes from all around the eastern Mediterranean. Recently *I. lazica*, a singing blue form from Turkey, has become more widely sold. The buds are frost-proof but not the flowers, a very good reason to pick them when the buds are like cinnamon sticks and bring them indoors to smell and enjoy. People mind the messy leaves, and so breeding work on this has produced *I. unguicularis* 'Mary Barnard', whose leaves are shorter and flowers a toga purple, as are those of 'Abington Purple'. But the most heavily scented is the opalescent 'Walter Butt'. These irises require patience. As Bowles observed: 'Patience seems to the only manure these irises need.' They will not flower until they have formed sizeable undisturbed, unshaded clumps. But for this reason, they're useful at the bottom of a sunny wall, somewhere forgettable. Noel Kingsbury suggests growing them with nerines, which also hate disturbance and flower on naked stalks at the opposite end of the year, in autumn. One could, I suppose, make a sunny 'Job' corner with them both to test out one's patience.

Started frosty. Picked gold-laced polyanthus and *Ribes odoratum* and mixed them in a small lustre jug. The sunny stars of the ribes flowers are spriggy and humble. You would not believe what waft they have. In the warmth of lunchtime their presence hung in the air: cloves, pudding spicy, warm as saffron. Still planting crocus and iris. About four this afternoon the sun broke through the beastly Tupperware sky; the turf breathed out and I breathed in, lying on the bank.

BUFFALO CURRANT

Ribes odoratum has one of the few smells that drifts a hundred yards. Now that *is* desirable. The buffalo currant comes from around the Rocky Mountains and was introduced to Britain in 1812. The genus includes true currants and gooseberries, plus *R. laurifolium*, which has no scent and inedible fruit, but its green dangling racemes complement anything from corylopsis to primroses in a jug. *R. odoratum* is a Mr B favourite. It is deciduous, of lax habit, spineless, with young shoots minutely downy, leaves singing green. If you are lucky it can grow taller than you, but it is wilful and can sulk. Flowers are bright golden yellow, each a lobed simplified daisy, like Mary Quant's logo or Marc Jacobs' perfume, on semi-pendulous racemes the length of a finger. *R. sanguineum*, the pink flowering currant, is a childhood familiar, with rosy red dangling flowers and a very strong catty smell that is both pleasant and rancid. Bean calls it a 'deciduous, glandular, unarmed bush' and surprisingly he rates it 'in the very front rank of all spring flowering shrubs' – but it is very unfashionable now.

Moaning March gales. Picked loads of daffodils and brought them in, plump and firm for smelling. It is affirming to smell them, even the ooze from their cut stems. Looking out from a distance I mistook daffodils on the bank for an outbreak of tennis balls. The designer and gardener David Hicks condemned the common yellow ones as like splurges of sick, but indoors even the ugliest orange choirboy types are a pleasure. I was in London this week and it smelled mean, of nothing, and I thought: daffodils are a Good Thing.

Yesterday felt for the first time truly springy, not just imagining it. The pug sat in the sunny window and sniffed at the air, his nose-parts whiffling and wet. The pug loves smells. He loves the kennels for entirely this reason – it's like Times Square for him.

Crushed the myrtle into the east wind, on a bright but bitter dry day. By association it released a capsule of far pavilions and bitter oranges, a sweet Alhambra in my pocket.

Wallflowers still smell of Parma violets. They are *Cruciferae*, members of the 'cabbagey' family, like rape and broccoli. They are, and smell like, homely kitchen things – vegetal – clove and vanilla. Wallflowers were the first seed I can remember sowing. I pushed them into the chalky lime mortar of the garden wall between soft ruddy Berkshire bricks, under the direction of my patient father, never thinking they would grow. How pleased I was by their lanky legs and velvet, warm-smelling flowers next spring. If you buy seedlings, plant them as soon as you buy them bare root, cut them back if they droop badly, and cut back hard after flowering to get woody bushy plants for next year – occasionally they just go on forever like the old and native *Erysimum cheiri* 'Harpur Crewe'.

WALLFLOWERS

Erysimum cheiri (formerly *Cheiranthus*) was once known as the 'yellow violet' because the first wallflowers to be introduced from southern Europe were yellow. It has a heart-easing smell, warm and powdery like mignonette, but the scent and also the plants are stock-like. It is known as *giroflée ravenelle* in French. *E. cheiri* is native to the eastern Mediterranean where it grows on cliffs and rocks, hence its happiness in the walls of

Roman and mediaeval ruins, growing wild throughout much of Europe. A small-flowered yellow double-leaved wallflower was rediscovered by the Rev. Henry Harpur-Crewe (before 1883, and before he hyphenated his surname) and is now named after him; *E.c.* 'Harpur Crewe' is very sweetly scented.

Garden varieties mostly have boring dark green leaves and form shrubby small bushes about knee height. If cut back hard after flowering they can go on to flower for a second year. The flowers and the smell are velvety, warm and plush, coming in colours ranging from blood red, burnt orange, bright orange, mottled orangey pink through to cream. They remain stalwarts of the garden for their companionable colour in early spring and their drifting friendly smell. Shrubby perennials, they are generally grown as biennials, sown in May and June for flowering the following spring. Most of us buy them because somehow it is difficult to sow things in May when one is so busy and distracted by other gardening things. But I often try to grow varieties you cannot easily get ready grown, unusual colours more than special smells, and I often sow them very late and get away with it.

Smelling wallflowers resurrected other memories. My brother Charlie and I made my mother rose water, re-using her wide oval Diorissimo perfume bottles with their houndstooth-check band across the middle. We filled a jar with brown green sludge; it looked like dishwater, but it did smell of trampled rose petals and earthiness and decomposition. Not unpleasant. My mother, not usually one to dissemble, looked touched and pleased.

Talking of childhood smells, my friend Katie tells me about the smell of squashed caterpillars. I must try it come the summer. Together we remembered the repugnant but magnetic attraction of our pretend cabbage-white 'farms' full of nasturtiums which all got devoured the day the grubs hatched. We wallowed in the smell of heaps of hot grass clippings and the making of those miniature gardens with moss for lawn and mirrors for ponds. We could still feel the velvet sandpit, summer afternoons playing, naked, cool and silky.

Everyone could smell *Prunus mume* but me today. Smell is like that, subjective, unpredictable and capricious. For once it was me asking, 'What are you on about?'

The Ides of March

It was my birthday the other day and we had lunch outside in champagne sunlight and drank champagne – which I don't like, but it's churlish somehow to celebrate any other way.

Went down to the wood and the garlic oozed from sharp young blades underfoot – rather marvellous, after the odourless winter months. It is pungent and cleansing. Stephen Lacey says that the best reason for choosing a plant is that it creates rich, primal, three-dimensional sensual encounters, stirs emotions and deepens pleasure.

The flowering currants, *Ribes sanguineum*, smell, in the words of Laurie Lee, 'sharply of fox'. A whole group of things smell like this, crown imperials most especially and much to my delight, but not to everyone's. When we moved here we knew we had to plant things like this – crown imperials, euphorbias and *R. sanguineum* – because it wouldn't be spring without their hot, close scents enlivening the garden. They do very well here.

Sir Richard Grenville plaque with a *Rhododendron* 'Fragrantissimum'

CROWN IMPERIALS

Crown imperials, *Fritillaria imperialis*, come from Kurdistan and places east. They are sublimely designed-looking, architectural divertimenti, and hence, I find, difficult to place in a bed. They are better in a pot, it seems to me, and best in a vase when picked. Mr B once found the decorator Robert Kime lying on his back with a straw sucking the nectar out of one, a bit like the montbretia sucking we used to do as children. But though the nectar may be sweet it is completely overpowered by the smell of the whole plant, which is foxy and skunky and something I would not be without in spring. It is like a mad March hare that boxes you on the nose and says: 'Hey! Spring is here!' Choose any of the three luxurious Silk-Road colours and plant in a hole with lots of gravel, placing the bulb on its side to drain any water from the curious hole in the ivory-coloured starchy mass that stores the food that makes those flowers.

Cornwall is famous, of course, for daffodils, which are loveable and spring-laden, but also vulgarised and overexposed. The daffs already ensconced at Trematon seemed not have been chosen for scent at all, but for glaring cheerfulness. There were old fragile and scented ones lurking round the back of the motte – *Narcissus* 'Amabilis'. And gradually Mr B rooted out the 'King Alfred' types with a strength and tenacity I was unable to summon up. My attitude was: let's just ruthlessly pick bunches of them every spring, because they all look great in a vase, every single one. But jonquils, John Clare's 'jonquil fair, that sweet perfumer of the evening air,' are the ones for smelling.

With the coming of the railway in the nineteenth century, an industry developed in Cornwall – particularly here in the Tamar Valley, Land's End and the Lizard, and also in the Scilly Isles – producing winter cut flowers for London, Bristol and other urban markets. Violets, anemones and, especially, daffodils could be sent up by train from October until May. There is a fabulous BBC documentary *The Flower Fields,* which can be rooted out, interviewing the few growers left at the end of the last century, and also those who could remember times when everyone grew whatever they could for a bit of extra spring cash. They would take their boxes of buds to the train, labelled up, and the cash would come back from the traders at Covent Garden on the down train by the end of the day. How extraordinary and how simple.

DAFFODILS

The tonnage of daffodils that I might begin to write about is anxious-making. In the middle of the nineteenth century, Dean Herbert 'Crossed a Trumpet with a Poet' in order to prove that wild narcissi might actually be hybrids; he was very suspicious that species such as the primrose-peerless, *Narcissus × medioluteus*, were in fact hybrids between species, and so it proved to be. This opened the doors thereafter to a wave of breeding of yellow daffodils that possibly got out of hand. Bowles laments that breeding is 'degrading daffodils' as early as the 1890s. But of the pheasant's eye he says that they were traditionally called incomparable, 'Nonpareille' and 'Nonsuch', and they remain so. Their porcelain perfection is captured by Margery Fish thus: 'the petals … have that same glittering quality that one finds in nerines and begonias, as if each tiny cell was encased with lenses to reflect light.'

When it comes to spring daffodils Mr B likes the native ones like *Narcissus obvallaris*,

Iris 'Harmony'

48

the Tenby daffodil and *N. pseudonarcissus* (syn. *N. lobularis*), the Lent lily, which is only a hand's height in the grass, the earliest wildling to flower. The Lent lily likes cool heavy soil; the wild colonies live in meadows such as those at Dymock near the Forest of Dean. Being species they will naturalise if the conditions are right. They all smell daffodilly and with the same modest charm as their looks.

TAZETTA NARCISSUS

For intense scent you need Tazettas and jonquils. It seems that small is generally more smelly in the narcissus world. Mr B likes some Tazettas. *Narcissus tazetta* is a native of the eastern Mediterranean, with small cupped flowers that are carried several on a stem, familiar to all as the 'Paper White Grandiflorus' that we grow for Christmas. Like the species, paperwhites are not really hardy here, which made them especially highly prized for winter flowering in cool glass and ideal for forcing as cut flowers. Originally the species were shipped from Turkey, but all the breeding and forcing went on in Holland for the cutting market and garden bulbs. Probably the smelliest cultivar is called *N.* 'Cheerfulness' and, if you needed to turn up the volume, 'Yellow Cheerfulness', with a robust sugary and captivating scent. Like all the narcissi this scent is an admixture of a jasmine-flavoured nectar with something of orange and then an earthy faecal or fungal (gardenia-like) element which can unbalance the beauty of it. The shallow cup of Tazettas is an adaptation, making life easier for invertebrate pollinators drawn in by the powerfully magnetic scent. *Narcissus tazetta* var. *orientalis* has a long history, grown in ancient Egypt and Israel for ritual, and in China it is the New Year's flower. I think, fashion victim that I am, I prefer the look of the milk-white 'Ziva' and 'Silver Chimes' and particularly 'Thalia' – a well-known classy favourite since 1916 which is also an excellent cut flower. Despite being the colour of strong Bird's Custard I love the name and smell of 'Scilly Spring' – one of the daffodil delights the Blue Box Flower Company will send you from their farm on St Mary's all winter long.

The double, cream-flowered, *Narcissus* 'Bridal Crown' – jasmine-scenting and long-lasting in a cool room – is good too and it is an odd thing that in the case of these narcissi the doubles turn out to be the more scented. 'White Lion' has an earthy depth, gardenia-like in smell and in looks – but the double flowers are too heavy for itself, making the stems collapse after rain, so best to pick it. It is arguable that they all smell better out of doors – the old wives believed they would give you a headache if in a room – but I love them in jugs in the kitchen; you just have to throw them out in time. For the garden, *N.* 'Sir Winston Churchill', similar to 'Bridal Crown', a double poet's narcissus – almost an anathema – with larger, loose flowers like a cream egg, performs well and is good in pots or little corners of open ground. It is gorgeous to smell but I would not spoil the native look of my orchard with it. Varieties of *N. tazetta* are grown commercially in the South of France to produce the essential oil; this smells different from the flower, more obviously of neroli, but none the less I would call it addictive.

The highly scented, prettily named jonquils are a world I would like to know more about. Although there is a species of narcissus that specifically relates to it, *Narcissus jonquilla*, the term jonquil is used for any short, multi-headed, often yellow single-flowered narcissus with strange rushy leaves almost square in section, with a sugared smell which can be powerful to the point of recoil. *N.* 'Trevithian' is a legend of a neat scented daff, and another cultivar, 'Baby Moon', though horribly named, is deliciously scented. *N.* 'Double Campernelle' is a jonquil with narrow leaves, bright green flower stalks and small, double, golden-yellow flowers with a powerful fragrance which I would say equates to a northern version of orange blossom. *N.* 'Pipit' is said to be one of the longest flowering, knock-out smelling, with multiple stems carrying multiple heads of flower.

POET'S NARCISSUS

Narcissi with tiny, flattened cups are known as poet's or Poeticus narcissi; the early flat-faced heavenly flower is *Narcissus* 'Actaea'. The true pheasant's eye, or poet's daffodil, is *N. poeticus* var. *recurvus*, one of the last narcissi to flower. The pheasant's eye is more graceful than 'Actaea', with creamier petals and is possibly more scented. It is one of the oldest narcissi in cultivation and is grown in the Netherlands and South of France for the production of perfume. The scent is reminiscent of jasmine and hyacinth, heavy and less orangey than *N. tazetta*. A plant of mountain meadows, it likes the cooler conditions provided by dappled shade or in borders where the leaves of other plants provide shade around the roots. It has a sweet but spicy scent. Of all spring bulbs these rank very high. They throng beneath the leafing birch, larch and poplar; they smell of shade and water, honey, apricots and a wisp of something more robust, musk perhaps. This strength gives them mystery as well as charm. Fragments of them have been found in funeral wreaths of the ancient Egyptians. The power of the scent is reflected in the name; the 'nar' part has the same derivation as narcotic – a flower with a scent that causes numb lethargy. They rarely perfume the air outside, it usually being too cold, but when brought into the house, they puff a festive note. In the still uncertain, spring-blown garden they must be sought out and picked, stems oozing, then pressed, cool and watery, to the face to experience one of life's deep pleasures. Vita Sackville-West describes the moment when the straight *Narcissus* 'Actaea' begin to flower, around the equinox, when the 'grass beneath the Worcester Pearmain blows with narcissus … all in a hurry in the wind of March'. She remarks on their generosity producing 'two score' progeny where you planted one. Probably grown in England since Roman times, they have countless, delightful common names including 'sweet Nancies' and 'none-so-pretty'. There are wildings found in Japan, and in Chinese paintings a double, but best for wild colonies are Spain, Portugal and North Africa. In the high Pyrenees, even as late as July, there can be found meadowsfull of very lovely, narrow twisted petalled *N. poeticus* var. *recurvus*. The leaves, however, are poisonous to cattle.

St Patrick's day today which is almost always bright. It is usually biting cold as well. Planted 'Tête-à-tête' daffodils from a bowl bought all out and smelling in a shop for my birthday three days ago; they quickly faded in the heat of the kitchen.

Spring cleaning

House full of the smell of washing. Spring cleaning, sort of. The sun shows up the grub on the loose covers and I overdose the washing powder. In the old days, Omo and Daz smelled of sneezey happy ozone, but now Ariel and co. have such a punch of cleanth, it is too much and too fake. The washing machine clanked all day merrily. I can remember the worship accorded our first 'automatic' washing machine, high in the house near St Mary's Paddington where I was born. My mother, superstitious about technology except for her love of open-topped coupés and her Atco mower (though she loathed gardening she loved mowing striped lawns and hoovering carpets), was in love with this move forward from the tub-and-mangle way of washing of the lino-London of the fifties. Washing was still draped all over the house on pulleys and clothes horses, set before gas fires, as there was no central heating and it usually was too wet and too far to take out to the back garden. The smell of washing, although a bit dank, was a good clean smell to muffle the many smells that permeated the house: bleach and polish, the smoke of coal fires, the pong of town gas.

Four days after my birthday. Getting older is tough. I am getting more angry, less cynical, but more wistful and sometimes urgent with the sands running out. Realise more than ever the fragile nature of a garden – beyond stone and water. Here and Hanham Court will slip away, the detail barely discernible after a decade, but we will have been lucky enough to have been holding the fort for a moment in their story. Each garden is a temporary larder for our daydreams.

Milky frost melted into a day as intense as any in July. Stillness stopped everything. Primroses have an enchanting way of sunbathing, and they smell of Devon lanes, green yet powdery. Someone has kindly lit a fire somewhere with hazel twigs, a sweet-scented polish to the peerless day. I got too hot in the greenhouse pricking out 'Cupani' sweet peas, and yet a week ago it was winter.

Pheasant's eye in a bunch. The smell has a hold on me. Crisp, laundered, powdery, and crystalline in purity like the petals. Tearing ivy off a wall, I realise that it, too, has a smell. It is strong and strange, bitter and dust dry. It is is most likely smelled when one is climbing clandestinely over a church wall, into a deserted garden, filled with resilient and scented grape hyacinths.

GRAPE HYACINTHS

Muscari are great for lost corners. Small hardy, spreading bulbs, they really start flowering in March. They were grown by the Turks and Greeks before the sixteenth century for their musky smell. This is much more the point of them than their untidy bed of leaves and odd blue pointy turbans. They need to be well drained but not too dry such that they will thrive in the dark root-ridden places under large trees. *Muscari azureum* is perhaps the best looking, but super scented is the white *M. botryoides* 'Album', which is a good cottagey edging for any bed. *M. moschatum* is a bit dingy but with a strong almost pure musk scent; it turns a dull yellowish olive colour, very smart in a 1950s kind of way, as the flowers age.

Smell is so often in the conscious periphery, taken in obliquely, almost through the body. The neurology of smell is fantastically complex and unlike the workings of the other parts of the brain. The experience of smell, each of our private and subjective experiences of smell, is a direct chemical exchange in the receptors which pass through the cibriform plate in the skull and into the thalamus. What we smell are actual chemicals, translocated from outwith our bodies to within, right deep inside the brain, the signals from which are myriad and, once decoded, they trigger detailed conscious and unconscious responses.

Passing a spot something brushed my synapses again today like yesterday. What is it? Casting about, my eye falls on the briar rose 'La Belle Distinguée'. There are leaves out already, scanty but lettuce fresh, and these are the source. Only then do I realise that the benign feeling is a smell. Even now, with this realisation of the source, the feeling is numinous: it smells of woody apple, of baking and somehow, oddly comfortingly, of horse piss. So easy to miss and so strange a thing.

The *Clematis armandii* smells today – hooray. It is doing exactly what was intended, which is so rare in any garden planting. Through the porch it permeates the house and down the stone steps into the kitchen on a slipstream of cooling air. Better still, this one does smell truly of the courtyards of the Umayyads to me, of almond and orange blossom. Planted by the front door so that the scent is sucked

Parkers mixed tulips in front of the house

52

into the hall, its tendrils grow with stop motion speed. You can never be sure what kind of a clone of a plant you have bought, and whether a particular version has the sought-after scent at its best, unless you buy one in flower.

CLEMATIS ARMANDII

A lanky, large, evergreen fast-growing climber with tapering leaves, this clematis ticks many a box but often looks unkempt and unpleasing, especially when I grow it. It can climb to the top of a high wall. It comes from a wide geographical range in China through Burma so is very adaptable and needs no pruning and only minimal spring feeding. There seem to be many differing clones, some good and flowersome, others ugly and disappointing. Good scented cultivars include the pure white 'Snowdrift' and the more rosy 'Apple Blossom'. Mr B's mother had one which was enchanting, filling a tiny back courtyard with smell and big white blossom settled in flocks on top of a wall in the sunshine. But its feet were in damp shade, which is often most pleasing to clematis. Weirdly it is toxic to dogs – but why would a dog eat it? Even Popeye the pug, who eats everything, would hardly stand on his hind legs like a goat for a good munch of *armandii.*

Hooray also for the *Ribes odoratum*, puffing away for the past three weeks, belting out hot-cross-bun smells from little lime-and-soda flowers. The *Elaeagnus × submacrophylla* has a very similar effect in September. Heat is the trigger, hence yesterday, when I found that the *armandii* was smelling I quickly realised the whole garden was buzzing like a radar station of invisible waves of smell.

The heavens are burst with spring, anticyclone skies and gangs of boisterous birds battling over territory. We cut back a mound of frost-bitten rosemary and barrowed it into the front hall and on to the fire where it crackled and blazed, smoke streaming up the chimney like fish spawn, smelling of Passover.

The warm coconut of gorse flowers is another scent of my childhood. We grow the double-flowered version (*Ulex europaeus* 'Flore Pleno') at home as doubles are usually more scented. It flowers for a long time, while being shorter and more compact than regular gorse.

WINTER'S BARK

Drimys winteri is a tall evergreen tree, rather conical in habit, with greyish highly aromatic bark. It is beloved by plantspeople. 'Leaves entire, oblong, elliptic, inflorescence umbellate or fascicled', says Bean. I had to look fascicled up as it made me think of the inflamed plantar fascia I have been suffering from. It means bundled together, and is related to the medical term for sinews, but here it means the leaves and flowers are crowded together at the end of the stems in clusters. The individual flowers, produced in late spring on pedicels, are ivory-white, flavoured with jasmine; the whole experience if you pick some is a pleasant mix with the aromatic pungency which comes from the bark. But somehow the overall effect is not, to me at least, joyous.

Hailing from damp woods in southern South America it loves the South West of England and has been grown in Europe since the sixteenth century for medical use. Brought back as a medicinal herb from South America in 1579 by Captain John Wynter – who had accompanied Drake on his round-the-world voyage, but whose ship had had to turn

Crown Imperial, *Fritillaria imperialis* 'Maxima Lutea'

back despite successfully rounding Cape Horn – it was effectively used as a preventative and cure for scurvy. Drake came here to Trematon and stowed the gold from the *Golden Hinde* in the keep for three days.

EARLY MAGNOLIAS

Magnolia salicifolia, also known as willow-leaved magnolia or anise magnolia, originates from Japan. It is a medium-sized upright deciduous tree, with a willow look owing to the narrow (compared with most magnolias) leaves. Hardy and fairly lime tolerant is the cultivar 'Wada's Memory', with double white scented flowers. They grew really well at Hanham Court where we planted a grove of them not really knowing what they were but having bought them as a bargain. They turned out to be full of charm, good growers and generously covered in scented flowers in early spring before the leaves. The leaves and bark are fragrant when crushed, as with all magnolias, but perhaps more pronounced in this case and noted in the common name anise magnolia.

The *Magnolia stellata* types, the star magnolias, are ubiquitous for good reason. They are the earliest-flowering, hardiest, smelliest, most floriferous of all magnolias and yet tidy and manageable as well. It is sad that we have become perhaps blasé about them. The smell is definitely lemony, and the best ones can scent the whole garden on a perfect early spring day. They don't mind shade and unlike most magnolias they are lime tolerant. *M. stellata* 'Royal Star' is exactly that, a delicious creamy white and very smelly.

The loebneri magnolias such as *Magnolia × loebneri* 'Merrill' are similar and scented. 'Wildcat' has many, many petals which give it a dahlia effect and yet it is scented. 'Donna' is slightly pink and smells strongly of lemon and turpentine while 'Leonard Messel' is much pinker but less scented.

MID-SPRING MAGNOLIAS

M. 'Galaxy' is hardy and grows to be a big tree which flowers generously and early in late March and early April; it looks and smells a little like *M. liliiflora* 'Nigra' with a rosy scent. Of similar parentage, *M.* 'Susan' is a very hardy medium tree whose flowers are purplish red in bud paling upon opening, but with a rosy floral smell which is good in an April-flowering magnolia. *M.* 'Heaven Scent' flowers when young, being a Gresham hybrid (developed in the 1950s in California); it flowers in April and smells of lavender, which is perhaps the case with other magnolia flowers, lavender being related to turpentine which is so much part of magnolias' makeup. It grows quickly into a flowering tree. *M.* 'Yellow Fever' is a really lovely newish hybrid from Louisiana with flowers of Chinese yellow in bud fading to cream and highly scented.

The Jury hybrids, raised by the plantsman Felix Jury in New Zealand, have produced my favourite fast-growing early-flowering scented magniloquent magnolia, *M.* 'Atlas', which has blooms as large and decadent as *M.* 'David Clulow'. It is worth checking out Jury's selections as he is obviously a man with a good eye and a lifetime's determination and devotion.

Two wisteria flowers have come out high in the battlements, emerging like butterflies from their grey scaled chrysalis. They are early, it still being the time of blackthorn, damson blossom and early magnolias. Balsam poplar hangs like incense under the crucible of a still March sky. The bee colonies are very active suddenly, and the mowed paths round the newly planted broad beans and potatoes smell of drying elderflowers.

Magnolia × soulangeana

Overleaf: Campion and bluebells on the motte

Lilac Time

What is all this juice and all this joy?
A strain of the earth's sweet being in the beginning
In Eden garden. – Have, get, before it cloy,

Gerard Manley Hopkins SPRING

The sun rises on April Fool's Day at six fifty-three, almost due east over the dockyard and the incinerator chimney. Each morning is yawning and stretching, extending itself by nearly four minutes daily. The incremental increase has reached the top of the curve and the sun sets at a very civilised quarter to eight, almost due west over Port Eliot up the Lynher.

We were mowing through sycamore blossom and balsam poplar husks, whose sticky gum is a key constituent of bee propolis. Propolis is one of the three major ingredients of the hive along with wax and honey itself. Bees make propolis as a glue, defensively bunging up all holes in the hive to keep out invaders such as wasps. It smells antiseptic, deliciously so, and is thought to have remarkable anti-microbial properties. Dark brown, like marmite, it's resonant of turpentine polish and Dettol. Bees collect all sorts of amber and aromatic oozings from trees and plants. When you open the hive, or even go near it, you are assailed by the smell of propolis more than the smell of honey. It is the smell of the apiary and smells of security, that protective working sisterhood of bees nursing their young.

This is the tawny moment, Robert Frost's 'Nature's first green is gold / Her hardest hue to hold.' This is when all the balsam poplars are stinking of Johnson's wax polish; their fledgling leaves are ruddy, muddy brown like the oak and the field maple. All the dingle dangle flowers of oak are singing if you look and listen.

BALSAM POPLAR

Every April, as the leaves unfurl through the resin-coated bracts that sail off stickily on the spring easterlies, a glorious incense fills the lanes. Balsam – the word – is derived from ancient Hebrew roots, *bot smin* 'the chief of oils' and *besem* 'a sweet smell'. Its use from untold times as an antiseptic and soothing balm gives us the derivation of the word for healing influence or consolation. Known in the perfume and health trade as 'tacamahac', this oil is made by boiling leaf buds in water – something anyone with a cold can do to clear the head. A good-sized western balsam poplar tree will reach 30 metres/100 feet in the wild, but they are rarely more than half as high. Most of the plants grown under the name *Populus balsamifera* were in fact *P. candicans*, explains Bean; he says that true *P. balsamifera* 'is a poor grower in this country'. The great charm of *P. balsamifera* is the balsamic odour of the unfolding leaves in spring which fills the air around, but, says Bean, *P. trichocarpa*, its western ally, is just as fragrant and a more satisfactory tree for us. It can be nosed out from a hundred metres away on a spring day. The leaves start off heavy with gum, shiny bright green on top, washed white below. In winter, this grey-barked, weak-limbed, unambitious shaped tree is like an outsize sapling. But the winter buds are formed

Syringa vulgaris 'Prince Wolkonsky'

61

viscid with fragrant gum from October, and from then on buds about an inch/
2 or 3 centimetres long will scent a room with a warm, fuzzy healthy smell, and by the
end of February the wands of the swollen sticky buds will unfurl their leaves and, if you
wait long enough, roots spring from the submerged parts.

Some notes: *Euphorbia* × *pasteurii* is better than *E. mellifera* and smells of lychees
they say. I cannot vouch for this myself. Both smell of honey, hence the *mellifera*
epithet – a rare nod in the direction of the olfactory defining qualities in a Latin
name. Perhaps this is because euphorbia generally have a skunky pong; the fact that
this particular smell is so delicious captured even the namer of names' imagination.

In the lean-to greenhouse, *Jasminum polyanthum* is in full flower suddenly. I
inhaled it deeply in the dark turning out the light and, turning aside, pinched some
scrunchy leaves of verbena that have just appeared on the scraggly bare branches
where, in truth, I had given up hope. Just this morsel was packed with lemon
spangles and spangled sunlight.

JASMINE

Many of these evergreen climbers have scented white or yellow flowers which are easily
cultivated in a sunny position and in a good loam. They need little more than a general
seaweed feed in spring. There are a large number of species, of which only about a
dozen are cultivated in the open air in Britain, the best perhaps being *Jasminum officinale*,
the common jasmine which Mr B loves to grow on a north wall. It is nearly deciduous, may
look totally finished in spring, but bounces back, making slender, angled long shoots.
These break into white, deliciously fragrant bloom in terminal clusters of cymes from June
to October. Although a native of the Caucasus, Iran and across the Himalayas into China,
it has been cultivated from time immemorial in Britain. The jessamine or gelsomina has a
place in our gardens and our hearts as secure as lilac or lavender.

For the cool unheated greenhouse there is no more joyous plant than the pink jasmine,
J. polyanthum – the specific epithet meaning 'many flowered' but called by the common
name on account of the rose colour of the flower exterior, which is more profound if grown
outdoors somewhere like the South of France. An evergreen whose young shoots are
slightly warted, not downy, it flowers in great panicles, in as many flowers as the Milky
Way and is very fragrant. It is a native of Yunan in China, discovered in 1883 by the
French Jesuit plant hunter Père Delavay. But it was George Forrest who found it flowering
between May and August 1906 eight thousand feet up in the mountains and returned
with it to Britain. However, it did not become known to gardeners here until the *Botanical
Magazine* illustrated a spray sent by Captain de la Warre from his garden on the French
Riviera – this plant was said to be a present from Lawrence Johnston, who owned and
made a garden at Menton as well as more famously at Hidcote in the high Cotswolds. It is
undeniably one of the finest of climbers for a cool greenhouse.

HOLBOELLIA, THE SAUSAGE VINE

Stauntonia, *Akebia*, *Decaisnea* and *Holboellia* might be described as scented cousins,
smelling a bit like jasmine but more fruity and liquid. I do not know *Stauntonia* or
Decaisnea, and *Akebia* simply took over the front of the house at Hanham without being
really all that scented. But *Holboellia*, a genus of five species of evergreen climbers,

Syringa vulgaris 'Madame
Lemoine' with cordyline

62

native to China and the Himalayas and introduced in 1840, is in my sights. Sausage vines are so called because of their bright purple or pink sausage-shaped, edible fruit, only they generally do not manage to fruit here, although the *Holboellia latifolia* at Dartington Hall has been known to. *H. latifolia* is the most usually grown, and is a luxuriant climber. It thrives exceedingly well in the South West, with twining shoots and dark glossy, leathery leaves. The flowers are fruitily fragrant, a tiny capsule of melon and cucumber, and similarly subtle and cucumber coloured. Whether the smell comes from the tiny male flowers with minuscule pistils or the female flowers, which have the nectaries, fleshy sepals, and are a much paler bruised plum greenish white, I am not sure. The pollen parent is less likely to smell than the nectar and fruit bearer. Resist the urge to chop them right back if they grow wildly. Cut back tendrils to the first few leaves of a season where the subtle but scented flowers will come next year.

Honesty and tulips have been flattened by wind and rain. Leaves, dust and petals are blown apart under bright light but it's a scentless day. Pug hides where the sun slides under the tractor.

Coffee outside. Outside makes everything taste and smell different. Tea is quite different outside. Quite special. This morning it was coffee on the terrace. Birds sang like they only do on mornings abroad when there is time to notice. I took the time to notice. Noticed the coffee, the wallflowers, the wisteria and the flowering currants.

Spangled spring day. Stood in the orchard watching the breathless drying up of snowdrop leaves, narcissi and fritillaries shrivelling. Violets and lily of the valley are pretty and soapy in smell even in the dry air. Everything is shifting in the spring breeze, and melting on it the smell of *Viburnum carlesii* fresh with overtones of new cowpat. *V. × carlcephalum* and *V. carlesii* are 'must-haves' in our garden, because, following on from the *Ribes odoratum*, they emanate for several weeks a similar smell trail, noticeable at a distance, but thicker, creamy like they look, and loaded with vanilla. They are good shrubs and easy to grow. They also have the great quality of being somewhat self-effacing. You don't really notice them during the rest of the year and, like ribes and wintersweet, can all have a clematis or a perennial pea grown up them.

Puffs of cherry laurel flowers fill unimportant places. Like the leaves, the scent is coarse; it drifts powerfully, spreading thick sweet honey, which is pretty good. But nothing beats the draughts of early wisteria flowers through the gateway in the heat, perfectly peppery. Sweet woodruff is smelling in the dell.

SWEET WOODRUFF

Sweet woodruff is *Galium odoratum*, a low-growing woodlander from Europe and North Africa. A stoloniferous invader for cool shade. Leaves are scented – particularly when dried (this is a chemical reaction commonly occurring with certain leaves especially those rich in coumarin like the woodruff) – bright green initially in whorls on numerous slender stems which spread across the woodland floor. All parts of the plant are aromatic and more so when dried. Flowers are tiny, white but almost unnoticeable, appearing in clusters in late spring/early summer. Meadowsweet has the same scented qualities, and it flowers with the cowslip in pasture. The aromatic scent of its leaves drying was treasured by Elizabethans and strewn about their chambers. It is still easily found on verges and field edges.

Bird table and Mexican orange

Michelia (*Magnolia*)
doltsopa

Garden notes to self. Finish supports. Plant out *Lathyrus* 'Cupani' and tie up all peas. Plant more peonies. Plant salvias. Cut back salvias. Chop yews back. Mulch front lane border. Mulch peony beds and sow cleome.

New box growth shone toxic green, almost a mould. Everything is changing hourly. The purity of winter is gone, and the profusion of scent is muddling suddenly. Warmth brings a depth and copious variety to the air; primroses peppery, cowslips too, singing out in irradiated yellow. Lilac time at last.

The lilac scent is fabulous today – which is supposed to smell the most? *Syringa vulgaris*? It is an overpowering and wafting scent that doesn't disappear in the nose like violets but becomes rank. For this reason, it is best in wafts as you walk by or better still, if your bushes are big enough, is to snap off big branches to take indoors – the definition of luxury. 'Prince Wolkonsky' smells and looks fantastic just now. The tomb of writer and aesthete William Beckford, above Bath on Lansdown Hill and made from hideous pink granite in the Egyptian style, was on his instruction surrounded by a grove of lilacs. An earlier eighteenth-century writer and aesthete, Horace Walpole, is buried at Houghton Hall in East Anglia where lilac probably grows best in this country. Walpole was a lover of 'lilactide' as he called it, once putting off a trip to Paris rather than miss the moment at his house at Strawberry Hill. Mr B is exactly of this turn of mind.

To those who don't love it passionately it is too much, assaults the senses and the sense. 'Too sweet, troubling and molesting the head in a very strange way,' wrote Gerard in the seventeenth century. It is not a scent in which to wallow, but

Rosa primula, the incense rose

in wafts it surpasses anything in the tropics, perhaps because lilac contains the extraordinary 'well-being'-inducing compound known as indole, more bewitching than the 'stove plants' such as tuberose and stephanotis. Vita Sackville-West finds solace 'in the distilled scent of every dew-drenched lilac you ever smelt', a quality like that of drinking the absolutely finest white Burgundy. Lilac somehow encompasses the louche and the homely.

LILAC

Lilacs are a group of small trees and shrubs, consisting of a couple of dozen species whose origins are not confined to the Old World – Europe, the Himalayas, East Asia and Yunnan in China; *Syringa vulgaris* and *S. josikaea* (found in Hungary) being the only two natives of Europe. *S. vulgaris* has been affectionately grown in England for around five hundred years. Species have been cultivated and collected since Persian times and by all the great names in plant hunting. They generally flower by May. Notable also for their prettiness are their heart-shaped leaves, silky and emerald upon opening. They make a handsome shrub, a better small tree, and they can also be cut and laid in a hedge to fabulous effect. They do take kindly to shearing, but in our climate they make you pay for it by not flowering for several years. The wood needs to ripen thoroughly to reach flowering point. This I suspect is why old ones in front gardens tend to get massacred, flush back in green regrowth but then don't flower, and get taken out after two seasons, just when they would have showered the street in blossom. The pity of it. Hereabouts I feel their beauty and evocative scent are less and less understood or lauded. In America, with its continental climate, none of this is a problem, and you see them as standard lollipops – something I long to do, but I certainly would fail doing it in Cornwall. They 'stool' them in the cut-flower trade in Holland, lopping them to the floor after bringing them early into flower by heat, the only sadness being that they are scentless, understandably resentful of such treatment. They were made to trumpet the coming of summer to the fluted echo of the cuckoo. Vita Sackville-West writes, 'If you pick a few green shoots three months before flowering you find either a pair of leaves or an embryo floret, like roe in a prawn, pale greeny white.'

In the nineteenth and early twentieth centuries the family Lemoine of Nancy, France, was gripped in a fever of breeding, creating, from the humble but delicious common lilac and its cousins, plants with shocking plumes of immense weight loaded with scent, the names redolent of a lost world: Necker, Lamartine, Vauban. They also extended the range of hue to depths of rich crushed mulberry and heights of iridescent stormy slatey-violet blues. Nineteenth-century Europe's drawing rooms were entranced by the shrubs and, as Proust put it, the 'starry locks that crowned their fragrant heads'.

Seriously scented species are *Syringa pubescens* subsp. *julianae*, and *S. vulgaris*. All lilacs benefit from generous treatment. Happy in full sun or light shade, they can grow to several metres round. The saintly gardener would deadhead them all, at least when young and getting established – which takes two or three years. Most are very hardy, hailing from the steppes and plains of Russia, Central Asia and Eastern Europe. (Russian trains make unscheduled stops to allow passengers to jump out and pick lilac from the trackside.) They thrive in well-drained limey soils and hate very acid soils. The colours are bewitching but it can be tricky to meld together the dark with the pale ones in planting a grove of them. Of the *vulgaris* named varieties the most scented suggestions are 'Katherine Havemeyer' – packed with dense saturated lavender purple

Primroses on the motte

heads of flowers which fade on opening; 'Prince Wolkonsky' – globby pointed plumes of plum-coloured buds open glowing violet; 'Madame Lemoine' – like Ambrosia Creamed Rice; 'Congo' – luscious reddish purple in thick thunderous heads; 'Firmament' – stormy blue-grey lilac heads fuming with muddling fragrance … to name but a few. Less for scent but for the mix as eye-catching are wine-dark 'Volcan' and the white-laced lilac petals of 'Sensation'.

In Hampshire working in a heathy place today, smells were sandy and sharp. Bluebells among the birches were a mirage with a grandiloquent scent. Bluebell scent operates on a finer, more astral level than hyacinth, having the same benign power to uplift, but somehow more youthful, energised and pure. Markedly stranger in the woodland is the scent of the yellow azalea *Rhododendron luteum* – curiously exciting and exotic. Mango-coloured and mango-scented, with melon and papaya, also watery with cucumber, 'finished', as they say, with a powerful flush of peppery spice.

From one acid garden we went to another totally acid place, Caerhays Castle in Cornwall. Here there is so much to wonder at: forests of magnolias covered with flocks of cockatoo flowers – and there is wonder on the smell side, most particularly, for, hanging over the rugs of primroses so thick they make you trip, are chandeliers of michelia, burst from their ferruginous casings into lily-white bloom, billowing perfume.

MICHELIA

Named after a Florentine botanist, Pietro Antonio Micheli (1679–1737) michelias are now reclassified as *Magnolia*. They are daintier than most magnolias, having smaller leaves and flowers on slim twigged branches. Michelias come from China. They have an artificial chocolate smell, a bit like a whiff of Terry's Chocolate Orange, with some sense of aniseed – exotic but maybe ersatz. At Caerhays they are the size of birch trees (whereas the *Magnolia campbellii* there – well over a century old – are the size of beech trees and truly grandiloquent) as almost nowhere else in this country. Their scent embraces you at some distance. They are eye-wateringly expensive plants but the preciouses I would chose would be the very smelly *Michelia* (*Magnolia*) × *foggii* 'Allspice' and also *Michelia* (*Magnolia*) *doltsopa* – by their own reckoning one of the most stunning and scented trees at Caerhays Castle gardens.

Orange is such an important smell. Orange blossom makes Mr B swoon. He longs to live an orange grove rather than an apple orchard for all his yeoman tendencies. And yet, he is sniffy about skimmia, already discussed, pittosporum and Mexican orange, all flower-bearing shrubs that waft the smell of neroli. Neroli is an essential oil produced from the blossom of the bitter orange tree (*Citrus* × *aurantium*), very orangey but with perhaps a leaden metallic quality. The smell of orange blossom, however, is indescribably beautiful, narcotic, and so elusive it can only be plausibly extracted by 'enfleurage' – the laying of the individual waxen flowers on to a soft fatty wax which draws out the scent, inhales and keeps it prisoner.

The gatehouse from the orchard

PITTOSPORUM TOBIRA

A dense evergreen semi-hardy shrub for growing in sheltered parts and London. Flowers in late spring – April around here, although in the Mediterranean you may be assailed by cuffs of its orange smell much earlier. Terminal clusters of creamy flowers almost smell as good as real orange blossom, but it is mixed with some of the bitterness of orange leaves. Despite its fragrance, the bush in general is somehow unpleasing to me.

MEXICAN ORANGE

Someone told me a very good thing: it is not particularly necessary that all parts of your garden should work all the time – something I also have always felt; they said that gardens should be like a Mexican wave, different bits standing up and then sitting down again. However, Mexican orange, *Choisya ternata*, is one of those all-time 'do-ers'. It is a super-shiny, bright green, evergreen small shrub, having fistfuls of leaflets that have a strong, pungent, sappy, but almost repugnant smell, nevertheless somehow pleasing to sniff. This strange aroma is mixed with the orange neroli-like quality which gives it its name. It explodes from oil-glands in the leaf if you pick and separate the pretty white flower clusters in late spring, when they look great in a jug. Native of Mexico, yet hardy in the British Isles, it was introduced at the very end of the nineteenth century and county councils have never looked back.

Return from working in Norfolk, stopping off to buy bundles of asparagus too delicious not to eat on their own. Poplars flashed and shone after the rain. A matchless evening falling under a full moon. Wisteria follows us in through the front door; the house still harboured the cold of several days ago, stony in its must.

The meadow is turning into a salad of vetch, juicy moon daisies, dandelions and crisp young thistles. Weeds are very important 'smellers' in their earthy distastefulness. The recoil from elder, the stench of slashed nettles, chickweed and goose grass, all smell of sap and chlorophyll. It seemed to me I could smell the essence of plants, so utterly different to us, the chemical processes turning sunlight into sugars; sugars that feed, sugars that smell. It is a long-laid-down layer of our consciousness, perhaps long lost, and for some never experienced: the rubbing of stings with acrid dock juice, bitter daisy juice recoiling in the mouth when chain-making, blenching when assailed by the unexpected draught of fermented moist silage under the fresh grass clippings – central olfactory experiences of the world, vivid and embracing.

Everything is so new. Wet-look leaves. Filmy fog early in the morning. Everything is pumping, dividing and replicating. I truffle around weeding fast through dusty iron nettles and tangy thistles, cardamom of fennel, myrrh-flavoured geraniums, marvellous mint; the low-down smells.

There is a rosy smell hovering in the air which must be lilac and viburnum. Close to, the viburnum is more medicine cabinet, but way out it is there assailing only the subconscious with something so floral and full of sun.

VIBURNUM

Viburnum carlesii seems to me to be among the best to grow for the scent of its flowers; together with the deciduous *V. × burkwoodii* 'Anne Russell' and also *V. × carlcephalum* (whose leaves are less downy and colour red in autumn), these are the ones. There is also

V. × burkwoodii 'Park Farm Hybrid'. Deciduous and rather gawky but rounded in habit, they are all very hardy and accommodating medium small shrubs about head height. Dull green leaves are made duller on the underside by starry down. Bean describes the flowers as 'well filled' terminal rounded clusters and as 'fertile' (as opposed to being false and infertile as some 'flowers' are) and 'charmingly fragrant'. I would call them 'milky' coloured, sometimes stained rose. The trusses of *V. × carlcephalum* are pink in bud but rather lumpy, later than *V. carlesii*, which starts flowering in April from buds visible from autumn. *V.c.* 'Aurora' has red buds opening light rose and those of *V.c.* 'Diana' are slightly mauve, with young leaves slightly chocolate coloured which can be off-putting.

Viburnum farreri was said by Reginald Farrer to be the best-loved and most widely grown of garden plants in China, which explicitly reminds one that we did not 'discover' any of these plants, but we were excited to collect and propagate them. It is extremely hardy here and flowers from November through winter. Walking round a garden with a friend she said, as we were almost knocked over by the emanations of a huge old viburnum, how integral it was in her head to the warp and weft of her growing up, year after year; that smell, so domestic and its returns so happy. Bean describes first seeing seed collected by Farrer flower at Wakehurst, Sussex, in the winter of 1920, and it having a 'very charming heliotrope fragrance'. Bean is astonished that it was not introduced sooner; a dried specimen at Kew is logged as coming from St Petersburg in 1835. He sounds a note of caution, however, about its variability from seed leading to very inferior varieties getting abroad. This, and the dingy brown-purple of its leaves, may account for my disappointment with it. I have never consciously planted it, for all its smelly reputation.

Wind coming from the east this morning. My dawn window panorama is rolling backwards, left to right, bearing a lowering chill. Soon after seven this morning the gash of electric red opened above the dockyard as the sun's chariot prepared to rise over HMS *Bulwark* as she glittered under the working lights as she has for nights and months. The stars melted as light intensified in the arc above the Navy when, cartoonishly, a submarine-shaped cloud came forging south, from the left, stubborn with concentration. Half an hour later the morning halo had shut down, the day clamped in battleship grey.

Blossom time
Lopped dead lavender and rosemary, creating clouds of turpentine, a studio smell, clean and astringent; this effusion continues even while cutting back the caryopteris. Return of the pleasure givers: swallows and blossom. Savour the moment. Apple blossom – Eleanour Sinclair Rohde says individually apple blossom has almost no scent but, in the mass, in the great orchards of the pre-war southern Britain about which she writes and which she nominates as one of the unspoken wonders of the world, the blossom creates an 'invisible soft cloud, exceeding sweet although delicate'. Where have all the flowers gone?

Picked the first German iris, and inhaled another sort of art-room smell: inky, pencil shavings and smelly rubbers while eating illicit sweets. Then there is the root, the orris root smell that comes when you are weeding and digging around the *Iris pallida* beds. Almost impossible to define, in the scent business it is used as a fixative of scent as well as for its smell, which is chintzy, vanilla sugar, sunshine, earth, white chocolate, sperm even.

The wisteria, azaleas and a Portugal laurel are in flower – the last almost stinky sweet, but rather good dilute, and unexpectedly embracing and comforting in an urban side street, just as boring old cherry laurel can be.

Do people dream smells? Not I, and not that others tell you so. Research regarding people's reaction to fire suggests that nobody smells smoke whilst they are asleep. They wake up because they are suffocating, and then they smell the smoke which hangs low by your face in bed. For this among other reasons fire officers insist upon smoke alarms. You don't taste in your dreams, do you? But I think you do touch.

WISTERIA

The many species and hybrids of wisteria, whether they come from China or Japan, are all scented to some degree and divinely beautiful. Monet was transfixed, and I return with undiminished awe to a black-and-white photograph, in one of Miss Jekyll's books, of Japanese ladies beneath curtains of long-tailed *Wisteria floribunda* trained over water on bamboo. The Japanese have a total affinity and understanding of wisteria, akin to their feeling about cherry blossom, which makes our suburban houses clung with mauve seem almost tawdry. In Japan the arcades and pergolas are acres wide and furlongs long. The leaves of wisteria are almost as appealing as flowers; thus, it remains a great plant when the flowers are gone.

Wisteria floribunda is native to Japan; you can imagine it like old man's beard cloaking streamland woods, and it's hardy and deciduous. Interminable racemes of flower hang down yards or metres in the cultivated form. The choice of colour in wisterias is for me uncomplicated: I like them wisteria-coloured and not pink or even white. So often the idea of white is great, but in this country the likelihood is that bits of it will go brown and, as with lilac only more so, this disturbs the purity and beauty of the overall effect.

Wisteria sinensis, Chinese by name and origin, is to my mind the supreme scented climber. It will grow up a house or structure however high or long. Here at Trematon it swags for 30 metres/100 feet along the battlements. To flower best it needs to be treated like a vine and pruned to a framework stem with flowering short spurs. Flowering earlier than the Japanese, the flowers of *W. sinensis* are more susceptible to frost damage, though rarely in these climate-altered times. Frost can turn the grape-like bunches of violet flowers into dirty old nylon tights overnight, and that year's smelling is all over. Valiant second flowerings in August are more often produced after such a setback, and the following year is likely to benefit from this natural pruning and be superabundant.

In the oldest specimens, planted around the time of its introduction at the beginning of the nineteenth century, the trunks and stems become colossal twisted reptilian monsters devouring masonry and ironwork. The Chinese twist is anticlockwise whilst the Japanese is clockwise.

Today's pick of addictive scents is lilac, pheasant's eye *Narcissus poeticus* var. *recurvus*, and the first rockii tree or moutan peony. The peony, with the deep mulberry splotches, at first smells of cream cleanser, leaving a keenness then a rose sensation. Mr B says the white tree peony we grew at Hanham, *Paeonia ostii* 'Feng Dan Bai', the white phoenix, is superior, smelling of cold chocolate paper. He also thinks that the later-flowering pheasant's eye has a more compelling scent than the

Motte and bailey, honesty and euphorbia

74

earlier *Narcissus* 'Actaea' and is a better meadow plant, being more understated and better timed to flower with the apple blossom.

So hot today. It is a thrill to see cowslips bejewel the high field where there were none before, returning by themselves, through husbandry not sowing or planting. In five seasons of hay-making, raking and taking off the small bales in high summer they have multiplied tenfold.

Got back at the end of an exceptionable hot spring day after interminable motorways and roundabouts, to find the house nestled in the gloaming, stone warmed. Poured a drink, rolled a cigarette and went for a roam round the garden. Much on mind, much anguish, friends in peril, garden silent but for an owl in the dell. The dell darkening. The magnolias faded and fallen. Everything lowering into cool blue-black green, only white tulips, tree peonies and *Viburnum carlesii* surface in the gloom. The orchard floats mysteriously above, apples and crab apples, and, returning to the right angle of the house, the stone radiated the captured sun like a night storage heater. Clock ticks in the bathroom and Bacci the Patterdale barks at a dog fox.

Last night we talked of the first summer that we planted tobacco plants in the small dusty beds we made under the south-facing windows at The Ivy. (The Ivy was a derelict, crumbling, magnificent baroque pile of a house near a roundabout in Chippenham, Wiltshire, which Mr B had bought and in which we used to squat whilst in the process of restoring it in great romantic discomfort, without electricity or running water.) Two old 'Souvenir de la Malmaison' roses and a couple of old blush Chinas had survived all the depredations of the house being boarded up and left to rot by developers. These stalwart plants responded gratefully to our attentions by flowering their socks off once we had remade the beds about their feet, adding compost and manure. And in these beds for our first summer we put tobacco plants grown from seed. No tobacco plants planted by either of us since have given back in the same way. The combination of our first summer growing things together, the sunniness of that year, the laze and escape from a long winter in Edinburgh, all combined to fill these beds with childish hope. There was no other garden, only mountains of earth dumped daily by eight wheelers and pushed about occasionally by a herculean digger. This was a garden made without cynicism or flourish, a garden built on hope. Or so we saw it. Our nostalgic conversation ran on to the Chelsea Flower Show and how it reminds us of school: the same dread competitiveness, gang-yness, same show offs, same herding and herd instincts.

Mr B smelled the wisteria and felt filled with a wonderful warmth and well-being that sprang up inside him.

Good Friday

The bees are happy. No colonies lost over the winter. The air is humid and heavy with scent, the garden a salad of rising sap. Pink cockatoos of *Magnolia* 'Star Wars' squawk on their boughs, slight foreigners in the woodland now that the floor is a mirage of campion and bluebells suddenly. The bluebells have doubled up each year since we sacked all the sycamore seedlings and let the light in. Somebody somewhere has lit a slash and burn bonfire; it smells of abandon, bin liners, mattresses, papers.

Easter Sunday and the crab apples are flowering madly. *Malus floribunda*, a super-floriferous crab apple, has notes in its delicate blossom of mock orange but also a gym-shoe rubbery quality, a characteristic of fruit blossom. It's a white

Syringa vulgaris 'Monge'

smell, one of the 'powdery' smells. When I was little there were acres of cherry between us and Didcot, grown in industrial straight lines on flat ground, quite boring most of the year, but we would walk them in blossom time and, I now remember, on Easter Sunday.

The artist Angus Fairhurst once enlightened me as to the reason we love regimented orchards so instinctively. He said it was the geometry: that way that the still points move as you move through the matrix, like viewing the terracotta army; the fruit trees slide and fold, vanish and emerge, swing round and move up. Angus ended his life in a wood.

Last night I walked out to collect the rugs from the tent and noticed for the first time the waft of cow parsley, which slides on the cooler air from beneath the walnut tree, down through the bars of the golden gate, down the steps and into the garden. This is a smell that anyone would recognise and connect with this time of year if you were able to bottle it, and yet we are barely conscious of it. The scent of cow parsley is comprehensively there. It comes to you through car windows, not distinguished or striking, but understatedly insistent, and it sits in the lanes and lowlands. Just as the day length alters incrementally and affects our lives substantially but invisibly, so too the content of the air in our nostrils changes daily, sometimes suddenly, sometimes blindingly. On Friday the cow parsley was only half grown and today it is broadcasting from its Jodrell Banks of umbels, sun-tracking, heat-seeking. Christopher who was with us said of the smell of cow parsley in the orchard that, whilst he cannot like the smell, its association with late spring, early summer, an upbeat mood, was so potent that he could not help but love it.

To Tetbury, which was *en fête*. Returning home, we burst through the wicket gate to be assailed by the smell of sponge cake just wrestled from the oven. It was so powerful, the sweetness, the sponginess, that seemed to come from the wisteria, but maybe it was just our lust for a strong cup of tea. Smelled the honesty this morning. Tangible as a cobweb brushing one's face.

CANDYTUFT & SWEET ALYSSUM

The happily named and easy-to-grow annual candytufts, *Iberis umbellata* and *I. amara*, are out of fashion but shouldn't be. *I.a.* Hyacinth-flowered Group, *I.a.* Giant Hyacinth-flowered Group and *I.u.* 'Iceberg' can be done from seed sown where you want them to flower next summer, if sown early, or under glass from September. These knee-high bushy plants are from the same family as wallflowers and stocks and their pink, white and lilac corymbs smell similar – a warmly powdered icing-sugar smell. Another old timer, sweet alyssum or Alison, *Lobularia maritima*, is a perennial usually thought of as annual, of the same group, to grow from seed. Good for children to grow, and as edging.

Back to bluebells, the smell of young girls, of the shimmering of the sky under trees. The inestimable scent of Keats's 'darkest, lushest blue-bell bed' from *Endymion*.

> 'Tis blue, and over-spangled with a million
> Of little eyes, as though thou wert to shed,
> Over the darkest, lushest blue-bell bed,
> Handfuls of daisies.

Pear blossom and greenhouse

Overleaf: Oak obelisks, 'Pink Perfection' cherry, honesty

This Whole Experiment of Green

Soon will the musk carnations break and swell,
Soon shall we have gold-dusted snapdragon,
Sweet-William with his homely cottage-smell,
And stocks in fragrant blow;
Roses that down the alleys shine afar,
And open, jasmine-muffled lattices,
And groups under the dreaming garden-trees,
And the full moon, and the white evening-star.

Matthew Arnold THYRSIS

May Day, and the sun rises just before six over Wistman's Wood on Dartmoor in the north-east, working its way round all day to the north-west and the highest point in the Tamar Valley, Kit Hill.

There is no lovelier sight in the half-light of woodland than lily of the valley. Pollinators of the Lepidoptera find comfort in the still meads and wooded valleys where scent is captured; they follow the scent molecules closely, flight unbuffeted in the protected and relatively still air. The very imagining of early-summer sunshine and cool north-facing banks awakens a yearning inside one for those very English days when the summery-ness is as fragile as a new-spun line of web, tensile and treacherous. These are the vibrant moments, fed by all those desires of which one is mostly so oblivious. You realise that earlier in the year, when 'elsewhere' thoughts invaded the brain, it was not a place you yearned for, not Tenerife or Tucson, but a time; time for lying in the sun, on a bank sniffing at the wild thyme, the vigour of the earth. *Convallaria* is a native gem, a lover of light woodland and possibly poor soil or else it will run all to leaf. 'The Conval-lily is esteemed to have of all others, the sweetest and most agreeable perfume; not offensive or overbearing, even to those who are made uneasy with the perfumes of other sweet-scented flowers,' wrote John Lawrence in *The Flower Garden* (1726). All variants are inferior in scent to the common form.

LILY OF THE VALLEY

Convallaria majalis is one of the most loved of scented perennials, spreading underground by rhizomatous roots. It grows in drifts of pointed edible-looking fresh green leaves in pairs. Flowers are crisp cotton white, bell-shaped and lobed, like fairy night caps, up to thirteen of them on a long arching stem. Native of light sandy or limestone woodland in Europe and North America, it is contrary as to how it grows, what it likes, and getting it established seems more to do with luck than attention. It should like partial shade and a moist soil with added leaf mould ... but, having failed to get it going in just such conditions, we are trying it at the base of a hot wall, as Mary Keen had it in her

Lily of the valley spears

garden at Duntisbourne Rouse, the opposite of woodland conditions. Whatever it is that it likes, if it likes you it will spread in mats, into your paths and your paving. I think that this capriciousness makes for its abiding allure.

The smell of *Euphorbia mellifera*, the Canary spurge, is akin to the moment in beekeeping when, upon lifting the lid of the colony, the smell of honey can rush out, strong and singular. The plant is gawky, and old plants here are unpleasing but Mr B says it is not a priority to take them out. If only they were the honey spurge, *E. × pasteurii*, which is miles better looking. I like the sound of one 'Phrampton Phatty'. Spurges generally smell skunky, to deter predation by goats in limestone hills of Istria, Dalmatia and Greece, homeland of my favourite *E. characias* subsp. *wulfenii*. Neither Mr B nor I liked this plant when we started gardening: we put it in the 'Star Trek' bracket of plants that look too alien. Now we 'boldly go' and plant it wherever we can. We must have become more 'plantiferous', a dangerous condition where the botany becomes more interesting than the aesthetics, which is absolutely legitimate, but not what we are after. With us the picture we paint and the mood created always rank above rarity, collectability or curiosity. But after a while a fondness grew for the irradiated green bracts and that smell in spring. None to be found at Trematon when we came here; we planted them in several different places and some were simply blown out of the ground. Come spring it was heartening to smell them, filling the air and foxy like a den, something of roast chicory about the whiff – not that it is smoky, more a smell of throbbing life. And the plant is so handsome. Remember to cut off their heads after flowering if you want the plant to bulk up rather than produce seed. I like them to seed in the gravel so I leave a head on each plant, but remember also that they are all violently poisonous – for spurge think purge – and the milk is caustic to touch and hideously painful in the eye. In Cornwall it is best to grow them in well-drained gravel; we even dug trenches so that they and the yew balls we planted could avoid the drenches and the torrents would run away.

Unconsciously we made a gravel garden: with euphorbias we put *Iris pallida* subsp. *pallida* and *Dierama*, angel's fishing rods (a fantasy of mine rather frowned on by Mr B), as a broad extension to the peony beds. People's reaction to the suggestion of more gravel in their gardens is, understandably, muted horror. Who wants to wade through acres of sterile Chesil Beach like most people's front drives? First get the gravel right: it should be compacted hoggin with a dusting of tiny pea gravel or washed shingle if possible, and then plant stuff in it. Plant verbascums, euphorbias, box, dieramas, irises, eryngiums, all sorts of things Beth Chatto-ish which will self-seed and dance about. Better still if scented.

Back on the euphorbia front we have been also been trying something quite different with them in the wet wild meadow bits here, copying the garden at Spilsbury Farm, Tisbury, trying to grow *Euphorbia palustris*. This euphorbia once established can compete in long grass, coming up like mouth-watering bolted lettuces along with bulbs in early summer. They can be completely cut down at the end of the year. Christopher Lloyd wrote that 'the whole inflorescence sparkles, especially towards sunset. It loves a heavy, wet soil, and will outlive us all as a perennial.' Well I hope he is right because they take a long time to get going.

The woodland path down
to the creek

84

SPURGE

Euphorbias can be annuals, perennials, shrubs or succulents, with milky sap and small flowers held within cupped, often electric green bracts. The apparent flower of *Euphorbia* is a condensed inflorescence known as a cyathium, but it is the whole plant that smells.

Euphorbia mellifera is a woody species from Madeira and the Canary Islands, with brown, honey-scented flowers, opening in May. It is tender but commonly grown in the South West. In Pendrea near Penzance it has been recorded as growing as high as a first-floor windowsill, so really a tree, and indeed it is allied to *E. dendroides,* the very beautiful tree spurge which grows on the dry rocky hillsides close to the Mediterranean Sea. For the bee-, wasp- and hoverfly-attracting scent and much less woodiness, *E.* × *pasteurii* is the more handsome of its forms and the cultivar 'John Phillips' is an erect, robust, evergreen shrub as big as a one-person tent. People like it for its red tones especially in autumn.

Euphorbia characias and its subspecies *wulfenii* are widely distributed in the Mediterranean, including North Africa. We like *E.c.* subsp. *wulfenii*, but there are innumerable cultivars called 'Humpty Dumpty' and other indicatives. It is a sub-shrubby evergreen plant waist to head height, and forming a dense thicket of erect unbranched stems, more herbaceous than the woody nature of *E. mellifera.* Native of Istria, Dalmatia and Greece and introduced here some time previous to 1837, in which year it flowered in the Horticultural Society's Garden at Chiswick.

The marsh spurge or milkweed, *Euphorbia palustris*, is a bushy herbaceous perennial that grows to waist height. Native from southern Scandinavia to Spain, the western Caucasus, western Asia and western Siberia, it dies down completely in winter but is truly hardy. Pushing up come spring it has straight, electric-green, leafy stems topped with terminal clusters of buttery lettuce-green bracts. These look luscious for months and bow out to form a sort of basket in winter, like a round woven hide or nesting ball for some marsh bird, unless you top it, which you can.

It is boom time today. Pinks are about to burst and blow scent along the path, peonies about to clot the head with cold cream and comfort. New-turned earth. Sap rising relentlessly. Bluebells, bloody hell! The homely, cottage smells of early summer. There are others, michelia, magnolias and *Rhododendron luteum*, but none so good as the bluebell. Easy to miss, the almost imperceptible smell of blossom floats from trees flowering madly everywhere. Below the orchard trees are the sun-tracking recurved faces of *Narcissus poeticus* var. *recurvus* and primroses lie abed with the cowslips. I lie with them trying to get the dog to settle for a moment. The dog smells good.

Arrived home late last night, wind had dropped, rain had stopped, full moon and the back yard bathed in the almond whiff of cherry blossom. The good old flowering cherry 'Pink Perfection'; poofy pink snowdrifts on the gravel, the sheer wet quilted quantity of petals smelling sweetly in a mass, almost as good as the lost orchards of the West Country, one of the wonders nobody even noticed whilst they disappeared.

My friend the VMH gave me some *Narcissus* × *medioluteus* dug up from her own garden. She is passionate about old varieties of daffodil, rescuing them from oblivion, and has made a huge collection. VMH has lost her sense of smell, a misery, but is interested in my scented plants project and wondered what I thought

Dryopteris and hart's tongue in the woodland

of the scent of *N. × medioluteus* – which means 'mildly yellow' indicating that it is much more cream coloured than the poet's narcissus. It is a naturally occurring hybrid between *N. poeticus* and *N. tazetta*, known here since Gerard as primrose-peerless; it was found initially in the west of France. They are indeed primrose yellow, more like a tiny dancer, but as late flowering as the *recurvus*. I told VMH that it is deliciously peachy smelling, like a top bath oil. *N. × medioluteus* is not offered by many nurseries but Christine Skelmersdale of Broadleigh Gardens offers it and writes about finding a small wild belt on Lundy Island. The Tazetta sold as *N.* 'Canaliculatus' is similar and easier to get. VMH is also fascinated by the 'Tamar Double White', which was one of the mainstays of cut-flower production in the valley here. It flowered at Whitsun, so late, so lovely white, so highly scented, that it was perfect for bridal bouquets. After the Second World War it became affected with eelworm, the scourge of all commercial growers, and died out.

Lily of the valley and single stocks: what a knockout. *Matthiola incana* are possibly my favourite thing. I can reliably grow masses of them from seed, which feels like a triumph to start with. But now you cannot ignore it, when they sound their smell horn on misty May mornings and again in the evening; it is their call to worship for bees and moths.

STOCKS

Matthiola incana is a form of the wild stock that is easily grown from seed, forms a branching subshrub with rosettes of slightly cabbagey grey leaves about 80 centimetres or 2½ feet tall, which can last more than three years. Flowers cover the plant in April and May, either snow white – 'Pillow Talk' – or those sold as Ten-week Rose and Ten-week Crimson, which are a mauve pink and a deep purple. Collect your own seeds and sow with heat in winter for flowering the first year. I no longer bother with growing annual double-flowered Brompton stocks because perennial single stocks are handsome, live for several years and smell even better. *M. longipetala* subsp. *bicornis* is the night-scented stock which I would not be without, although it is contrary: sometimes a huge success for no trouble and sometimes a rank failure. Scatter in cracks and gravel and in a few weeks you will have knee-high straggly grey plantlets with deliciously scented night-opening flowers for months. The old trick is to sow them with Virginia stocks, which have slightly more showy flowers that open in the day.

An enormous number of common names of wild flowers are smell pointers. Sweet woodruff, sweet cicely, honeysuckle, sweetbriar, meadowsweet, clove gillyflower, dame's violet, remind us just how much the unknown countrymen who named these beauties valued their nose-able qualities.

DAME'S VIOLET

Hesperis matronalis is the dame's violet or sweet rocket, a short-lived perennial about waist high usually. Leaves form a hairy basal rosette up from which come the flowering stems. Evening-scented single flowers appear in terminal clusters on the branching stems in May and are most often white or shades of lilac. A cottage garden plant with a cottagey old-fashioned smell.

HONESTY

If you don't like the sugared-almond shades of white and pink through to violet, the bulk of scented flowers are not for you. Recently, strains of honesty, *Lunaria annua*, have been selected for their intense purple-ness with a lot of red in it, and for strains which are much nearer to clear blue known as 'Corfu Blue'. These are even lovelier than the common flower, but I like the common best where it just springs up in a farmyard or driveway. There is no gardening can improve upon it. Mr B thinks the colours are most enjoyable when mixed up so that the variations are evident and remarkable. The perennial form, *L. rediviva*, I have always found capricious and disappearing. I love the biennial more for its generosity of flower, variation in colour and big moon seedheads. I like the mix, all the diverse shades from white, lilac, periwinkle, mauve, plum, mulberry, scenting the air about it better, I think, than the perennial. Ours are all hybrids and mongrels which may be why they smell, and the smell is very similar to other spring-flowering *Cruciferae* such as dame's violet, wallflowers and stocks. The seeds are prolific and their cases beautiful; the common names often refer to purses and money (*monnaie du pape* in French) as well as the moon, for they are silver, and moon shaped. They self-seed with loveable determination.

Old friends

A tap on the shoulder: the first summer iris – I think it is called 'Blue Satin Ruffles' – snuck up behind me this morning and breathed an efflux, totally unexpected and utterly familiar. As if hugging an old friend, I sank my nostrils into the lustrous blue. Like a very famous painting it almost thumped me with its familiar genius, with the soufflé smell of life, heart, southern heat. If only one could paint the pelt of its braided beard, the sulphur heart among azure falls, but at least one can smell source of the savour.

Returned from trips to Norfolk and Sussex late to find that the freshly baked sponge smell emanating from the wisteria, even after weeks in flower, is not over yet. Each inflorescence is in the 'stormy skies' moment, lowering grey and mud violet. Wish there would be a storm. Norfolk was parched and windy, Sussex heathy and hot. Dropped my bags and trotted round the garden. Early philadelphus has come out. The Banksian rose sprigs the ashen walls with foliage and buttery pompoms. Lilacs are still good but only just. They are phenomenal in Norfolk where one imagines the more extreme and continental climate suits them, as it does irises: baking and freezing.

Treat beyond treats, *Magnolia sieboldii* is out at the end of the long walk, covered in lanterns and smellable at a distance, all the more refined, more lemony and less rubber sole. Also, *Hesperis matronalis*, which makes the heart leap with a homely sweet smell, like violets in the heat. Irises are massive and peonies about to come out in a rash. Mr B has conjured up a winning, flaming combination of French lavender and rusty orange rock roses whose corten petals spot the gravel as leopard skin. All so different from where we were working near Haslemere, whose woods and copses still swoon under sweet chestnut with bluebells and reek acidly of fern and moss, the iron bark of rhododendrons and azaleas.

Occasionally I open the door of the Shepherd's hut, a redundant den, just for the waft of endless possibilities that you get from such neglected places; old hay, camp bedding, fallen glasses, guttered candles.

I was just now stunned, almost knocked sideways by *Rhododendron luteum*, by the snuff-like pouf off it which immediately fell away to nothing. I put it in water to come back to … desiring it ardently. I want to plant a passage, a sunken lane, a hollow of it in which to wallow like a hippo. Mr B says it is a river smell, rusty and elemental. It is all these things but for me they are mingled with guavas and melons in the gutter.

I have an abiding problem with rhododendrons, stemming from the only real time that I have spent among them, at St Mary's Convent, Shaftesbury, Dorset, in a landscape dominated by their brooding evergreen presence. They grew in such immense quantity, all the way down the drive, which was a full half mile, all through the two combes between which the monstrous Hogwarts towered, and all round the north side of the school, the kitchens, the gym, the labs. Some rhododendron flowers smell of nectar and honey but the overall effect of massed plants for most of the year is what I call the iron smell of the bark, the leaf litter, the deadness underneath their swampy mangrove branches, where we made our dens. Flanks of high rhododendrons made outside the school dark, and just as the inside smelled of polish and cocoa, the outside smelled of the Himalayas – I suppose (I have not been there). The other day I remembered – maybe it was after smelling rhododendrons – that we wrote AMDG, an acronym for the Latin *ad majorem Dei gloriam*, 'To the Greater Glory of God', on everything. Every single spelling test and maths equation pencilled in chequered exercise books was dedicated thus. And in 'Handwriting', a timetable 'period' every afternoon from the age of ten to fourteen, we did it with a flourish. I think I lost faith when I took up physics, chemistry and biology, when magic became less potent, or at least turned into an interest in extrasensory perception, very much a fascination in the era of Uri Geller and Gary Glitter. As teenagers we described ESP as being 'deep' – the ultimate accolade, and what I would now perhaps call being intuitive. We had a lot of time on our hands, television being restricted to a few glorious sweet-sucking hours in the common room at weekends – the original *Poldark* with Robin Ellis and *The Professionals*. We never grew out of den-life in the Rhodo-den-drons, because they simply became places to smoke and drink and talk about 'deep' things. I loved school, so this rhododendron thing shouldn't matter, yet it is very dominating still, and not in a good way. When it comes to rhododendrons, I am caught in a time warp. I know other people have this about lilies and death scenes, about pine woods or heather.

Never seen oaks so bearded as they are now, dripping with flowers frilled by miniature fists of leaves. I brought some in to put in a jug on the table and shed-loads of pollen soon blanketed the surface, a luminous mud green.

At Trematon, we have a 'smelly tunnel', so dubbed, lovingly, not because it is rank but because it is a conduit for the 'smelly' planting on either side of it. The tunnel part is a stone vault my height and the length of a bus stop which runs under the bailey wall between gatehouse and motte. On the side facing east is the orchard and it is early warming but cool thereafter, and the other side is a sort of canyon between house and motte where the drive curves round. Here we found and extended some good planting beds, cool and dewy until the sun comes over the curtain wall, sun-trapping and radiant until late at night. The cool side we have to work on; the unusual philadelphus are possibly not warm enough and sulking, but we inherited a rhododendron labelled 'Polar Bear' which is flowering hugely.

Matthiola incana 'Pillow Talk' in bed with *Erigeron karvinskianus*

I wondered whether it was actually this cultivar because the books say that it is a late flowerer, from July to September. I did not realise that any rhododendron flowered in September, but I have smelled it in July and recorded it in my diary notes. Each flower is a monumental trumpet and eerie white. The smell drifts in all directions and it has a slight toffee or caramelised aura. I was confused by it at first, dazed by its force, although is very ladylike and smells of rustling dresses. I find it magnetic, drawing me in with its lure of lemon and peaches, almost ersatz, like instant creamy puddings from a packet. You think it is a boudoir smell: grown-up, sophisticated, but soft as swansdown. Close to, however, it gets a bit fairground: cheap perfume and candyfloss. I cut some and brought it indoors where three days later it is still pretty, apple-blossom pink and white, scenting the room spicily with added levels of pepper and nutmeg. This year, though, I have realised that we must plant more smellies from the Rhodi family on the east of the smelly tunnel by the gunnera and the Black Prince's long-drop. We should plant a grove of them, extend the flowering time, and then we can swoon amid the white wings floating on its pheromonic scent. Maybe they will work down the drive and in the dell; maybe it will end up like St Mary's, only they will all be white, and all be scented.

Trematon Castle has spilled itself so thoroughly everywhere in the garden that the naturally acid rock soil has been neutralised by the lime mortar, yet there is a discernable *terroir* of acidness. And you can smell it. Just as you can on Fernden Hill outside Haslemere where we are working, or in the New Forest. This is a very significant thing. The geology of one's chosen plot, one's daily environs, is a nuance somewhat lost on city dwellers.

I remember that the potting shed by Grandmama's veranda smelled of blood fish and bone, of paraquat and diquat. My father said to be careful of paraquat because it looked very similar to Robinson's Lemon Barley Water. Parents, however well-intentioned, are very odd in their thinking, for after that I was forever afraid of lemon barley in case it was paraquat in disguise. I think what he meant – because in those days everybody, quite rightly, re-used everything – I think his real fear was that the paraquat might have been put in a Lemon Barley bottle by Dickinson the gardener. Fear of poisons lies deep in the cerebral cortex, deep in the sense of smell as a warning system. We all twitch at the admonitory smell of arsenic that is bitter almonds, the smell of gas, the smell of sulphur and ammonia. I used to get up in the night and check that the warfarin, used for rat infestations, was in a safe place when the children were small.

Mid-May

I am reading Nabokov writing about the smell of butterfly wings on his fingers. A lepidopterist, he was regretful about his collecting, about the destruction involved, but he was clearly driven by this and other less savoury compulsions. His powers of observation are what make what he had to say worth listening to. His writing is very good on the subject of smell, and as a scientist he noticed and recorded much with a gimlet eye. That the powdery scales of butterflies, the scales that make the wings opalescent, also smelled of lemon and vanilla was a finding he published in the 1930s. This was between the first reference to it in science, at the beginning of the twentieth century, and the scientific corroboration of his observation in a full-blown study at Oxford, using many butterflies, ten years later in the 1940s.

White *Allium nigrum* with stocks and Dalmatian iris

The scent of butterflies is now, over fifty years later, beginning to be understood in evolutionary terms.

The first burnet rose bud opens, one of a million buds, with the purity and strength of rose scent. When the *Rosa spinosissima* (now *pimpinellifolia*) 'William III' is fully open next week, if the sun shines, it will irradiate the kitchen garden and the helium balloons of its scent will knock into you as you get out of the car. Mr B says this 'William III' would be astonishing if you were growing it in the South of France, because of the unlimited sunshine and heat. There are so many roses, and I think one might include many David Austin hybrids, that are best in a Mediterranean climate, Californian equally, where the pellucid summer is over very quickly but its glory and scent are all the more intense. There is an argument though that the occluded humidity and gentle warmth of a slow Cornish summer nurtures scent and, of course, lasts longer.

The *Iris pallida* subsp. *pallida* spears have been open since the weekend. Already the first ones are curling up into tricorns or blue samosas. Unopened, they stand ready as blue lipsticks or rolled umbrellas. The scent is almond, Italian cakes, clean, uncomplicated as the flower itself which has lilac tongues like gas flames, hiding chrome-yellow bristles on its falls. Up close where the bee sucks, this understated flower offers a purple zebra-skin 'Welcome' mat.

BEARDED IRISES

Rhizomatous border plants with familiar and invaluable sword-shaped fairly evergreen leaves, irises have been much developed by breeders, particularly in the last hundred years, to produce prodigious variety in colour and 'remontant' qualities, which mean they can flower again in autumn. Scent, as in most plant breeding latterly, has not been a priority and I feel they have lost much elegance even since the days of the artist and iris breeder Cedric Morris.

Their origins in the limestone hills of the Mediterranean give the biggest clue as to what they like. Drainage above all, lime, gravel and scree. They are fabulous in almost anywhere on our eastern seaboard, but they sulk rather in the wet south west and can be a struggle to keep going. We have to scrape the winter crop of moss from their root stalks every spring.

Iris pallida subsp. *pallida*, however, is generally easily grown and such a delight. Flowers of the surest, clearest blue emerge from papery white bracts and come in a daily succession for as long as a month with rigorous deadheading. This is no hardship for five minutes on a May morning; gazing at them, inhaling the smell, is a pleasure in all weathers. Gerard says the scent is much like the orange flower but more vanilla. I think that it is much lighter, but it induces the same heady hedonism. Its older subspecies name, *dalmatica*, explains its origins. The root is one of the forms of orris, which means it was once grown in acres and acres of Tuscany and Croatia. Sadly no longer, although it survives as an escapee in many Tuscan gardens. The pharmacy and perfumery of Santa Maria Novella, established by Dominican friars in Florence in 1221, gained notoriety for its use of the rhizomes of iris. They were not the first – Greek and Roman writings mention it – but their perfumes, cordials and powders contained liberal doses of this rare and precious substance.

The value of orris was not so much for any scent that it harbours, which contains a compound called irone that is faintly violet smelling, but as a fixative, holding other

Wisteria sinensis

fragrances or flavours in place through chemistry. The irone contributes a missing atom to the lightweight compounds that constitute other scent volatiles, thus slowing down their release into the air, holding it to the skin. Many people are allergic to it. But none of this chemistry was understood by monks or Romans; perfumers and distillers would only have understood that the rhizomes had to dry for two to three years before they become effective as a fixative. We now know that it takes that long for a slow oxidation process to occur, bringing about the organic chemistry (in the technical sense) that causes irone to form. Only about 173 acres of orris are grown today in the whole world, either *Iris pallida* subsp. *pallida*, grown in Italy, or *I.* 'Florentina', grown in Morocco, China and India. *I. albicans* is also used in orris production. To extract the orris, the rhizome must first be pulverised and steam-distilled to produce a waxy substance, *beurre d'iris*, from which an absolute (a fragrance substance produced via a solvent) is extracted using alcohol. Orris absolute is used in the making of gin, and in many other spirits. The resurgence of artisanal ethical production for the luxury market has seen a tiny rebirth in the orris fields of Italy.

Of the bearded hybrids, a group chosen for scent over and above colour and form might be 'Before the Storm' – deliciously dark with a fitting chocolatey smell; 'Champagne Elegance' – ruffled peachy with orange blossom smell; 'Clarence' – delphinium blue, very smelly; 'Dusky Challenger' – glamorous loads of iridescent scented flower in violet from the very end of the spectrum; 'Immortality' – a seemingly endless succession of glistening white scented flowers; 'Rajah' – late flowering, and like a mulberry-coloured velvet waistcoat embellished with gold frogging, wafting in a cloud as exotic and spicy as an Indian prince should smell; 'Red Rider' – a very tall flowerer in plum red with purple midribs and mustard beards and just as show-off-y in smell; 'Titan's Glory' – the deepest lapis colour. For those who crave mahogany brown, 'Natchez Trace'; and with it 'Sultan's Palace', which looks and smells akin to a fruity claret.

Iris graminea, the plum tart iris, is a May-flowering bulbous iris. A curiosity I have not yet grown. It is a tiny thing, rich damson blue in colour, and smells of August and

95

warm greengages. The clumps of upright leaves look like its cousin, the winter-flowering Algerian iris. It is equally undemanding, even thriving in grassland and meadows, but endangered in its wild habitat which ranges from Spain to Russia.

Rosa 'William III' was playing hard to get. I thought maybe we had been imagining its scent, exaggerating the memories, and then this morning I was dashing up the ramp to the car and it punched me in the face. It boxed my nostrils and my brain. It is like fancying someone: when they are not there you begin to think you are imagining it, and then when you see them the response is like falling overboard. Some smells ambush one with unexpected intensity and force.

Peony 'Rubra Plena' (*Paeonia* × *festiva* 'Rubra Plena') has a dispensary smell but without the rose-like hints in the scent of other herbaceous peonies. But the pleasure is all in its being the first to flower, along with the acid yellow Molly-the-witch (*P. mlokosewitschii*), which has a curious non-smell, by which I think I mean that very many flowers smell of florist shops, vegetal, green, cucumber and this is pleasant but perhaps it isn't 'scent' which, practically speaking, is a combination of nectar and pollen designed to attract pollinators.

I go out in the twilight because Mr B is pulling out goose grass in the gloaming. It has rained all day, finally petering out about an hour ago, light washed, greens saturated. Smells everywhere of fresh-sawn applewood, like the eglantine rose but with bark. I join the goose-grassing, irresistible as well as essential if we are not to be inundated, drawing the threads out, desperate not to miss any. As the light diminishes, the bluebells become inkier and the greens meld into black. Birds banter on, but less urgently.

Pulling goose grass all the next day with Nicola, who gardened so hard with us for three years I think we exhausted her; god she was a worker, never a break or even a cup of tea in her routine. The hazy sunshine brewed into a Burmese sultriness by the afternoon. Smells pumped up; hawthorn on the brink, cow parsley clinical as the smell of propolis mingled with smoke and honey when checking the bee colonies. Tearing at the squidgy green goose grass I'm unable to identify a smell for it other than that 'non' but vegetal smell I just mused on, but when herb Robert comes with it a clementine zest is released, a green tangerine smell of some deliciousness.

Magnolias in May

Two magnolia things. One is that we are planting them again now; this is the best time, for they respond and recover from any damage we may do to their fleshy roots much better when they are in active growth and sap flowing. We planted *Magnolia* 'Heaven Scent', a huge hardy late-flowering one for May, and *M.* 'Apollo', which has had its rose-smelling violet-purple-turning-rosy flowers already; Also a popular recent New Zealand hybrid called 'Star Wars' which is big, scented and flowers young. 'Juvenile' flowering has been an aspiration of magnoliophiles since forever. Until recently many of the best ones made you wait thirty years to see a flower – not really the modern person's timescale. But in recent decades New Zealand breeders have cracked the problem. You can now have huge exotic flowers, such as my favourite *M.* 'Atlas', on a three-year-old tree. Pungent is the scent of their roots, gaseous shellac and turpentine exuded when we damage the

Rhododendron luteum

96

scented roots in spite of all our efforts at care. Presumably if one plants them earlier, in the cold, this smell is not so evident.

The second thing was a visit to the late Dr John Naish's garden, Algars Manor, at Iron Acton. So rare to see untouched barns, honesty, lilac, garlic, bluebells invading, despite perhaps it being a bit too much 'aboretum' trees for me and Mr B. We don't like 'tree zoos' and I was really chuffed to find out when reading Colin Tudge's *The Secret Life of Trees* that trees don't like being in a tree zoo either. They like to hang out with their relations, in clumps and gangs of botanical families. But the magnolias were stellar, and the stars were *Magnolia × loebneri* 'Merrill', *M.* 'Pinkie' and a *M. obovata* (syn. *hypoleuca*) which was huge. *M. liliiflora* 'Nigra' smelled so good; we have it at home smelling of gym shoes and putty mixed with rose essence. Oddly if you take a bud and open it up slightly, put your nose inside and smell, it's gorgeous, but it doesn't smell when fully opened or on the air at all. Ungenerous flower.

First grand rose, 'Climbing Etoile de Hollande', which I picked and put in a bowl with *Magnolia sieboldii* – a great combination of weird and wonderful; these hanging lanterns of May.

Picked the first opening sprig of *Philadelphus coronarius* and put it together with a sprig of lemon verbena, which I now am supposed to call *Aloysia citrodora*. They complement each other well, the sweet sherbet lemon and the mango fruitiness. Picked the big black iris called 'Sable'; it smells like old French houses or hotels – is it lino or something like it? Then the rice-pudding bowl of a 'Festiva Maxima' peony, milky with a tang of dispensary, cleansing and compelling. Finally picked for Mr B a rose, *Rosa* 'Climbing Devoniensis' that he planted by the front door. We took it in turns to bury our faces in its quartered papery petals; weary from work, the experience was something akin to entering an air-conditioned diner by the side of a hot dusty highway. It was instantly cool, and its breath was watered and smelled of apple pie, floor cleaner, starched table cloths, paper napkins, gleaming surfaces. All in a rose? Mr B agreed: all that and much more.

Because the family is quite old, magnolias have survived many geological events (such as ice ages, mountain formation and continental drift), and their distribution has become scattered. Some species or groups of species have been isolated for a long time, while others could stay in close contact. To create divisions in the family (or even within the genus *Magnolia*), solely based upon morphological characters, has been a nearly impossible task but recently, using DNA sequencing, phylogenetic studies have proved that, scattered as they are, the bull bay in the US and *Magnolia obovata* in Japan, not to mention their ostracised cousins once banished to the name of *Michelia*, are in fact very closely related. Dating back 90 million years we can see the similarity now proven by the electron microscope but we can also smell that they are related. The theory is that, developing before the arrival of insects let alone flying insects, their attractions are focused on the fruity fermentatious smells beloved by beetles and ants. *M. sieboldii* attracts me greatly. Today it has a smell that is watery lemony but fruity and exotic, powdery and warm; mahogany red stamens and a rough mahogany smell of opening drawers. There is definitely a 'through leaves' forest-floor-ness about the smell, almost fern and bracken at its heart. It is a tennis-shoe scent of rubber plantations which speaks of heavy rain in an exotic forest.

Magnolia grandiflora begin to open now. To bend a woody flower stalk and bury one's face deep into the huge, cool, alabaster bowl, and to draw down the first draught of its fruit cup, is the end of the beginning of summer. An intangible watery quality rushes from it, quenching the mind. They are magnificent, stupendous, profoundly exotic and primeval. Robin Lane Fox writes of the scent that 'it has an ingredient all of its own'. He claims he 'cannot describe the strength of the resulting mixture,' but he does so brilliantly: 'the smell of stone – like a great pillared church, so cold it makes you shiver even in August.' The fact that it is both torrid, yet chill, lissom and waxen yet adamantine, makes it beyond compare. Clearly beyond my powers of description. Like so many voluptuous smells it is fugitive, fleeting. I cannot get enough of it. One moment it is aqueous, deliquescent, close to the waterlily, the next it is spicily fruity, citrus, guava, melon, fig and banana left in the gutter at the end of market. At the same time, it is woody, new-cleaved mahogany and leather and wet limestone. Picked on the point of opening it will unfurl, in a progression of strange jerks, over two or three hours, sitting splendid by the bedside looking like a foghorn. What can it be like to be a beetle in this cathedral of sensuality? Vita Sackville-West describes the texture of magnolia petals as 'dense cream', 'ivory suede' and 'thick paste'; endlessly fascinating even as their perfection bruises, browns, creases and ceases. Bean rates it the finest flowering evergreen tree; he says that the bark when crushed emits a 'pleasant aromatic odour', something noted in all magnolias and their roots.

LATE MAGNOLIAS

The most scented magnolias are the summer-flowering ones. Of the group that flower first, and which I would describe as having white lantern-like flowers and this remarkable but rather rubbery scent, there is much confusion. The differences are subtle and botanists must forgive my ignorance. From my understanding of Bean this group includes *Magnolia sieboldii, M.s.* subsp. *sinensis*, and what my friend David Vicary called the 'Watson and Wilson Mags' of which *M. × watsonii* – and you need the brain of Sherlock Holmes to get this straight and remember it – is now called *M. × wieseneri*. But nobody in the trade bothers to be so specific and you are lucky if you can find any of them in nurseries but the *sieboldii*. I love the habit of all these as shrubs, love the flowers, which hang more or less pendulously, like Lalique lamps, and love the smell. I find it compulsive. The genus was named after Pierre Magnol, Professor of Botany at Montpelier until his death in 1715. More than half the species are tropical, but all the hardy ones have been triumphantly brought from Asia and the New World to hybridization in England.

Magnolia sieboldii can grow to the height of a small house and is hardy and smelly. I have grown them with enormous pleasure; they grew fast at Hanham, which means that they seem reasonably lime tolerant, and then one day they died. But I have seen huge forgotten ones not only in acid Cornish gardens but also in the middle of oolitic Bath. The most distinctive characteristic is the glorious maroon-crimson disk of stamens. Native of southern Japan and Korea, probably first introduced to Britain around 1879 by Messrs Veitch of Exeter – who sent the Cornish brothers Thomas and William Lobb, as well as many another including Ernest Wilson (of *M. wilsonii*, 1908) on plant-hunting expeditions in the wild. Bean explains that the 'flowers are not always borne in one crop but appear often a few at a time from May until August on the leafy shoots'.

Magnolia sieboldii subsp. *sinensis* is a very similar shrub, friend of cool woodland and native of western Sichuan in China and is perfectly hardy; it was discovered and introduced to the Arnold Arboretum by Ernest Wilson. I think it more beautiful and fragrant than *M. wilsonii*, which is more often found in British gardens, but it is hard to tell them apart. They should all be planted more because *sinensis* even thrives on chalky soils. A very similar shrub is the cultivar named *M. wilsonii* 'Highdownensis', received by the late Sir Frederick Stern at his arboretum at Highdown in 1927 from J.C. Williams of Caerhays. They were seedlings from a pan whose label had been mislaid, so the seed-parent of the Highdown plants is unknown. Bean says that 'Dr Spongberg reduces *M. sinensis* to the status of a subspecies of *M. sieboldii*'. I love this: 'Doctor Spongberg will see you now!' – but am I any clearer?

Magnolia × *wieseneri* is a thing of loveliness. A deciduous shrub or small tree like the others but of stiff habit and – here's the point – flowers like side plates, with a strong aromatic odour. This magnolia is probably a hybrid of *M. obovata* (a staggering thing) and *M. sieboldii*. It first appeared in Europe at the Paris Exposition of 1889, when it was exhibited in the Japanese Court. Bean is sniffy about these plants: 'like many imported Japanese plants, those originally introduced were badly grafted, and many of them died'. Hence they gained a reputation for being difficult when they are not, he says. In the wild of the Hokkaido forests the *M. obovata* are the height of our beech or lime trees with ginormous leaves and powerfully scented goblets of flower in July.

Magnolia 'Summer Solstice' is another child of *M. obovata*, a hybrid which is sensational in the gardens at Caerhays in late May and on into June right at the end of their opening season. The whole concoction is a pudding; thick suede-textured ruddy buds open to a clotted creamy bowl filled with rich crimson stamens with yellow anthers, and the whole smells of exotic guavas and tropical fruits. Although never one to enthuse, Bean calls it 'one of the most beautiful of all northern trees both in leaf and flower, this magnolia is also quite hardy. When young its habit is open and sometimes rather gaunt.' It is deciduous and often the leaves are barely out when it begins to flower in late May.

Magnolia liliiflora 'Nigra' looks like all the early magnolias, but flowers in May and June. The flowers are a dark deep purple, hence the specific epithet one would imagine, and also clearly lily-shaped, and freely given on what is eventually a medium tree. It is very hardy and reasonably lime tolerant.

Evergreen magnolias, locally know as bull bay trees, crossed the Atlantic from the southern states of America in the early eighteenth century, *Magnolia grandiflora* being the most famous. Polished dark green leaves are intensely reflective when healthy, with snuff-brown felted backs. They are hard as leather boots. *M.g.* 'Ferruginea' – meaning in a sense 'iron-clad' – is even more rusty and fudged with felt. The flowers are bisexual. They flower from high summer until October, singly at the end of a shoot. In late summer, particularly in a good hot summer, seed pods like bulbous warty cucumbers split to show red orange beans attached to the carpel by a silk-like thread. The evocatively named *M.g.* 'Goliath' really does bear gargantuan pearly white flowers, beauteous beyond belief and just as pungent as the species. *M.g.* 'Exmouth' is said to be the earliest to flower and possibly the hardiest. Its story is worthy of repetition. The original seedling tree grew in a garden at Exmouth in Devon and, at the end of the eighteenth century, was a rare sizeable surviving specimen. Almost all of the first *Magnolia grandiflora* planted in Britain in the early part of the century were struck down by the great frosts of 1739–40. Demand was way beyond attempts at re-introduction from the wild, and nurserymen came to the 'Exmouth' tree to 'rent' it for layering, selling the new plants for a whacking five guineas a piece (in 1768; this would be equivalent to about £680 today). The tree was accidentally felled in 1794.

White honesty and broad beans

On a great May morning, drinking my way round this garden has the trippy-ness of religious ecstasy. The Holy Trinity of spring for me are sweet rocket, honesty and single stocks. All three are of simply no interest to plantspeople but were always cottage stalwarts. Some dislike the preponderance of mauve that spreads across the beds, but we are not fussy. We are happy with everything lilac-coloured. Along with white hawthorn, fruit blossom and narcissus, what salmagundi could smell better?

Hawthorn is deeply superstition-ridden. Its rose-like flowers being hermaphrodite, this allows for easy transference of pollen by small flies drawn in by the scent. This is a heavy, complicated scent; it has in part a clinical, dispensary smell, the distinctive element of which is triethylamine, which is also one of the first chemicals produced by a dead human body when it starts to decay. On the other hand, triethylamine also smells like semen; hence the positive association of hawthorn with wild springtime romps in the fields. In the open it is a bright and breezy smell, almost like background noise, when confined noisome maybe, but sharp and clean.

HAWTHORN

Hawthorns are trees and shrubs, nearly all deciduous, and they nearly always come more or less armed, formidably, with spines. *Crataegus monogyna*, the common hawthorn, consists of two very distinct forms now usually regarded as separate species. No other tree or shrub is better suited for stock-proof hedging; it fills a unique place in the English landscape as the fundamental constituent of tens of thousands of miles of hedgerow. The naturally grown hawthorn 'has a singular beauty of habit', says Bean. 'When in blossom no object of our waysides has greater beauty, and its charm is heightened by one of the sweetest of open-air perfumes.'

Picked some *Silene vulgaris*, the bladder campion, for Mr B and agree it smells of hot metal on sheets, and something more plant based which is perhaps starch. It smells of hot ironing: it smells sweetly singed. We call it the 'ironing plant'. It is also very pretty, having fimbriated white flowers set off against very verdant foliage. It can be propagated simply by pulling up rooted sections. Also blooming in May and June, the white or evening campion, *S. latifolia*, has pure white flowers that – while not completely closed by day – expand at night. This and the fact that they are sweetly scented at night make them more attractive to nocturnal Lepidoptera.

Down at the apiary, a firestorm of activity. David, my ninety-four-year-old bee-keeping mentor, and I divided the colonies. David lives bees and all his things smell balsamic retsina-ish, of propolis.

Today was rain in May, and all the world smelt of cow parsley and tarmac. With tree peonies it is the petals that smell, which is unusual although rose petals smell too. The smell of *Paeonia rockii* is rose and satin, its buds are gorgeous and leaves handsome. The smell of *P. delavayi* I like but it has a rank element not unlike those May-flowering magnolias *sieboldii* and company, a rubbery aromatic oddness. The big blowsy tree peonies hardly smell sometimes, especially if they are seedlings, but the best *rockii* ones smell delicately of rose, with something like guava, taking one again into a realm that is almost sweaty.

Cistus × argenteus 'Silver Pink', *C. × purpureus*, Dalmatian iris

103

Balsam poplar is still ponging away. This point in May is like an ebb tide, spring flowering almost over and summer not started bar the *Philadelphus coronarius*, which is the best and earliest of the mock oranges.

The evening fell as a moody blustered dusk; the house is at peace and outside irises iridescent in the shadows – who cares what colours we chose, or the nursery sent? The watering is done, and the dog is fixated by a stoat in the wall.

Lit the fire tonight with it being so overcast and blustery, and the 'smell bath' of the 'William III' rose is nearly over. When it started two weeks ago it opened from a million pert buds. The pinnate hands of tiny leaves I would call 'ferny'. The whole effect is miniature perfection, like a doll's tea set. The smell has the purity of attar of roses and the strength. I never knew until recently that the word 'rose' is thought by some to come from the Celtic adjective 'rhos', which means 'ruddy' or 'red'.

The rose 'Climbing Etoile de Hollande' has been out for ten days; it's an early-budded bird along with 'Albéric Barbier' and I love it. Mr B thinks 'so what?'. Odd that we should react so differently to some things. The magnolias – *Magnolia sieboldii* along with *M.* × *wieseneri* 'William Watson' and *M. wilsonii* – have to my mind something mineral, sandy, mossy and man-made in their curious olfaction. They smell, as things do, of their *terroir*, sunny, sandy woodland, acidic and mossy. The anthers start, when vacuum-packed, a deep crimson exactly the colour of 'Climbing Etoile de Hollande'.

Found lilac still scented though mostly browned off of one side – maybe by yesterday's wind? It makes me feel 'planted' even in its mustiness. It's the indole (or indol) in the chemistry of its smell. Indole occurs naturally in human faeces and has an intense faecal odour. At very low concentrations, however, it has the flowery smell of many of my favourites such as orange blossom. But what is really interesting is that indole is thought to have similar properties to the neurotransmitter serotonin, and to melatonin, hence its 'well-being'-inducing qualities. Concentration is very important in flower smell; for pollinators it makes the signals very specific. A moth can smell one molecule of bombykol – the female pheromone – at a time. At our crude level of perception concentration makes the difference between the foul and the fragrant.

London in May smells quite fruity in the rich bits, the parks and the leafy streets. Paddington Station was empty at dawn. It is a grand space, one of the greats. Paddington smells of diesel, steel on steel, asbestos brakes, salty and acrid, with dust, sandwiches, newsprint, all wafted with bad coffee. My garden sleeps in my head.

Everywhere in the lanes and the garden hedges are great whorls of honeysuckle; wild woodbine, *Lonicera periclymenum*, primrose and pink fading into green, deck the walls and other shrubs. The smell is boiled-down hedgerow, liquid meadow, an encapsulation of wild flowers of open grassland and of sunny glades. A day smell, and a homely smell.

Up in the refined acid woods of the Sussex–Hampshire borderlands we remark on the finer mossier nature of the woodland grass here, making one think of Japanese gardens and pools of gin-clear water. And then there were the simple yellow azaleas pitched into the livid intensity of spring woodland. Back at home the rain overnight must have brought on all sorts; the delphiniums and Cooper's

Burmese rose (*Rosa* 'Cooperi'), awash with flowers suddenly from unnoticed buds – charming but scentless. But *R.* 'Rambling Rector' has opened a few buds, and the scent of myrrh is just detectable. Everywhere is flushed with scent, philadelphus rippling wafts across the border. Somewhere nearby is fennel, I must have brushed against it, a green smell, awakening, anise, cardamom.

Whitsun

Suddenly the lovely month of May is drawing to a close. Whitsun weekend is early. The year's most perfect moment. I stood this morning after rescuing a winter-planted *Magnolia sieboldii* from a flush of four-foot-high wild flowers which offered a ladder to the schmoozing monopods, the slug beasts, gaily munching my very expensive birthday presents.

My 'studio', which would be better described as a small primitive submarine, smells delicious tonight. I have honeysuckle laid out on white A3 pads waiting to be photographed. I have become more aware of nature's details through photographing plants this way, through this prism of the scanner. My fingers are jammed with the sticky ooze of honeysuckle in which I can see tiny flies and bugs caught. Pollen and propolis, gums, milks and powders are all part of the biology, engineering and chemistry of plants. Pollen stains so strongly that picture restorers tremble at the thought of it. For evolutionary reasons it is the finest and most potent disseminator and, no question, it smells. This I know from the beehives. It is strong powdery protein smell.

Came in this evening pockets crammed with smellies. So much burgeoning out there. Looked around for something in which to empty them, and found a great use for Tupperware. Opening it now in the quiet of the night I am assailed by the smell of apple mint. Rough stuff, hirsute and thuggish in a bed. It is a childhood smell though, chewing on gritty hairy leaves for hours. Delicious in flavour next to the mint is an astonishing peony, 'Duchesse de Nemours', with its cold, creamy, gypsum nature; the smell is flashed with lemon and utterly enveloping. Then petals of *Rosa* 'Roseraie de L'Haÿ' smell of citrus sugared with raspberry. *R.* 'Rose à Parfum de l'Haÿ' was bred from *R.* 'Général Jacqueminot' and *R. rugosa* for the rose-water industry of southern France and though not commonly found in gardens it is the most powerfully scented rose, with an old rose scent along with its cousin 'Roseraie de L'Haÿ.

Honeysuckle has been swooning in my office all evening, pearly moonlit buds I have been photographing in the dark along with the 'Devoniensis' rose. If you were to do a blind smelling of this rose, you would know by the smell that it must be the colour of clotted cream, gill-petalled, and washed with apricot, with, like many roses, a gin or fennel subtext.

On my desk for photographing are *Nectaroscordum* (formerly *Allium*) *siculum* subsp. *bulgaricum* – astonishing green alliums exploding in May and ageing gracefully throughout the rest of the year; they are a bit like trendy lampshades in the 1970s – but they do pong, being from the garlic family, and garlic is all over my hands: meaty, sulphurous, rancid. E.A. Bowles in *My Garden in Spring* (1914) wrote of it: 'A curious plant grows at the corner here … a tall, strange looking thing … one of the Garlics. It possesses the most pungent and evil smell of any plant that I know, and I enjoy breaking a leaf in half and getting my friends to help in deciding whether it most resembles as escape of gas or a new mackintosh.'

Dalmatian iris

Then I photographed angelica, a plant I return to regularly for photographing on account of its architectural engineering. It is also great in the border, although it self-seeds madly, but it is easy and delicious to weed because it smells so good. Today weeding fennel next to the perfectly pinkly cupped rose, 'Baronne Edmond de Rothschild', I noticed they both smelled oddly of star anise.

Cistus today smells hot, of turpentine and dark wood. It comes from thirsty hillsides growing in schisty scree. It employs a gaseous carapace of balsam, not only to fend off grazing animals but also, it seems, to protect it from the heat of the sun. The aromatic oils on the surface of plants like these evaporate into the air about them, which reduces dehydration in the leaves.

Everywhere smells of late spring, hawthorn and cow parsley almost over. I had forgotten how gluttonous the feeling of wanting to smell the outdoors can be.

Rosa primula, the incense rose, smells of Orthodox churches, shellac and incense when you crush the leaves. Sometimes it is reluctant, but after a shower on a hot day it will fill the air with a much more green, leafy smell, like the eglantine rose (*R. rubiginosa*). The pale lemon cups are luminous in bud, the scented foliage is feathery like a miniature fern.

My simple ambition is to pick a sweet pea on the 1st of June. I could improve on this with October planting and of course by doing pots-full in the greenhouse; that way one could probably have bunches in April. I think the autumn sowing thing is worth doing and I feel stupid and lazy not to do it. If one had masses of room one could experiment with extending the season from April until, when? Late October? Without full spectrum lights plugged in that must be the limit. But at the moment the first on the 1st of June is looking unlikely. Some years are hopeless, and better pea growers than I put it all down to light levels.

Back home everything is moving up a gear, summer almost here yet there is still lilac; Beauty of Moscow (properly, 'Krasavitsa Moskvy') is particularly wafting, a rosy white double with sparse flowers that picks and smells well and is so late.

Honeysuckle can be a source of disappointment in planting: so often they don't do very well, or they do well but they don't smell.

Rosa 'Albéric Barbier'

Today might be a July day, it is so hot and blustery. High hot winds from the south and westering clouds below. Garden pullulating with smell: the pulsating myrrh of *Rosa* 'Rambling Rector' on the ramparts; the swirling mock orange; mystic with the incense-laden moss of roses; the spice of differing pelargoniums; iris and orris; clove-laden stocks and pinks; French lavender. This storm of smell is topped with honeysuckle. Iris petals, known as 'falls', are flimsy, fluttering like bunting, and these petals are scented. Yesterday's spent *Iris pallida* blooms smell as I collect the dead heads to bring on successive buds. I sometimes wonder if this fierce training, this enforced flowering, might exhaust the iris, but it seems not, and we do cosset them with wood ash and bone meal both after flowering and in the spring run-up to it. *Rosa* 'La Belle Distinguée', a briar rose, plays with your sense of smell like a trailing veil, now to the left, now to the right, now full in the face like a hot towel, applewood scented. It is strange the smell of sweetbriar roses, it takes people differently, but to me it smells of apples and vinegar, acetylene and horse pee, along with something alluring with a warmth a bit like heliotrope.

Planting in the kitchen garden, I went among the salvia sweetness of the blackcurrants. They give off a bitter, leafy, compulsive but repellent smell which reminds one of Ribena mixed with tomato, sweat and guava. In this instance it came to me mixed with calendula, a smell attractive to white fly, repellent to green, but impossible to describe other than noting that it is oddly compulsive.

First pink and white 'King Edward VII' sweet peas, the essence of summer; lazy days, salad days, sweet pea days. In the apiary the 'flow' is on, and bees are working frantically – not that they use sweet peas for nectaring, but bean flowers and related clover, which they do love, are also out in force.

A gear change

It is warm in a different way. Definitely the beginning of summer, not the end of spring. There is a compound change in the smell factor; this is in a higher gear also. At last. The warmth is wholehearted.

Roses abound. We have grown *Rosa* 'Madame Ernest Calvat' because we read that it was as or more scented and more beautiful than 'Madame Isaac Péreire' – and it is. The first two are out today and gorgeous. Their scent reminds me of 'pressed silk', it gives one a giddy feeling, like falling in a dream. It was bred by a rose grower named Schwartz in 1888, the year my grandmother was born. Unlike my grandmother who survived the Spanish flu, Marie Calvat died of pneumonia in 1896 at the age of 37. I pick a first fist of roses; 'Albéric Barbier' has the scent of green apples and glowing warmth upon sniffing; 'François Juranville' has a rosy smell with apples, fizzy and fruity; 'Climbing Etoile de Hollande' smells of satin impregnated with lemon zest.

Mr B says hedgerow honeysuckle needs to be bashed to bits somehow to release the scent. He remembers picking armfuls on a camping trip to Wales when young. In a hostel that stank of disinfectant, everyone was so grateful to him. In the wind, at the right temperature, honeysuckle's breath of honey nectar is beyond compare. There is a newish honeysuckle called 'Scentsation'. Mr B says the smell is 'hedgerow near Hay-on-Wye'. It is proper woodbine. Honey thick and shiny and watery, bursting with bean field and pea scent. The flowers are huge and luminous, green-white in bud, like Pontic azaleas, deepening to

Rhododendron 'Lady Alice Fitzwilliam'

butter, almost plastic in their shiny robustness. They have massive rubber-glove fingers; these lobes wave at you, it is prodigious in flower now, and the scent drifts on the evening breeze for a long way.

HONEYSUCKLE

Beauty of the hedgerow, woodbine – once, laughably, the name of a cigarette brand – *Lonicera periclymenum*, is a deciduous or sometimes evergreen climber, usually with twining stems and peeling bark. Used since the Bronze Age as rope. Honeysuckle is the smell of summer in the hedgerow. The southern European *L. caprifolium* has a long nectar tube only fit for night-flying Lepidoptera, whereas *L. periclymenum* – hailing from northern Europe and the British Isles – has a shorter tube, and as observed by Shakespeare there 'the bee sucks' and the day-flying butterflyers and hence it scents the daylight hours. John Parkinson (botanist to Charles I) in his *Paradisus* (1629) thought that 'although it be very sweete' it was best in the hedgerows 'to serve the senses of those that travel by or have no gardens'.

The flowers are described by botanists as pentamerous, a succinct word meaning having five parts, and appear in axillary pairs, or in whorls (another great word) subtended by bracts and bractlets. This means that part of what we think of as the flower is in fact a modified leaf, while the actual flower is the corolla tube, most commonly forming two lips at the opening, and changing with age from white to yellow. The nectar is to be found right at the bottom of this confection and often only a night flying hawkmoth with a long proboscis can get at it. There are species from all over the globe, in rainbow colours, generally scented. The leaves can be shared with the larvae of white admiral and marsh fritillary butterflies. Being woodlanders they like their feet in the shade and heads in the sun. Sometimes I have been disappointed by honeysuckles I have planted – this may be the reason: their feet were too hot. Placing them needs thought because, if they get hour or two of sunshine in late afternoon, come evening they will emanate warm fruitily scented oils. *Lonicera periclymenum* 'Graham Thomas' is the old favourite, and the modern one called 'Scentsation' does what it says on the label. The hirsute Etruscan one is good – *L. etrusca* 'Superba' – very smelly flowers turn into gleaming red berries. All honeysuckle fruit are poisonous to us but good for garden birds. *L. periclymenum* 'Belgica' or the early Dutch honeysuckle flowers sooner with a watered sugaredness. Later comes the more spicy *L. × americana*. The Japanese honeysuckle, *L. japonica* 'Halliana', can overwhelm the back door on a summer's evening.

Pulling weeds in the Magic meadow, Mr B comments how often 'weeds' smell meaty and unpleasant.

Big downpours; everything shining; wet lawns; barley waving; ashes fully out; all the wet tarmac smells of summer. The next day smells of cucumber skins and radishes torn from cakey warm earth and the bearded iris smells of furl, furrow, limpid wateriness.

Philadelphus coronarius is really flowering. The loveliest of the mock oranges to my thinking and it flowers for a month. It is truly orange-blossom scented, and the tooth-yellow petals hold the smell just there, nearby the plant, but driftable, so it is great on a corner or near a draught coming through a gate or a doorway or a slight tunnel made of plants. To begin with it awakens a thirst for orange water, makes me think of a lighter version of the more sonorous smell of *Magnolia grandiflora*. There is a hint of the finest fresh white pepper, something like lily of the valley, an aldehyde, definitely the old sophisticated kind of smell of scent made from real flowers. I have a bowl of *P. coronarius* with *Rhododendron luteum*. I had never realised that they flower together – partly because they generally grow in such different types of garden. But this bowl of mango and orange blossom is quite as delicious looking as it is knockout smelling.

Scent hunting adds another dimension to life: it's the quarry, the flowering moment, the collecting thing that the magpie brain unsettles for. However, the search has added jeopardy: the flower may be there, your timing may be perfect to admire the beauty or bashfulness, but you may not be allowed in after dark when it chooses to scent the air. The garden is fuming with philadelphus today. The border is a laundry room of peony smell about my feet.

RHODODENDRONS & AZALEAS

Three different groups of rhododendrons are renowned for their scent: the deciduous azaleas; the tender scented rhododendrons with large white flowers, often called Maddeniis; and the tree-like evergreen rhododendrons with pale flowers, of which the most familiar are the Loderi Group cultivars. The Maddeniis are especially useful in areas such as California and Australia, as they are more heat and drought tolerant than the other groups; they also make excellent pot plants for a cool conservatory. Part of the charm for me of the scented rhododendrons, and particularly azaleas, is that scent does not predominate in the bonkers-coloured ones – thanks to the preferences of moths and other invertebrates, the scented members of this family are white, pink, buff and mango coloured.

The Pontic azalea, *Rhododenron luteum*, is a hardy, deciduous, medium-large shrub which can be the size of a bungalow. The species is most memorably banked along the Moat at Sissinghurst in an unforgettable scented mass planting. It is easy to grow, it can be almost invasive, as it runs underground, but only if you have the right conditions. This I remind myself after every failure, and I have had a few. In our latest attempt here they all turned black, as if burnt in a forest fire, but so did other things in that part of the garden. It clearly likes sandy acid soil, but I have seen it in neutral soil where there is plenty of humus. The azalea *R.* 'George Reynolds' is a cultivated large variety, with globby large heads of buttery-streaked orange flowers. To my eyes and nose this is not a patch on the species.

I think the names of all the conservatory rhododendrons, grown for their gorgeous smelly white flowers in winter and early spring, give a clue to the cossetting they require. Of the half-hardy ones who really need to be under glass, except in Cornwall where people do it just to get them to flower for Christmas, *Rhododendron* 'Lady Alice Fitzwilliam' produces masses of pink buds opening fully florally scented and white and probably the best behaved. There are many of these 'Fragrantissimum' hybrids with lots of posh names. They have never kept going for more than a couple of years in our house; one day perhaps there will be time to re-pot and nourish them, take them out and show them a good time, and give them the high maintenance and treats they demand. *R.* 'Countess of Haddington' makes a shrub taller than me, with the usual dark green scaly undersides to the leaves of her class. Her flowers in April and May are big funnels of fruity scent, porcelain-white of complexion with a rosy blusher and mascara-ed anthers. She is irresistible. *R. fortunei* subsp. *discolor* is a huge 10-metre/33-foot hardy evergreen with monster leaves like paddles, hailing from central China, which means it is tolerant of neutral soil and more heat. It is later flowering, and the clusters of tannoy-sized trumpets give off a sharper medicinal witch-hazel-edged scent that carries. *R. fortunei* was crossed with *R. griffithianum* to produce the Loderi Group hybrids which, as intended but not always achieved, feature the best qualities of their parents. The flowers of *R.* 'Loderi Venus' are the colour of a cabbage rose in almost embarrassing abundance, especially given the light frame and shy leaves of the plant. Eventually an enormous rounded shrub, it has a clinically refreshing fragrance. It is choosy though, needy for moist, rich, acid humus and delightfully dappled shade. All rhododendrons and azaleas do best in acid sandy soil and do best in pots if watered with rainwater and stood outside in a cool shady place in summer.

Yesterday we were in Somerset, sitting on a lawn thick with chamomile, drawing in that smoky, peaty smell, like a single malt whisky in a green meadow.

The Oriental poppy called 'Raspberry Queen' has made me a great picture. I notice in the 'submarine' whilst scanning it that Oriental poppies do have a smell, not a scent but a distinctive smell. As a gardener you know it well and you realise that it must be a pollen smell; those incredible anthers, weighed down with soot powder pollen, smell earthy and odd emerging from the furriness of bud.

Crambe smells like my morning drink of hot honey and vinegar. To encounter its discordant undertones of cabbage amidst the succulent mix of peony, rose and mock orange is not altogether pleasing. But there it is and it looks absolutely incredible. It is much harder to grow in Cornwall than at Hanham where it would have taken over. The bubblegum-scented *Philadelphus maculatus* 'Mexican Jewel' mingles with these other smells. Today's heatwave is providing the perfect conditions for the pungency of roses, a dream of the Riviera, all the aromatics in the wings – stoechas lavender, cistus, rosemary. We live in paradise regained, only we cannot seem to recognise that we are destroying it.

May Bank Holiday
Of course it is miserable. Windy with tin pan skies. The few visitors who came to the garden looked bravely cheerful in their puffa jackets and carried brollies. Mr B is in Dorset, planting all day. By the time he had drunk his tea upon returning, the sun was pouring into the kitchen window and we took some trays of tobacco and cosmos plants to the delphinium bed to plant together. It was sunny and muggy after the rain. Weeding can become a pleasure if you treat it as a treasure hunt. The smells are often absorbing, verdant sprays of goose grass, a musty spike of creeping thistle. The undercover agents are the Himalayan balsam seedlings, looking like legitimate border fellows. Turn your back and they will take over, but pinched and pulled out, even when small, they reek of watery autumn balsam. Cohorts of creeping buttercup smell bitterly as you rip out the running threads. Damn them! Fingers work faster, made furious by the audacity and effectiveness of hairy bittercress,

Today I went to London. Riding the Tube, I smelled the 1980s. I cannot tell you why.

Magnolia sieboldii subsp. *sinensis*

Overleaf: Battlement border

112

Summer Pudding

Cut grass lies frail
Brief is the breath
Mown stalks exhale.
Long, long the death.

It dies in the white hours
Of young-leafed June
With chestnut flowers,
With hedges snowlike strewn.

While lilac bowered,
Lost lanes of Queen Anne's lace,
And that high-builded cloud
Moving at summer's pace.

Phillip Larkin CUT GRASS

On June 1st, the sun rises behind the great belly of the Motte, above the walled garden at just after five in the morning. Even before Radio 4. The World Service is gurning on but there has been dewed light for some time before and all my garden bird friends up and about and trilling along; the finches, the tits, the jackdaws, the robin and the wren were not wasting a moment. At the other end of the day the gardening goes on forever, late into the evening, but on the first really warm evening we can stop, sit out and drink, drink it all in, and consider what Emily Dickinson called the 'old–old sophistries of June.' It is eighteen degrees at nine at night, pink cirrus in the north-west sky. I have dreamt about 'summer evenings' for seven long months. Henry James said that the two most beautiful words in the English language were 'summer afternoon'; perhaps he was right, for having time to do nothing earlier in the day is inconceivable. That is why these evenings are so precious, and so particularly Northern. For ten days from the solstice the sun will set after nine thirty and all the way round at Kit Hill, place of Kites in old English, only fifty degrees west of due north, beyond Callington, behind which lies Bude and the Atlantic Highway. It is still not dark when, just before bed, Mr B calls me out to see the moon borne on a chariot cloud in the west, inching over the house like a court masque. I walked the border, silent clouds of white stocks calling moths with wafts at my feet, and in the dripping long grass where the air is cooler there comes a smell which is green in the dim violet light.

Picked first 'Matucana' sweet peas in the eternal exhaustless freshness of the morning. They were self-seeded seedlings from last year, sprouted in the autumn where they fell by their teepees and got a head start. I popped them into my ponytail where the scent nudged me all afternoon. I gathered a bunch full on June 4th, the sweetness all the more intense after a ten-month wait. Sun-warmed water, soap suds, marzipan, marshmallows; treats of all kinds come to mind on sniffing

Paeonia lactiflora 'Peter Brand'

sweet peas. The first *Lathyrus odoratus* flower of the year is like the return of a great friend, usually alone and fragile, who has made it to your doorstep. A couple of days later, you might be able to pick six and proudly put them on the kitchen table. A week later the house is filled with them in every sort of vessel, like paint pots, like a flower show. The wait, the patience, the frost fingers, grappling with hazels, mania about mice, all becomes worthwhile.

SWEET PEAS

The Sicilian sweet pea, *Lathyrus odoratus* 'Cupani', named after Franciscus Cupani who sent it to England in 1699, and the larger, similar, *L. odoratus* 'Matucana' – whose origins are unclear – have, respectively one to two and three to four flowers on a raceme, winged, standard purplish red, keel and wings purple. These are the sweet peas for the ultimate nosing. So plush is the scent that it could be said to smell like a cousin of the gardenia, with which it shares an earthy, truffled undertone, a curious muffled mushroom flavour, unlikely and yet bewitching.

Research into the scent of sweet peas at Stirling University isolated six major constituents and twelve minor ones, but they could find no single note which makes the smell distinctive, which must be why it is impossible to bottle. All the ingredients have to work together: ocimene gives basil, hops and tagetes; linalool gives lavender, daphne and jasmine; phenylacetaldehyde gives rape and honey; geraniol gives roses and geraniums; nerol gives orange, and magnolia; citronellol smells of Damask roses.

Sweet peas, for all their familiarity, are not part of the old English world, not the world of Chaucer, nor Gerard nor Shakespeare; they came too late. The story differs, but it is thought that sometime in 1699 Cupani, a Sicilian monk, sent a few seeds to Dr Robert Uvedale of Enfield near London. Amongst the plants that came up, most remarkable was a twining pea that produced reddish-blue and deep-violet flowers and had 'quite an overpoweringly sweet smell'. Mediaeval illuminations show pea flowers but clearly the degree of perfume in this Sicilian pea was unheard of in late-seventeenth-century Britain.

By 1724 the Cupani type was being sold commercially and shortly a pure white version, now lost to cultivation; a pink and white version, known to us as 'Painted Lady', was growing in the Chelsea Physic Garden by 1737. Uvedale's plant collection was sold, upon his death in 1722, to Britain's first First Minister, Sir Robert Walpole, for his garden at Houghton Hall in Norfolk. Here they are still grown to this day from seed collected every year.

The familiar cottage-garden image dates from the early nineteenth century. In 1813, Keats captured the fragility of the small early plants, almost certainly writing of 'Painted Lady'.

> Here are sweet peas, on tip-toe for a flight:
> With wings of gentle flush o'er delicate white,
> And taper fingers catching at all things,
> To bind them all about with tiny rings.
> Training the trailing peas in bunches neat,
> Perfuming evening with a luscious sweet

There were five varieties by 1800, only six by 1837. By 1883 William Robinson rated sweet peas as 'perhaps the most precious annual plant grown', and the last quarter of the nineteenth century saw a wave of sweet pea hybridisation. Henry Eckford began seriously to select and cross strains to produce larger flowers and a wider colour range: the Grandifloras. In 1899 the wavy-edged father of the since dominant Spencer type was discovered by Silas Cole, gardener at Althorp House, who named it 'Countess Spencer' (though the plant may have emerged at other locations at around the same time). The Spencer type were subsequently bred over and over for the show bench. They were the sweet pea Royal Family, their scent apparently diminishing, though not their popularity, throughout the twentieth century.

Eleanour Sinclair Rohde's excellent book *The Scented Garden* (1931) does not mention them except in a reference to arranging them in vases with mignonette, about which she writes pages. Fashion is a fickle thing: mignonette languishes now almost unmentioned. A 'humble little weedling' having 'a certain wistful delicacy' and a scent beyond astonishing was Vita's verdict on the pea and in 1970 in *The Well-Tempered Garden* Christopher Lloyd said that 'the scent [of Grandiflora peas] was of a voluptuous richness, such as one had forgotten a sweet pea could possess'.

Scents of childhood

We have been working in an eastern county, back in acid woodland. For us both the smell is all wired up with the useless houses that harboured us at school. My convent was a Vinegar Baron's Edwardian fantasy of smoking rooms and endless tiled corridors beyond the swing door, where fittingly the nuns, the servants of Christ, lived in mysterious seclusion. Mr B was sent to broken-down establishments, run by broken-down men, recommended to his valiant father by venal priests. For him, the bits of prep school that he has not blocked out are ponds, chalk tracks, dens and gardens. In the smell memory a rich mix remains all redolent and golden, mud, stinky slow worms, grass snakes and grass tennis courts with their smells of creosote and whitening. He harbours a profound smell memory of some sort of white gumption for cleaning chrome; for polishing the Monseigneur's Jaguar. The Monseigneur was a high-ranking holy man who visited in a great flourish of leather-scented car – a smell Mr B still drinks in with happiness, poking his nose through the quarter light of any old parked up Jaguar. It was suggested that the boys might like to clean the gleaming British-made bodywork using a special polisher that was fluffy and soft and which they dipped into a tin that was extracted from the glove compartment (tabernacle of confined smells, boiled sweets and leather). It smelled acrid like the swampy azalea woods from which, filthy in their shorts, all the little boys had emerged at the purr of the motorcar. Such important visitation presaged a trip to the model shop afterwards, as a treat for the boys.

I feasted on the wild strawberries which colonise the concrete gutter along the back of the peony bed. Like a child I gorged on them, ripe and unripe, with handfuls of sorrel. My middle son can smell a single strawberry in a room, or a piece of pepper on a plate; we used to call him the super-smeller in a double joke which he groaned about. But it was clear that for him, particularly at the tender age of seven, the age when his father was packed off to boarding school, smells haunted and assaulted him, making him uneasy. He is very much a home bird; the one fateful skiing holiday we tried we ended up confined in the hotel for a week on account of avalanches, and Rex sniffed the napery like a gun dog, yearning for the simple white food he liked (rice cakes and edam).

Overleaf: *Rosa* 'Wedding Day'

119

I can only imagine that, for Rex, smelling strawberries must be a bit like my favourite thing about the Chelsea Flower Show, in the old days of the old marquee: when you entered at a certain corner you hit a wall of potent strawberry smell mixed, in the dimmer light, with the steamy smell of wet grass under canvas.

Sorrel, *Rumex acetosa*, smells and tastes tangy, citrus sharp and flutey green. Sorrel's filmy freshness means that it wilts before your eyes, before you can eat it. Sorrel could be cropped by my sister Fans and me from the beds and benches of the teetering greenhouse of my childhood home, as part of a morning's 'grazing'. How did we know what not to eat? A kind of children's lore. It was clear to us that the seeds of laburnum would taste disgusting and that only idiotic grownups would even think of eating them. I suppose my brother might have been tempted to boil some up on the enamelled cosy stove in our den, whilst we laboured for him scraping the beards of saltpetre from the walls for making his fireworks.

My brother's prep-school existence was a thing of fascination to us girls. It prepared him for a life of self-sufficiency and invention; there seemed less boredom to combat than our convent offered, although the whole thing was equally ridiculous. Being a scout possibly saved my brother, and made him Gandalf to us wide-eyed hobbits; we were his devoted serfs. In return we got danger and imagination. We built in brick and rummaged timber, rescued old stoves and used a pre-war vacuum to create a furnace in which we melted glass and lead and copper. We tried cooking snails and were disappointed. I had too tender a feeling for newts and frogs to want to roast their legs, but how plentiful they were. These days I get so overexcited if I see a frog. We skinned rabbits, fascinated by their full bladders and grass-soup stomach contents, which had to be excised, with noses held, before cooking in a pot with tulip bulbs. This was part of a game in which we pretended to be Dutch children in the war. Nettles were delicious and daring; that I could and did eat them was a good trick to subjugate cocky cousins and village boys. My memory is of being permanently peckish, which was why we smelled, tasted and ate everything we could. It was a world without 'snacks' – amen. Summer was therefore truly the season of bounty.

Summer pickings were infinitely better at our grandmother's because she had Dickinson the gardener and hence early greenhouse tomatoes, a fruit cage and a good variety of vegetables. Dickinson was the enemy: he was a veteran soldier and had long declared war on the grandchildren. Bent-backed and in a rage of pain, he knew that raw carrots and courgettes could be filched easily, but astringent goose-gogs, bloody currants and raspberries were enshrined in the fruit cage. Unguarded were the strawberries of the strawberry tree, *Arbutus unedo*, a strange fruit but palatable. The tree was the bearer of the tree house which we built under the tutelage of my brother, imagining we were on the River Kwai. At home my father grew marrows and artichokes which were less grazeable, but there were crab apples and sloes – both made you grimace – apples unripe and overripe, glossy red rose hips, especially the fleshy fruit of Rugosa roses which I still find delicious today. We ate rose petals, raw quinces, unripe sweet chestnuts, tiny green hazelnuts. We were wary of fungi, but again that seemed natural since they smelt powerfully weird and looked unappetising, except puff balls, which my father loved and fried in butter. He also taught us to make chewing gum by chewing ears of corn on our long walks along the Ridgeway. Deadly nightshade was an ever-present danger, just the idea of it. I only discovered recently that the reason it is dangerous is that every single bit of it is indeed deadly, yet tastes quite pleasant.

SWEET CHESTNUT

The sweet chestnut, *Castanea sativa*, is famous for its delicious edible nuts. The unisexual flowers are produced in long slender catkins, some of which bear one, two or three clotted creamy female flowers during July. The overall effect is magnificent, but many are off put by the flowers' semen smell. The whole plant smells softly musky in autumn as the nuts rot, halfway to the deliciously fragrant smell they give with cooking. As children, having unleashed them from their prickly burrs, we munched on them quietly for hours. The timber is not much used in Britain, except coppiced for fencing and turning. The remaining coppiced trees for this once-important harvest are still grown and fabricated into palings at Torry Hill in Kent. Veteran specimens are some of the most gigantic and characterful of parkland and hunting-forest trees, with distinctive twisting furrowed or runnelled bark. There are Japanese and American species of *Castanea*, but the sweet or Spanish chestnut loves the heat, being native to southern Europe, North Africa and Asia Minor. It was certainly in Britain before the Conquest, supposedly introduced by the Romans.

Completely connected in one's heads with childhood are sweet peas. Is it that they do smell of confectionery or on account of their being so easy to grow? Perhaps it is that the honeyed breath of all the pea family is simply filled with beatitude. The *Leguminosae* are a fantastic tribe. The wild peas are furze, gorse and broom. The agricultural peas are peas, clover and beans – 'Creamy bean flowers with black eyes and leaves like bored hearts', writes Sylvia Plath in 'The Bee Meeting'. The garden peas are wisteria and sweet peas. They have a 'day' scent that is uncomplicated and generous, best when it is dry and sunny, not in the evening.

BROOMS

The term 'broom' covers a variety of yellow-flowered species, many growing wild, all of the pea family and all scented, from our own gorse (*Ulex europaeus*) to Mediterranean broom (*Genista linifolia*) and Moroccan *Cytisus* (now *Argyrocytisus*) *battandieri* and also laburnum. *Spartium junceum,* the Spanish broom, is a hardy, vigorous subshrub. The stiff stems are green and rush-like, the leaves are narrow, few and evergreen, and it grows rapidly, and tall, resenting disturbance. It needs little attention, less luxury, and is tolerant of most things, growing well by the sea. Flowers come in fingers or clusters; they are chrome yellow, marzipan-and-coconut-scented and come better if it is cut back hard in autumn – imagine it has survived a forest fire. It is difficult to place in formal gardens but could be a good ingredient in a perennial prairie planting.

Another good ingredient would be *Genista cinerea*, one of the most desirable brooms, tall, hardy but deciduous with narrow rosemary-like leaves. Originating in south-west Europe, especially Spain in the Sierra Nevada, North Africa and the Canary Isles. It flowers in May and June in clusters scenting the air about. It is a legume, of the family *Fabaceae*, and smells like much of its family, broad beans, peas and clover.

Argyrocytisus battandieri is one of the first upright tree-like shrubs I grew as a climber at the base of a Bath stone bay at The Ivy, the derelict house we rescued in the 1980s. Being from Morocco it likes the warmth of a wall and the dryness, and the books say that it likes acid sandy soil. However, it romped away there, its yellow flowers smelling like pineapple fruit salad at the first-floor window. Its leaves are nicely downy, which gives the green a silvery tinge. It is quite awkward to place, but things that smell of pineapple are good to have around. I love the tender pineapple sage which smells of those cuboid boiled sweets called Pineapple Chunks.

Back home from London – which smelled great. Paddington Station is the best; those cast-iron vaults are never stale. To step off the train and smell London in this form of asbestos brakes, diesel, fluff, chewing gum, steel, paper and fast food is a heady metropolitan handshake. It will smell different when electrified. The Tube, oddly, was full of people reading the *Financial Times*, not their phones. Later crossing the Millennium Bridge, I smelled the sea.

June mornings

Dawn of incomparable lushness, everything loaded with the wet of the night and greyed over with dew. That absolute Madame, that mistress of a rose called *Rosa* 'Souvenir de la Malmaison', has arrived at last. Bury your face in this rose. Bury your nose in a bed of dew. When H.E. Bates wrote that gardens should be like lovely, shapely bodies, 'all curves, secret corners, unexpected deviations, seductive surprises and then still more curves,' he meant the whole garden I am sure, but he also meant the intimate world to be found within each flower. This rose is the perfect bosom, the décolletage, the cleavage of happiness, a cushion of silky petals, smelling of apples and pears warmed by the sun. You have to bow to it because it does not scent the air, but instead invites you in by its perfect seductive form, asking you really to eat it, creamy, fragrant, sweet and generous. It flowers on and off for maybe six months. It was bred and named for the magnificent garden of the Empress Joséphine. Clearly a sensualist, she had the walls of her boudoir rubbed with musk from the poor old musk deer because it was thought to be a massive aphrodisiac. This strange unguent continued sulkily to scent that room for over forty years.

There was a barren front garden on the way to the boys' school where Madonna lilies came up every year along a chain link fence. Bold and indefatigable. Mr B and I dream of getting them to settle in and clump up like that, as if in a Helen Allingham watercolour, but have never succeeded. And the smell is so much purer and more northern than any other lily, more like the native martagon lilies which have a great wild freshness, cooler, closer to melon rind and cucumber than their Asiatic cousins. 'It grew late. Through the open door, stealthily, came the scent of madonna lilies, almost as if it were prowling abroad,' wrote D.H. Lawrence. It pleases me in a mean way that the scent of all lilies is almost impossible to bottle, to harvest and commercialise. Mr B thinks he once made a potion of Eau Sauvage and Ambre Solaire which smelled like regale lilies. Their scent has an intensely narcotic aura, inducing a sense of receptivity and surrender, almost a feeling of being ravished as well as a longing for it.

Rosa 'Paul's Himalayan Musk'

124

Rosa Sir Paul Smith smells to me of cucumber – I wonder what the incomparable knight thinks it smells like. An Indian poet described a rose as 'a book of a hundred leaves unfolding' and this one fits the description. There is something about roses which brings out good feeling; their full-bodied beauty and their scent drive away melancholy, lifting the heart. I read that eighteen to twenty degrees is the optimum diffusing temperature for the scent of roses. This is why, in one's dreams, one would be growing roses in the South of France or Ninfa south of Rome where they would flower earlier at the time when this perfect temperature rarely falters. Here the gamble is much more dangerous, like a Thomas Hardy novel; rain, hail, wind, drought may all thwart your efforts and smash your precious blooms.

Geranium acts as a pick-me-up and wafts away fatigue, and jasmine is a shield against low feelings and an aphrodisiac, creamy, suave, and persistent. There is something about the smells of June being this fresh, grassy, dewy, leafy thing, whereas July smells are narcotic, hypnotic, sultry.

Though they generally looked battered and misplaced on windswept seafronts, I have discovered *Cordyline australis*, Torquay (or Torbay) palms, for scent. The inflorescence is huge, like loony candyfloss, and looks like it would never smell delicious. But it does. It smells utterly memorable, exotic, of hot nights and frangipani, night-blooming jasmine – the whole blooming lot in fact. And it drifts. It is astonishing, and I never knew it. Note to self: must get info about New Zealand and *Cordyline australis*.

The garden under rain smells musty but comfortable, of myrrh and wet fur, like many a dog room or lean-to. It is England at her *Black Beauty* best. The orange red buds of *Rosa* 'Albertine' are like 1970s lipstick, and the smell is a bit chapstick, with apple pie and melon. *R.* 'François Juranville' blooms in the same spectrum of fruity pink, but is very quartered. It has an intensified version of the 'Albertine' smell, less theatrical with more natural apple, and it flowers its heart out from now until forever. Tea-Noisette roses are lovable characters, being blowsy with scent, warmly stony in colour, and some of the best repeat flowering Ramblers. No wonder we smothered Asthall Manor with them when we did that garden. Throughout the nineteenth century, Noisettes were the only repeat-flowering yellow climbers. They were then eclipsed by shrill lemon and canary yellows, the fierce colours of the twentieth century, which are still difficult to use.

Philadelphus 'Belle Etoile' is flowering everywhere. It is the moment for all the 'philadelphi', among the most scented of all garden plants, at the top of Mr B's plant top twenty. His speciality is to use the little ones in beds and borders, such as *P. microphyllus*, small-leaved by name. *P.* Silver Showers (*P.* 'Silberregen') is another shorty, just above waist height, with strawberry-scented single flowers all over it like coffee froth. The great dew-drop flowers stacked on the stem end up weighting down the sprays, loading them with pineapple and bubble-gum.

Philadelphus 'Belle Etoile' and *P.* 'Beauclerk' are the large shrubs, their larger flowers have a plum blotch behind the anthers, their scent is more refined, spritzier, fly-away, delicious to nuzzle, it doesn't stick around in the air like the earlier-flowering tooth-yellow *P. coronarius* – the true mock orange with the inimitable smell so loved by Mr B. The most bing-bang-bongy of the bubblegum smellers is *P. mexicanus*. Everyone should try to find it and grow it. Mr B lights up at the strangeness of its smell, which is pineapple gone synthetic and haywire, and he loves also the gawky elegance of its habit, like a scruffy lurcher. Pruning can either be ignored or reduced to removal of the old woody stems to encourage new shoots from the bottom. In an ideal world the aim is to create a fountain effect using the arching stems, but most of us just let them grow into handsome bushes.

MOCK ORANGE

There are 65 species and cultivars, which I find muddling, but broadly speaking, these are hardy, drought-tolerant, deciduous, long-lived arching shrubs, and can form huge bushes or very compact ones. I always assumed that all philadelphus came from the deserts of the Americas, but it turns out that our crowned favourite, good old-fashioned *Philadelphus coronarius*, is native to the rocky hillsides of south-eastern Europe and has been grown here since the sixteenth century. The ravishing ivory single flowers can spread their orange blossom mixed with mango scent for many metres. It also turns out that species can be found in much of North America, including Idaho and Montana, and also in Asia and Japan. Carl Linnaeus, the Swedish botanist, physician, and zoologist, chose to call the plant genus 'Philadelphus', a word that translates as 'brotherly love'.

Philadelphus mexicanus (origins obvious) and its confusingly named types look rather spavined with few fine leaves on reed-like stems. Evolution has made them parsimonious for survival in the desert and they resent any chopping. Sadly, ours died here, just when they were getting really substantial, in last winter's cold blast. The small bushy ones such as *P.* 'Manteau d'Hermine' 'Snowbelle' and 'Sybille' are most useful in borders and beds, spangled with starry white double blossoms which drift pineapple fruity fumes all around them later in June. The RHS for once goes mad about the smell of 'Sybille' in flower: 'in early summer lashings of citrus-scented white flowers appear. They form in generous clusters, so the overall effect is very impressive – and the perfume is wonderful!' – their exclamation mark. I think this is the one Mr B got so excited about last summer. It has grown to waist height in the orchard, utterly blown away with blossom. I am afraid that we find it hard to keep track of all that we have planted – it is hard enough keeping them alive let alone remembering their names. Slightly larger and earlier *P.* 'Avalanche' is lax and graceful, a decent-sized shrub whose arching stems drip single lemon-perfumed blossom late in June and July. The flowers that are bigger than most are those of *P.* 'Beauclerk', which open flat, single, with a plum tinge at the base. The biggest flowerer, with creamy pompom roses, *P.* 'Monster', is worth tracking down. *P.* 'Belle Etoile' is an elegant shrub and I swear can grow as big as a shed – but Mr B disagrees – and it has large flowers with a strong purple central flash and scent. *P.* 'Lemoinei' smells better though, with dainty flowers in such abundance and ahead of the rest. I read but have no direct experience that *P.* Little White Love ('Snow Dwarf') is good in pots. But it's a good thought.

Mr B talked very touchingly about the forever powerful combination of arriving home for the holidays and breathing deeply the smell of philadelphus in his parents' garden outside the garage, a scent that he also remembers smelling at school, where it transported him briefly and full of relief, home.

From almost a lifetime observing Mr B, it seems that, for him, certain smells, particularly the scent of mock orange in early summer and any related smell such as orange blossom, act like a lightning conductor to the past, good and bad. He was lucky to have a truly marvellous dependable, wise, fearless mother whose protective care was always there until the time when she needed his – and yet she, like others of her age and class, sent him away to school, because it seemed the right thing to do. To my generation it is difficult to fully comprehend how such a loving mother could find it conscionable to send a seven-year-old boy to the sort of clapped out, cruel, ignorant dumps which he describes as his boarding prep schools and because of which, as a defence, he developed a passion for outdoors, hard work, oblivion and women. In his mother's hairbrush, he found the epicentre of her marvellous animalic motherly smell; Blue Grass perfume, skin, oil, hair, powder and it calmed him. School was like surviving on the Great Plains, awash with scatological and fear-induced smells, sweat, pressure, beaten bums, scratchy woollen uniforms, filthy boiled food, cloying polish, acrid ink. School, prison, hospital, gym, submarines, Tube trains, concerts, football matches, massed humanity awaken all levels of olfactory responses. We live in a world that inadvertently manipulates us, from scented bin liners and windscreen wiper wash to the nitrous-oxidised opening of bags of salad. The ozonic world of chilled distribution. But the earthy rooty smells and flavours are not only still there if you look for them, they are still prized in a shamanic almost absurd way – truffles, oysters and wine.

For me the smell of peonies, their smell of face cream, carries a memory like a missile of something, walking into a room somewhere – an institution, a school, some place now abandoned. The smell of this place is not unlike the smell of stationery and pencil shavings. The sensation is so strong, but it is also ungraspable. Leaves me lost. I bury my whole head in the biggest blowsiest beast of a peony, 'Monsieur Jules Elie'. It is the physical sensation of satin on a hot June morning that makes you want to die happily right there. It is anaesthesia at one remove and it came all the way from China. Peonies are the *femmes fatales* of the garden. They have a 'townie' fake-ness, the expensive smell of florist's shops, leaves, stems and wrapping paper. Binomial naming could have been so much fun; it is interesting how it focuses predominately on the person who found the plant, which is interesting and, if familiar, also gives you a clue to where and when it was found. But two hundred years later I feel the hairy, smelly, frondy adjectives stick better in the mind. The odder and funnier the epithet the better for my mnemonics, and because Latin is full of wonderful words, the losing in translation makes it endlessly surprising. I found out only recently that the *Paeonia lactiflora* 'Edulis Superba' – truly a magniloquent pongy pink dinner plate of a flower produced with liberality and reliability – is not so called after some French count or a wandering Jesuit priest called Edulis, but – although all parts of the plant cause tremors and a racing heart – 'edulis' is the same as 'esculenta', a straight translation from the Latin for 'edible', a term I use with affection for children and small creatures. On the whole the Latin words for weepy, creepy and sleepy (well, laid out cold) are sufficient familiar and yet peculiar to be memorable: *pendula, reptans, prostrata*. I find this way of looking at it helps.

Philadelphus 'Starbright'

128

Summer is for roses

The rose is such a huge and complex subject. It is hard to make a start. They come in groups which have slowly made more sense to me as I have grasped simple rules of thumb.

Albas have rather blue leaves, are upright growing and like a bit of shade. Pale flowers, pink and white, come once in early June. The scented ones I would choose have old-fashioned names: 'Great Maiden's Blush', 'Alba Maxima' – the Jacobite rose – and 'Königin von Dänemark' all of which smell blithe, airy and breezy, of midsummer.

Gallicas are the oldest garden group, native of southern and central Europe, east to the Ukraine, and of Asia Minor, the Caucasus and Iraq; cultivated since time immemorial. Gallica roses such as the apothecary's rose, *Rosa gallica* var. *officinalis*, were valued for the velvety texture and lustre of their tannin-rich petals, which preserved well and were astringent; they were put to various uses either dried or in syrups and conserves and the buds were used for making sugar of roses. June flowering and once only, they make neat shrubs without pruning, sucker a little, and put up with a lot. A rose pre-eminent in Mr B's good books is *R.* 'Charles de Mills': summer pudding fruity in sight and scent, it behaves and does well. Mr B also loves *R.* 'Président de Sèze' with a muddled velvet flower opening magenta, hardening king crimson in the sun, fading to a purple that is eventually brown. The smell is earthy, luxurious and robust.

Taller than the Gallicas, the Damask roses do not sucker. The flowers are semi-double, borne in lax clusters of up to a dozen with those curious elegant sepals that are twice the length of the flower bud, slender, sometimes slightly extended like a long-tailed tit. They have been in cultivation in Europe at least since the early sixteenth century, but these Damasks are likely to have been flowering in southern Anatolia since the Neolithic era. Also important in thinking about perfume is *Rosa × damascena* 'Kazanlik' (syn. *R. × d.* 'Trigintipetala') known since at least 1689 also as the Kazanlak or Kazanlik rose after the valley in which it has been grown – perhaps since Roman times. This and *R. × d.* 'Professeur Emile Perrot' are the roses from which they abstract rose oil, or attar of roses and rose absolute for the perfume industry still in Turkey, Bulgaria and Tunisia, and once upon a time in the Kabul region of Afghanistan.

Of the cultivated forms of the Damask rose 'Ispahan' is the ideal border Damask rose, smelly and sumptuous-looking, a beauty much loved by Mr B for flowering long and with a strength of scent born out of golden anthers on a blush cushion. 'Madame Hardy' is possibly the best white rose, a stately bush of unfading billiard-table green, a foil for folded flat upturned faces of flower which smell like a fruit salad, said Parkinson in the *Paradisus*, 'of the most excellent sweet pleasant scent, far surpassing all other Roses or Flowers, being neyther heady nor too strong, nor stuffing or unpleasant sweet, as many other flowers'.

Provence or Centifolia roses have nodding flowers, solitary or few in a cluster, borne in late June or July, clear pink, very double, goblet-shaped from the incurving of the petals, becoming more lax when fully blown, exposing the tightly packed petaloids. The sepals are spreading, longer than the flower buds and covered, like the pedicels and receptacles, with sticky aromatic glands. By the middle of the nineteenth century 'cabbage rose' had become synonymous with 'Provence rose', and *R. × centifolia* underwent a burst of evolution.

Sweet peas – 'Blue Velvet', 'King Edward VII', 'Prince Edward of York', 'Lord Nelson', 'High Scent', 'Noel Sutton', 'Aphrodite'

Left: *Rosa* 'Climbing Etoile de Hollande'

The Moss roses that I so love are mutations of *R.* × *centifolia* or *R.* × *damascena*. They have their habits and their problems; lax and mildew-attracting, many give up on them especially as I feel they need a Mediterranean climate. But for me the combination of Centifolia scent and the strange balsam of the mossy, parsley, glandular smell is irresistible.

The common Moss, *Rosa* × *centifolia* 'Muscosa', is a sport from *R.* × *centifolia*, characterised by the development of much-branched, moss-like aromatic glands on the calyx and pedicels and, as Bean puts it, 'the excessive glandularity of the leaf-rachis and branchlets'. In size, foliage and flower it is slightly less than *R.* × *centifolia* itself, but both the rich pink colour and the fragrance are the same. This mutation first occurred on the continent very early, before 1720, but became a great favourite here in Victorian times.

The crested moss, Chapeau de Napoléon (*R.* × *centifolia* 'Cristata') – at just over five foot about the same height as the great self-made emperor – is a sport which originated in about 1820, identical to *R.* × *centifolia* in every respect except the flower buds, which are as powerful a pomade as Penhaligon might have procured. Bean describes the mutation much better than I can: 'Sepals are extended into many divided wings or appendages; they frame the bud with a parsley-like frill of green. The French name recalls the cockade-like effect of these wings'.

Bourbon roses are the pick of the scented roses and the start, in breeding terms, of longer flowering in roses. They are much more modern in character, the flowers more globular and, particularly the leaves, fast growing, darker. 'Madame Lauriol de Barny', 'Madame Pierre Oger', 'Louise Odier': all those French-named wonders – 'Madame Isaac Péreire' is the most scented rose that I know. Their perfume is generally more berried, raspberry and blackberry. But none of them

Right: *Rosa centifolia* 'Muscosa'

132

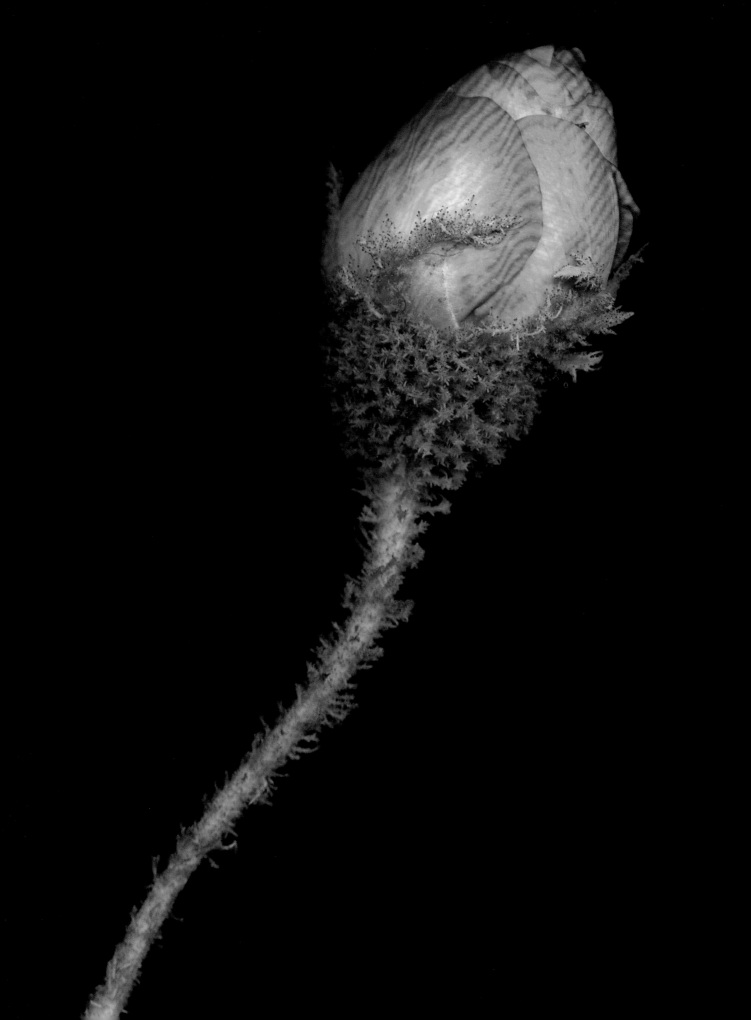

can beat for my money, for perfecting the beauty and repeating and sweeting with a smell that is what 'Perfume' should be, the imcomparable 'Souvenir de la Malmaison'. Like a piece of couture it was created in 1843 by Jean Béluze, and named after the Château de Malmaison, where Joséphine de Beauharnais, Napoleon's empress, created her paragon rose garden.

Portland roses are also 'remontant'– this is what rose growers call being able to flower more than once. 'Madame Boll' (long misidentified as 'Comte de Chambord'), 'De Resht' and 'Marchesa Boccella' (syn. 'Jacques Cartier') are three roses we never work without. We argue about which are the best and which the smelliest. But Madame is pinkest, 'De Resht' a great fuchsia smelly rose, the Marchesa the most remontant. The origin of the Portland rose, *Rosa portlandia*, is not known, but it was named for the Duchess of Portland and was in commerce in Britain by the 1770s. It is of historical interest as a parent of some of the truly repeat-flowering roses that were to come, and because there are two stripey ones (a trait I find enticing), 'Commandant Beaurepaire' and 'Variegata di Bologna'.

Hybrid Perpetual roses are more remontant and keep going in bursts. The best is a stripey job called 'Ferdinand Pichard', striking-looking, repeating and smelling of raspberry and rose sorbet. The 'Empereur du Maroc' has a dark chocolate scent and visage but is very weakly and apt to fail. Much more robust and as velvety as a damson or morello cherry and similarly scented is 'Souvenir du Docteur Jamain'.

By crossing the Hybrid Musk roses, the Rev. Pemberton of Essex founded a free-flowering, fantastically fragrant and handsome series of shrub roses at the turn of the twentieth century. 'Felicia' is my most useful and super-scented favourite, followed by 'Penelope', 'Cornelia' and 'Buff Beauty'.

Rugosas come from Japan and are very useful in Cornwall, therefore, where they like the damp and the acidity and repay it by infusing the air.

China roses are both ancient and repeat flowering but their importance is in the influence they had in making cross-breeds flower for longer. Old blush China (correctly, *Rosa × odorata* 'Pallida') used to be in all good gardens for it flowered continuously from spring until Christmas and bore silver pink flowers, on an almost thornless bush, which smell on the air of rose Turkish delight. I've seen it said that the fuchsine-pink and endless flowering China rose called 'Sophie's Perpetual' has a 'perfume-like fragrance', which is a bit lame. The point is that China roses repeat, and some smell delicious in that afternoon-tea way, because they are proto-Tea roses; it is the petals that smell and their petals make excellent rose water. *R.* 'Hermosa' is another reliable beauty, her scent not of the first order but good planted in threes as Miss Jekyll liked to plant less vigorous roses such as 'Stanwell Perpetual' – an absurdly pearly girly pink and smelling as such. These kinds of roses smell, and would taste if you were to munch on the petals, of apricot and raspberries swirled together. David Austin's Eglantyne looks a little too apricot and raspberries swirled together for me, but it does smell well.

ROSES

Roses are ungenerous, they produce no nectar. The smell is there to lure in pollinators of course, but only pollen is on offer. The scent of individual roses is very troublesome to classify and describe in its richness and subtlety. In general, the scent of the

Rosa 'Minnehaha'

Centifolia Damascena Gallica group of old roses and the modifying Earl-Grey-tea scent of *Rosa × odorata* is what anyone would recognise as 'rose'. In the early nineteenth century the introduction of the Himalayan *R. moschata* brought a spicy quality to many rambling and later climbing roses, whilst *R. arvensis* thickened the smell with honey. The Austrian briar – in fact a native of Western central Asia – *R. foetida* is so called because its fruit scent smells of boiled linseed oil, its unpleasance likened to the smell of bed bugs. It is a scaring yellow and is responsible for the chrome colour which it added to rose breeding from the mid nineteenth century and enabled the concoction of all those traffic-light roses, beloved of the Queen Mum and gardeners in Morocco for some inexplicable reason. They have perhaps a certain 'vintage' élan and the Austrian briar also added a different tang to the scent of modern or post-1900 roses. It is interesting to note that wild yellow roses are either scentless – like *R. xanthina* f. *hugonis* and *R. hemisphaerica* – or have a peculiar scent of their own, as in the fabulous *R. primula*, which smells of incense.

So varied are the smells of roses, ranging through tarragon, pepper, elder, leather, that they would make a book of scent all of their own. But for simplicity, the rich and subtle variety of the smell of rose may be divided roughly into five sections by the non-parfumier or humble gardener here: old rose; tea; fruit; musk; spice; other.

In the garden, old rose scent is found typically in the Gallicas and the Damasks and also in *Rosa rugosa* (though the smell is slightly different), the Hybrid Perpetuals and some Hybrid Teas. It seems to be linked biologically with the colours red, pink and white. Five essential rose-scented cultivars are 'Roseraie de l'Haÿ', which was raised by Jules Gravereaux and introduced by Charles Cochet-Cochet for the perfume industry in the Grasse region of France; 'Gruss an Teplitz', which has a special power for scenting the air and the fading petals smell of pot-pourri; 'La France'; 'Zéphirine Drouhin' (incredibly useful as it is thornless, pretty and well-behaved); and 'Ophelia' – with much honey in the scent. Of the species, all the Scotch briar, burnet or *spinosissima* roses smell light and deliciously of cold cream.

Many observers describe the smell of the Tea roses as not that of dry tea, as I would, but of ripe raspberries. This example of the subjective difficulties of smell analysis proves that, as Linnaeus thought, the vagueness of smell description is generally insurmountable and hence useless to science. I smell raspberries in plenty of roses, but the tea smell is particular, and to me particularly delicious. Be it Yorkshire, Darjeeling, Assam or Lapsang, tea is one of the great smells of existence and where we find it in a flower we should celebrate.

Of the tea-scented roses, 'Gloire de Dijon' was one of the first roses bred with the intense quality of Lapsang souchong and still one of the best. Mr B says it's impossible to grow because it has lost something even in our lifetimes in the quality of the stock. 'Mrs Dunlop Best', raised in Twyford (though surviving stocks seem to have returned from Australia) and registered in 1916; 'Yvonne Rabier', a tiny Polyantha introduced in 1910; and 'Mrs Foley Hobbs', the creation of Dickson in 1910, all throw a great tea party.

A fruit scent is deeply ingrained in our psyche as the scent of the wild eglantine rose of Shakespeare and Chaucer, *Rosa rubiginosa*. It has a pervasive apple smell, from its leaves as well as its flowers. It is a smell that carries a long way on a damp day and encompasses all that is summer in orchards, farm meadows and hedgerows for me, but conjures up horse pee for others. 'La Belle Distinguée' and 'Lord Penzance' are named varieties of these eglantines and I would hope never to be without them. Top roses in all respects, and more baked-apple-scented, are the reliable climbers 'Albéric Barbier' and

Rosa 'Rambling Rector'

Thalictrum flavum, Gallica roses 'Président de Seze' and 'Charles de Mills'

'François Juranville'. Other than apple, there is apricot, with the addition of a sharp note of orange. It is found in the species roses *R. bracteata* (the tender Macartney rose, a very prickly, simple, pretty white single rose best on a warm wall) and *R. foetida* hybrids, which have a hint of fresh coriander seeds and become more pleasantly fruity when diluted by distance or hybridisation. *R. helenae* is quite difficult to grow, even to get hold of, but smells hot and tropically of bananas, myrrh and musk and can swathe a tree. Although discovered along with *R. rubus* by Henry in the 1860s, it was collected from east Sichuan and Hubei by Wilson in 1900; it is named after his wife Helen who was killed in the accident in which he also lost his life on 15 October 1930. It is a parent of a climbing well smelly yellow rose registered in that year and called 'Lykkefund' which means 'lucky find'. Another such golden smelling and looking is the Rambler rose 'Goldfinch'. *Rosa rubus*, the blackberry rose, is wild rampant with single white flowers. We grow it over the ramparts for the charm and simplicity of its flowers, boosted by a great boss of stamens, bold fruity scented and late to flower.

Even the idea of true musk is too visceral and cruel for modern tastes, and the smell's meaning is therefore dissipating. As a secretion from the anal gland of the musk deer, hunted almost to extinction, musk smells unsurprisingly faecal. In perfumery it has been used for millennia primarily as a 'fixative' for other smells, as with orris, and its smell in massive dilution is warmly animal and familiarly fragrant. In the description of roses, 'myrhh' is now often used in place of 'musk' although the derivation from the Arabic 'murr' means 'bitter' (hence the gift of the Magi foretells of the bitterness of Christ's Passion), which is not a quality found in any rose smell to my knowledge. As well as being bitter, bitter myrrh – a gum extraction from scraggy white-flowered desert trees called *Commiphora myrrha*, native to the Arabian Peninsula and north east Africa – smells edible, dark, leathery, smoky, which is less difficult to equate with the smell

Honeysuckle and valerian

139

of rose. In terms of roses I think musk has come to mean something different, more akin to the smell of *Myrrhis odorata*, the umbelliferous herb sweet cicely, a smell that is beeswax and honey with, in perfumery terms, a whiff of ambergris – that magical ingredient that smells of sun on warm skin. I think I'd call it 'waxy'; it makes me think of the smell of beehives, and I believe the 'living' smell of it is the highly protein-rich smell of pollen – dry and powdery – which is abundant in such strongly myrrh-smelling roses as 'Rambling Rector', which also smells peppery. *Rosa filipes* 'Kiftsgate', the thug of all thugs, has this smell and if you have a dull wood or wild patch plant masses of it up trees or just plant it and let it mound up on the ground. *R.* 'Princesse de Nassau' (syn. *R. moschata* 'Autumnalis') flowers in late August, like a returning friend and is exceptionally pretty in bud. *R. moschata* and *R. brunonii* have a delicious clove scent allied with muskiness. But principally these roses emit drifts of smell on damp evenings. That is their glory.

Fruity myrrh with added cinnamon could be described as a quality found in another group of roses: the Noisettes. Favourites of mine, they clamber vigorously, clad in sprigs and sprays of buff yellow hue, highly scented and for a longish part of the summer.

Of the violet-scented roses, the dog rose (*Rosa canina*) and the white Banksian rose (*R. banksiae*) have a fresh clear scent like an intense mignonette or violet. The Banksian rose is a giant climbing shrub with slender, unarmed shoots. It is a native of China, where it has long been cultivated and was first noted in the West by the Russian traveller Porfirij Evdokomovich Kirilov (1801–64) in the gardens of what was then known as Peking. *R. banksiae* var. *banksiae* (syn. 'Alba Plena'), with white, violet-scented, double flowers, is the form from which Robert Brown described the species in the second edition of Aiton's *Hortus Kewensis*. It had been introduced by the Kew collector William Kerr from Canton in 1807. But *R. banksiae* var. *normalis* was already in cultivation in Scotland, as attested by E.H. Woodhall in a curious story in the RHS Journal of 1909. 'I found a rose growing on the wall of Megginch Castle, Strathtay, Scotland, which seemed to be a very slender-growing form of *R. Banksiae*. Captain Drummond of Megginch told me that it was a rose that his ancestor, Robert Drummond, had brought with other plants from China in 1796. This old rose had been repeatedly cut to the ground by severe winters, and had rarely, if ever, flowered. The impression, however, was that it was white and very small. Captain Drummond kindly gave me cuttings, which I took to Nice, and this year they flowered, proving themselves to be the typical single white Banksian rose so long sought for and hidden away in this nook of Scotland for more than a hundred years.' It was only after this that it began to be grown widely. The Banksian rose 'Lutea' has double flowers of Anchor-butter yellow, the most robust but the least scented; those of 'Lutescens' are single, yellow and bit more scented, still subtle, but helped in both cases by the sheer mass of flower. I would not call them smellers. I find they need no pruning and are much best left alone, as they flower on laterals two or three years old too easily removed by the tidy gardener; however, others recommend a little annual tidying. A similar-looking a hybrid *R.* 'Eugénie Lamesch' is very rarely grown now; it is a yellow pompom rose of 1899 smelling of violets, surviving in California it seems.

Rosa 'Katharina Zeimet' and *R.* 'Evangeline' are said by some to pong hauntingly of honey, very strongly, with a unique power of diffusing in the air. I will have to try them because Peter Beales (the rose nursery) says they have little or no scent at all. This is always the conundrum: one can only know through direct experience and, even then, one may simply have been unlucky in clone or circumstance.

Watered the vegetable garden after a hot windy day. Such a pleasant chore, the water playing on the paving and sending off a steam of warm stone smell just for the hell of it. Rescuing tiny transplants and invisible seedlings an unmitigated pleasure. Deep breathing. Earth and water. My fingers going numb for squeezing the end of the hose. Vegetable growing is particularly 'close work' always requiring pinching and feeling plants, which results in much contact with the scents of growing things.

The hay meadows have yellowed overnight.

We went to Penheale, which was enchanting. The chamomile lawn path is what it should be – an invitation to take your shoes off at the very least and stamp about on it, releasing an aroma of green tea, smoking yarrow and daisies. I really want to lie face down and breathe noisily with my eyes shut. But this is a grass path only and not a lawn, and there were lots of people blithely pushing their way through, completely unaware of the fragrant carpet beneath their feet.

Today I have been photographing since six this morning the impossible, impossibly delicious and sadly impossible to capture, wilderness of blossom, interwoven, intertwined, wreathy, garlanded and profuse beyond all profusion.

Opium poppies: what a weird smell that is. It really defies description. You don't grow them for scent, nobody picks them except children and painters, but their smell is so distinctive and part of the garden. It is important, along with elder and hawthorn.

This evening I was on the warpath, enjoying the scent of destruction, ripping out fuzzy-smelling dead nettles, sticky goose grass and Himalayan balsam seedlings. You can smell how fast the balsam is growing, see it in the luminescent cell structure, the red-tinged leaves and shoots. Now only hand high, they will look completely as fresh as this, and as thrusting, in three months' time – September, October – when they will be covered in poppable policemen's-helmet seed pods, striped and torpedo-shaped, tempting and tantalising. The mechanism for their seed dispersion, catapulting seeds from its photosynthetic trebuchet, is so mechanically show-off it makes a child of you again. The entire plant is glazed in some faintly balsamic sticky glue, and the bees love the grey autumn pollen.

Having ripped open some spaces in the borders, cutting back early bit parts like dicentra and hesperis, we filled the gaps with pathetic-looking annuals sown in those crackling plastic, polluting six packs. The plethora of plastic in gardening is very hard to control; shameful but practical, plastic dominates everyone's hard-pressed, do-it-yourself gardening life these days. There must be another way. Even some of the really great real nurseries where they actually grow plants from cuttings are swathed in trailer parks of baking plastic crumbling in the ultraviolet. There is another way: the beauty of compostable pots is that you plant the pot and the plant – so much easier as well as so much greener.

Crambe is taking over like aerial algae. I love it, but being of the cabbage family, along with wallflowers and gorgeous stocks, it has a problem with a back hint of sulphurous Brussels sprouts which gains potency as it fades. The branching skeleton will carry on looking good until winter, so I just put up with the smell, which goes when it dries out.

Rosa 'Madame Isaac Péreire' is the Queen of Sheba, Delilah and Jezebel rolled into one of the most scented and truly handsome double princesses of the rose kingdom. She smells like a boudoir should. Lady's bedstraw (*Galium verum*) mixes well with her, its scent a mixture of honeyed warmth and absorbed sunlight. The whole plant dries with a fruity lightness and hence was strewn about the bedchamber, and it was used to stuff mattresses as the coumarin scent of the plants acts as a flea killer. There is something of the hay-cut clarity of lady's bedstraw in *Matteuccia struthiopteris*, a fern worth picking as a foil for flowers and for the smell.

Coumarin is an organic volatile that releases the smell of new-mown hay that we associate with it. The name comes from a French Guianan term for the tonka bean, *kumaru*, one of the sources from which coumarin was first isolated as a natural product in 1820. Celia Lyttelton in her book *The Scent Trail* says that you really do want to lie down and sleep when you stand in a tonka bean field and inhale it. That sweet odour has been used in perfumes since 1882. Sweet woodruff and sweet clover also have this smell and were used for 'strewing' owing to their high coumarin content. When it occurs in high concentrations in forage plants, coumarin is a somewhat bitter-tasting and is therefore presumed to be produced by plants as a defence chemical against predation. Strangely both the synthesized and natural coumarin are powerful anticoagulants, vitamin K antagonists, used in rodenticides like warfarin.

Ferns are now fronded, unfurled and smelling fruity in a manly way which is all about woodland. On heathland, the bracken is pungent and compellingly toxic.

Primula florindae from Tibet are just flowering. The entire stem is luminescent, the tall umbels of the aptly named Himalayan cowslip smell just as their English cousins do in spring only lighter, brighter, more golden. They would make a better bath oil, being bolder, full of summer, more obviously floral and more peppery.

I left some white peony flowers in my scanning room overnight and returning in this morning I'm hit by a warm tender scent filling the room. Outside the first of the storm rain smells of potatoes just dug.

Summer solstice
Noon on the solstice brings Mr B's June joys. He picked the following: *Paeonia lactiflora* 'Duchesse de Nemours' – luminescent lemon white, echoed in the citrus scent, delicious and cold, womanly, rounded, whole but light; *Philadelphus* 'Minnesota Snowflake' – a starry double, smelling of pineapple, orange and lime. The sun rose at 5 am. John Snow, the cock in the keep, was crowing long before that. And the evening lingered and lingered for hours after the official sunset at 9.31 pm.

My journal-writing head is jostling with life, children, work, houses, gardens, and meanwhile out there has become crowded too, a riot of scents and fleeting sensations. The first refreshing filigree of rain for ten weeks made the smell bath explode and meld into something indescribably delicious. The single notes of winter and spring become hard to distinguish in the orchestral clamour of summer, the noise of things wanting attention, pollination, insemination. The garden has been throbbing towards the solstice and smells quite different from a week ago. As midsummer rises and then passes, something elegiac enters the soul of the garden. It stole up on me in my distraction. There is a smell associated with all things end-of-term, which might be recognisable, I would guess, to almost everybody. In the garden, just as it all reaches its zenith,

Philadelphus 'Dainty Lady'

142

some nausea sublimates, a rank note, a sense that summer, whilst it is only just starting, is also starting to be over, spent.

Now is the time for lime blossom, from the linden tree (*Tilia* species). Lime blossom tea is slightly astringent because of its high tannin content. Mr B said today that the lime was out and brought a bunch muddled up with sweet peas, which he says smell of marzipan and almonds – just because he loves marzipan. The two together, *Lathyrus* and linden, create an olfactory minefield. Lime flowers fog this moment of high summer. It hits in waves on hot days; you cannot think what it is, a brain assault, sensual, forgotten. Perhaps the drone of bees throughout the silver lime's drooping branches made me remember and realise what it was that I was smelling, or why I felt so benign; it was because of a smell that I wasn't even aware of smelling at first. Some say that something in the scent, or the nectar, kills the bees, and it does seem to make them drowsily drunk. Like the bees I remember lying about on their backs under the silver lime at Christopher Gibbs's house, Clifton Hampden, Christopher giggling and intoxicated too. When our friend David Vicary died we had a memorial for him in June at a chapel by Maud Heath's Causeway on the River Avon; it was so hot some of us went swimming after the service. Then we had tea and sandwiches in the tin hut at East Tytherton. The day before we picked branches of lime and branches of philadelphus. This was David's favourite flower combination for vast arrangements and he insisted, rightly, that all the leaves should be stripped away for a purity of effect. The night before the memorial we sat up half the night, a tide of stripped leaves rustling about us. It was a Tennessee Williams hot night, one that happens once in a decade. It had been the same a decade earlier for our wedding party. So hot were we that we sat in the cellar door and garnered the breeze, lit only by the iris sky. We also made trophies of all David's garden tools, painting them white, and for many years we hoed and raked like blind horticulturalists.

25th June

We got married on this night. It was one of those unsurpassed nights when the sky was a deepest lapis and never blackened. The party was a picnic in our ruined house without electricity or running water, and we spent most money on fireworks, bowls of sweet peas and cherries. We made pyramids of elderflowers, which flagged long before the revellers did. I still love the smell of elderflowers, their muscat grape waft, but the whole plant smells of pee and honey. Nothing wrong with either but the smell of elder is not good. It is malodorous and disturbing. Evocative for sure, but like a stuffy room; almost human. Perhaps it is the rank amino acids, the building blocks of life, protein, power.

Something about the ubiquity of elder, *Sambucus nigra*, makes it a marmite plant. Love or loathe it. Luckily for all man's attempts to root it out, it is a survivor, cropping up from seed whenever nobody is looking. The flat umbels or, as John Gerard delightfully puts it, 'spokie rundles' of flowers smell, when you can get away from the smell of its leaves (which Richard Mabey likens to the smell of mice nests), of a sweetness related to muscat grapes and gooseberries. Pliny wrote of the belief held by some peasants that the most sonorous pipes were made from elder wood, but only that which grew beyond earshot of a cock's crow. As a child I found elder sinister: it was the inhabitant of neglected places, which are rare now. It grew round the well and the old

Philadelphus maculatus
'Mexican Jewel'

privy, the fallen-down shed and the back alley. I always regretted making an elder sword or wand and ditched it for something less abundant and snap-able. I remember the bark and the pithy insides, all of it stinky. It has dirge-green leaves and then the flowers – so appealing, like cow parsley, a filigree firework, and, oddly, having that extraordinary champagne aroma that really can be captured and bottled. All that delicacy and filigree froth translates into one of the great drinks of the world, elderflower cordial. For me champagne is not a patch on the cordial mixed with fizzy water. Now we can buy it, but until I was grown up it was a seasonal treat, very quickly over, and hence the making of it was a high point in the year.

Later I was shucking furry broad bean pods; much of the pleasure of doing this is in that watery smell. I am convinced that the smell of summer alters dramatically around the solstice. It is five days later now and I could swear the hint of decay has perceptibly entered the mix; atrophy has arrived at the party. Night regains supremacy minute by minute. The dark forces are present underlying the still sweet swill of roses and pea blossom. The peonies are long gone, and it is noticeable how they simply come to a standstill at midsummer; they stop doing anything, neither flourishing nor failing. Whether the leaves are pumping sunlight back down underground or have done with that, I do not know.

Woke about twenty past four and full of thought. No light but perfect stillness, start of birdsong. Up on a current of air from the river comes the scent of a gas lighter and a newly lit cigarette, distinct, a thin trail five hundred yards long, materialising in our bedroom.

I went downstairs for a cup of tea and a cigarette and thence into the garden as day broke. Dawn lilies, 'Sander's White Rambler' rose – which is late flowering and thicker in scent than other roses – and honeysuckle all fuming quietly. The yew smells salient in the dark but box is indiscernible until the heat of the sun gets going. *Philadelphus* 'Beauclerk' and *P. mexicanus* emit pineapple and bubble gum as they have done for five weeks now, but their rotting leaf corners are harbingers of the end. Just through the archway, chlorine from the pool assails the nostrils and there's a lily smell in the air, like St Tropez without the money. This morning is a Roman or Tuscan morning: tobaccos are opening for business and Etruscan honeysuckle (*Lonicera etrusca*) smells a bit bosky. The briar rose leaf broadcasts cidery fumes, Moss rose flowers are gone but their sticky sepals still emit a *bibliothèque* smell of books and glue and aromatics. Accidental plantings, such as the white aquilegias amongst some flossy Timothy grasses in the paving by the pool, give my heart such a lift. The surround of the pool right now has attained just the level of *The Garden of the Finzi-Continis* abandonment, with wild strawberries and floating rose petals.

It is 7.45 a.m. and the early birds have retreated, leaving only a couple of pigeons murmuring disapproving gossip on the lawn. Salvias and caryopteris attract attention with their slightly sweaty notes. Caryopteris is in the turpentine family of aromatic leaves; salvia somewhere much more complex. The most bizarre and armpitty flavoured salvia is *Salvia sclarea* var. *turkestanica* (now *turkestaniana*), compelling in a slummy way, tangibly pungent in the nose. All salvias are turned up too loud; noisome, nettle, acrid.

The end of the party

A rank torpor. Browned goblets of unopened rose buds, dirty confetti-strewn gravel, black spotted hands of leaves, tawdry delphiniums. In hotter climes, the lucky escape dusty cities for lost demesnes and shacks in the sun. Shadows are deep, lettuces bolting, sweet peas are difficult to tear by hand. The broad beans blacken, oily when crushed in the picking, but still the smell is goodly green, pure pea, summery and savoury. Ants' nests have grown high, drily bristling with the finest grasses, vetch tangling through, and thyme, teaming with tasty bites for the green woodpeckers in the orchard.

Fig trees have such a potent place in visual history, the leaves such grace and the smell of the whole plant so fundamentally right. By the swimming pool we planted Smyrna figs in ignorance; they only produce mini figs early in the season which drop off. I am tempted to hang them with gilded casts of figs, but the plants are beauties, their fragrant deeply lobed leaves tropic green with geographic veining, and sensually scented. Fig is one of the great smells yet people don't plant them for their scent.

Mr B picked his favourite combination, 'Cupani' sweet peas and *Calendula officinalis* 'Indian Prince', marigolds fit for a maharaja. The combined smell is bewitching: unutterable sweetness and shimmering candour, midsummer nights, tropic and lucid.

Regale lilies still astonish. They are the perfect way to get excited about gardening. Buy the plump artichokey bulbs in December, plant and watch them flourish around Mr B's birthday into tannoy trumpets, white and yellow as Bewick swans, bellowing out perfume. How must Ernest Wilson have felt upon discovering them in the wild? We have continued to grow them religiously, even in the face of the scarlet lily beetle, which must be picked off vigilantly before they breed. The hideous, munching, mucus-making offspring are a deadly menace, their snot-green larvae can demolish any lily stalk in a morning.

LUPINS

Lupins are not what one thinks of scented, bar a childhood reminiscence of something peppery; most of these are herbaceous, but the tree lupin really is scented and deliciously so, pumping out bean-field green notes into the air all about it. *Lupinus arboreus* can reach the top of a window or door, laden with candle-like sulphur-yellow flowers in terminal racemes. One gardener I know has it planted in a bed along the back of an outdoor 'hangout' room and was I jealous. It looks enchanting, having that cool colouring which is a combination of lime green white and sulphurous yellow – very Enid Marx (the artist). Their introduction to this country from the coastal region of California is unrecorded, but they are quite hardy in the south of England. Being *Leguminosae* they smell of beans and peas and sweet peas, and I wish I could grow them successfully.

Walking through the orchard very early I was set upon by the scent of meadow, plunging and 'swardy', a miracle tapestry of smell threads, the breath of the Great Plains. The fecundity of fruit and berries, barely visible, is beginning to cloy the air. Peonies are swelling, roses rage with myrrh, deliquescent, but in the beds below petals are browning. Lusty summer is perceivably laced with chaos and entropy, which makes it even more urgent to enjoy. Early mornings are still sublime come July, but there is perfidy in the garden.

Overleaf: Roses 'Rambling Rector' and 'The Garland', philadelphus and *Elaeagnus* x *submacrophylla*

The Cloudy Swoon

Come into the garden, Maud,
I am here at the gate alone;
And the woodbine spices are wafted abroad,
And the musk of the rose is blown.

Alfred, Lord Tennyson MAUD

I walked into it yesterday, something like a wall, blindly unsuspecting and then whoompf! The woodbine spices and the musk of the rose. July is Tennyson's time. In the cocktail of the summer garden, hot roses remind me of lying on the carpet in the Big Room at home as a child listening to Marlene Dietrich singing Fats Waller's 'Honeysuckle Rose'. Her voice dripping a dangerous eroticism and stalked by the double bass.

The sun is over the solstice yardarm and now the days diminish inexorably. Sunrise is just after five on first of July, and sets still at a leisurely, Mediterranean, nearly half past nine.

July has become the domain of the strimmer, when the faded meadow and wild patches become shaggy hearthrugs of regrowth after a haircut. In the lanes, the flail has been merciless, chomping the honeysuckle wands. In the garden, the overgrown path has had the dusty order of municipality imposed. Smells of blitzed ivy, macerated reeds of hemlock and nettle exude an elegiac savour. July used to have a good spent smell; now to walk the back paths to the beach is a dance through the detritus of holiday-makers among the marram grass and the bagged-up dog turds. In the garden the currants are shiny wet red, though their leaves smell of nothing. Dusty bloom-laden blackcurrants are fat with smell, dissonant and dirty.

The thuggy *Rosa filipes* 'Kiftsgate' is foaming now, a draught of bees and hoverflies floating on the surf of its scent. *Synstylae* roses, the section of roses that have their styles joined into a single column, flower in 'corymbs' – even the word sounds celestial – and it is this way of flowering, the characteristic look which is common to them as a group, that means they are the ones I like best; the single or double white rambling species are generally smelly.

Rosa 'Roseraie de l'Haÿ' smells of cucumber, tea and laundered tablecloths laid at a table on the lawn. Such a moment, so carefully orchestrated, as almost no one would take the time and trouble for now. Call me old-fashioned, but to my mind this rose is by far the better smeller than *R.* 'Blanche Double de Coubert'. Mr B does not agree.

Honeysuckle hangs like camouflage netted above the vegetable garden, and thus descends in liquid essences of sugar and butterfly juice. I grabbed it down, tugging at the strong tendrils so as to smell it up close, like fingering stuff in a frock shop. How wrong I was to do this, because sniffing the nectar in the tubular flowers is prosaic compared to the mysterious wafting of it from above.

A rogue white rhododendron flowers in the shadows of the gunnera umbrellas.

Dianthus superbus

Nameless, huge and stickily oozing nectar now in sultry July, it smells almost repugnant. The melon freshness of *Rhododendron* 'Polar Bear' a month ago is gone, and this one smells of deep shadows and woodland litter where fungi thrive. Those things which grow on the chalk are somehow clearer and would never smell as foetid and rank as this anonymous rhododendron, but then I am, I think, a born calciphile, a chalk-lover. I used to eat it at primary school. It was one of my tricks, along with nettle eating, which I used as a weapon to keep my reputation kookie and thereby fend off any cheeky stuff from the village boys.

I smelled seaweed through the train window at Dawlish, and then a plunge into fairground candy and sweaty onions. Fairground smells! The thrill, the thrill of St Giles Fair in Oxford at Michaelmas when the nights had drawn in and a special family outing meant all five of us getting in the Papacar, the coolest, gas-cooled-suspension, Citroën DS Safari. Safari! Wow! The word conjured up the TV programme set on a game reserve called 'Daktari'! We all went, all dressed up warm in those first frosty nights, and all together. Even my mother would come, because it was Oxford and reminded her of her heady long-gone youth. The thrill and the smell-safari that was the fair, the Waltzers, the smell of the Wall of Death and our ecstatic giggling. We never really forgave my father for trading in the cool French Safari Papacar for a new Austin Maxi from the garage at Rowstock where we collected our Green Shield Stamps. But 'Look!' he said with such pride, 'You can fold down the seats and sleep in the back!' My mother turned away. She was never going to sleep in the back of any car. He had no understanding of styling or cool, although he had a great eye for pictures. We did all go to Ireland and he and I slept in the back of the Maxi while the others had to be content with tents. One morning we were woken by the car's gentle rocking motion, as if we, like the The Borrowers, were afloat. We sat up to find a herd of cows licking and butting the Austin on all sides. The Maxi was never called the Papacar. Fairgrounds smell like no other set-up. My special love is steam fairs because the smell of diesel and candyfloss, dodgy electricals and static manmade fibres is tempered by the smell of steam locomotives, anthracite and oily rags.

Never sleep under a magnolia
Dipping one's head into a *Magnolia grandiflora* in obeisance is like dipping into the yawning of a deep well, circumfused with iridescent green smells. One might be in a cave or grotto in an ancient and barren landscape, by a pool glassy green as an emerald. Water smells seductive in the heat.

'You Must Never Sleep Under a Magnolia' writes Alice Oswald

> when the tree begins to flower
> like a glimpse of
> Flesh
> when the flower begins to smell
> as if its roots have reached
> the layer of
> Thirst upon the
> unsealed jar of
> Joy

Phlox paniculata 'Eva Cullum'

Lost desmesnes

We inherited a fabulous book from David Vicary: *Lost Desmesnes of Ireland 1660–1845* by Edward Malins and the Knight of Glyn. The subject is the Anglo-Irish houses that have disappeared and the edition was mouse eaten and rotten sweet smelling. Empty and derelict houses are suffused with a peculiar addictive damp, toiletry, rotten sweetness. Utterly narcotic to Mr B and me; we get high on old forgotten places. The Grand Meaulnes complex. We sometimes get to look round empty houses for work, as we did the other day. Barn doors hung at crooked angles, swallows chattering like loose change, like Belloc's 'Ha'nacker Mill': 'Spirits that call and no one answers; Ha'nacker's down and England's done.' Such places are very rare now. Idle dining rooms, soaked in gravy smell, drinks cupboards redolent of bittersweet schnapps which itself harbours a memory of the heat of summer. Manly smells: study smell, cigar smell, leather smell and stationery smell. Womanly smells: clothes and mothballs, bathroom unguents, soap. Old people smell, which starts alarmingly young. Dogs, cats and assorted pets, coats and boots, dusty umbrellas and biscuits. Some houses attempt to smell unlived in, of steel and spotless carpets, but all empty houses smell the same, in the end.

I woke far too early and decided to tackle the euphorbias in torrents of tepid rain. Had to change my clothes three times. Had two baths, one at seven and one at nine. It was great. Piled the heavy heads of seed in the back of the Gator, covered and oozing with a milk like Copydex glue – very dangerous in the eye; a friend had such a horrible time by mistakenly rubbing some in his eye that he swears he will not have them in the garden. I'm sweaty under the protection of a big coat, and happier than in weeks.

Coming home last night, motes filled the air cleaned by a storm, the train station full of scurrying tourists in the lustred low light, the road home powdered with pollen, sifted with sycamore scurf. The gate smacked open in a haze of jasmine scent on the north side, the south side flooded with lily warmth, cosmetic almost. Fish fingers in the oven, and there was time to canter out into the garden, water on stone, petals pasted to shining pebbles.

Daybreak was shell-like, perfection pink, dewy with the promise of matchless heat.

I love pinks so much, their tidy manners, looks and smell. All the consolations of summer lie in a handful of them.

GARDEN PINKS, MALMAISON CARNATIONS AND SWEET WILLIAMS

Pick a pink as you go by very early in the morning, when a July day is hotting up for a scorcher – the best moment. Placed against the tip of the nose *Dianthus* 'Mrs Sinkins' exhales her warmed meady airs. Mr B taught me about these short-lived perennials. When we first met, we drove out of Edinburgh, east along the Firth of Forth to Eyemouth where my Scots ancestors came from, to see some pink-growers near Dunbar. David Stuart was growing them, and he has since written many books about plants and gardens which we have devoured. The garden there then was entrancing – I remember feeling great garden envy. It was years before I discovered again the shredded beauties we found there: the *Dianthus superbus*.

The carnation and the garden pink have long been domesticated, thanks to their prettiness and scent. Cloves, nutmegs, Keats's 'lucent syrups, tinct with cinnamon', there is a world, both outlandish and homely, in a tiny flower. 'Carnations and

Brugmansia × cubensis
'Charles Grimaldi'

155

gillyflowers for beauty and delicate smell and excellent properties, deserve letters of gold' wrote Parkinson in the seventeenth century. In Britain the truly native Cheddar pink, *Dianthus gratianopolitanus*, is as spicy as any cultivated variety and clings high upon Somerset's extraordinary limestone crags near Cheddar. Its charms led to so much pilfering in the eighteenth century that by the nineteenth it was gone from all but the most precipitous cliffs where it clung on, to become a protected species in the twentieth.

The history of the pink, from Holbein to Paisley to John Major, is all in David Stuart's *Plants from the Past*. At some time in the nineteenth century they became the archetypal cottage-garden plant. John Clare almost invented the cottage garden 'path with pinks and daisies trimmed'. Early writing talks of their wiry stems bearing 'crimped', 'fringed', 'blotched', 'freak'd', 'splashed', 'picotee', and 'bizarre' flowers. Most are very sweet smelling, although long flowering has taken precedence over smell in the breeding of pinks latterly. The old ones 'Mrs Sinkins', 'Laced Monarch', and 'Gran's Favourite' are among my favourites. A new white-flowered hybrid Memories has much of the scent of 'Mrs Sinkins' and carries on flowering all summer. It sounds a dream but somehow it does not have the same charm and abundance of Mrs S from Slough. She was developed by the master of the Workhouse in that fabled city and named after his wife. They all grow best in a well-drained, limey or limestone soil or gravel bed.

Dianthus plumarius and *D. superbus* are short-lived perennials that are best grown as long-lived annuals, as they are easy to grow from seed and they have become something of an obsession with me. They are fabulously fringed and febrile, like wild sea anemones in rose pink (Rainbow Loveliness Group) and white with a green eye (Spooky Group) that first enraptured me that afternoon in Dunbar in 1982. To my way of thinking they have a smell that is a velvety dolly-mixture or sugared-almond, tantalising only when you pick and sniff. I don't think they scent the air as much as the best garden pinks do, but they are special. They must surely be the ones that Vita Sackville-West refers to as 'summers draggle-tails' in *The Garden*.

Malmaison carnations are the best of all for scent, and they were the height of fashion in the days of plentiful garden labour, the time of Proust and Wilde. Malmaisons are descended from an old blush carnation *Dianthus* 'Souvenir de la Malmaison' which, like the most delicious of roses bearing that name, was raised in France in the early nineteenth century. 'Thora' is worth trying, but Malmaison carnations are tricky glasshouse dames to grow. They require 'disbudding' to reduce flowers to about three per plant, then they require shade and cool airy conditions in the summer. I have never even attempted to grow them but have swooned at the scent and haute-couture beauty of them under the tutelage of the greatest grower, Sue Dickinson of the garden at Eythrope in Buckinghamshire.

The bearded pink *Dianthus barbatus* is what we all know and love as the sweet Williams of the cottage garden. They are short-lived perennials native to southern Europe. I love the taller varieties – the scent is better appreciated when they are thigh high – but generally these are only available as seed. But they are easy to grow as biennials, I promise. The shorter ones generally for sale are less likely to fall over and lounge about all over the bed as some do, but properly they should all be staked and so you might as well grow the pretty taller ones. They are best grown in large swathes or rows for picking. The smell is happy and typically of cloves and warm baking, but not as good as the garden pinks.

The baler is in the next field, clanking and rattling. The meadow is pullulating with life and the smell of life, oozing good times, lazy long grass, chamomile smoky, wheaten like a muesli.

Walking back through the orchard in the gloaming it was as though the buildings and plants were moving and I was suspended still, my face brushed by the smells on the air. The back of the sky was tangible and lights on in the house advanced towards me, pushing the night scents through me. I felt like a vessel, and I would settle with being just that, just drinking in the night. Inside the house again the boiler had come on roaring, heating hot water. It was later than I had thought.

Rosa 'Madame Isaac Péreire' is out again with blooming *R*. 'Prince Charles'. They are the perfect couple because he is a papal purple Bourbon rose that smells of summer pudding, and she is just the most beautiful-smelling rose in the world. Summer pudding is all berries: raspberry; tayberry; black, red and white currants smashed up together and, when I used to try to make it, always all most on the point of fermenting. That coastal path smells of dust and brambles, fermenting berries, nettles, elder and something of pencil shavings in buddleias.

It may seem arch to quote Proust, but, for the smell diarist, there is no getting away from it, he just gets it. 'A gap in the hedge gave a view into the gardens; a border of jasmine, pansies and verbena which ran along the wide path, was interplanted with fragrant wallflowers the faded rose of old Cordoba leather. A long green hose snaking across the gravel sent up every few yards a vertical prismatic fan, and the multicoloured drops showered over the flowers in a perfumed cloud.' The vertical prismatic fans, seen from Proust's Paris to Hockney's Californian lawns.

CARPENTERIA

Carpenteria californica is a shrub bearing scented white flowers with masses of yellow stamens, like a rose or eucryphia, in June and July; bushy in habit it has pithy branchlets and evergreen leaves, which have a pale soft felt on the undersides. Native of California as its name suggests, it first flowered in Britain in the Godalming garden of Miss Jekyll in 1885. It thrives in good loam, but it needs low humidity and a warm wall – at its best in the South East, and I am not familiar enough with it.

A milky, sandblasted Californian morning. Left the house at seven. Half an hour later it was 19 degrees. Nothing smells at the job I'm working on; there is no sensuality in that garden at all. Arrived back after work in a cloudburst, iron filings in the clouds. Silently it stops. In shafting sunlight, we open car doors to draughts of lime blossom, almost a physical wave, a white-out. Too many summers ago, Mr B moved some lime trees from a car park in Bristol that was being redeveloped. They were late flowering and prolific like the silver lime, *Tilia tomentosa*, which is the best for flower scent, driving bees into drunken raptures.

In the kitchen garden – a Veg Too Far, I call it – the sweet pea teepees have grown into ball gowns which need preening. We can hardly pick fast enough to keep the flowers coming, so the house is awash with buckets of peas like paint pots of colours. In the twilight picking, spider's webs criss-cross the paths, all ticklish.

Overleaf: *Lilium* African Queen Group, pelargoniums, *Thalictrum flavum* and fennel

157

By the seat the *Lilium* African Queen Group blows cinnamon and apricot orange. House is musty with cooking smells in the July dusk.

Mr B's big triumph is his night-scented stocks. This year he has really got them going, trailing from the side of pots. Last night we sat out smelling them and chucking similes at one another. Chocolatey said I. No, violets said he. Devon violets. The smell of ballet shoes and powder puffs, something of patchouli. It is strong yet volatile enough to drift upwards to the bathroom, a weightless night scent. The smell of the regale lilies pours forth also, but the molecules are heavy and sit round the terrace, barely bothering to sink to the lawn below.

NIGHT-SCENTED STOCKS

These hardy annual stocks, *Matthiola longipetala* subsp. *bicornis*, are found in wild sandy places in the Mediterranean fringes of the Middle East, where their life is brief, and they need to get pollinated quickly by the similarly short-lived moths of the night. For this reason, they put all their efforts into making a far-reaching, night-emitted perfume, and are next to nothing plants to look at. Growing to about knee height these rangy, grey-leaved plants flower sometimes sporadically and sometimes in great whorls of individual cruciform flowers, very like the flowers on shot rocket plants, with slightly curled up petals. Cosseted, fed and watered until flowering time, in Mr B's gardens they get prodigious, and Mr B's Big Trick is to get them to trail over the edge of his Big Pots, like the mauve beards of aubrieta. Sow the seed in autumn, and again in spring if you can, to extend the season of delicious warm-clove and white-chocolate drifting scent, month after month and all night long.

Buddleia has its charms, and a curious not-quite-right scent. I think the ordinary one in abandoned places is the best, with that the warm sickie smell, by the railway lines and brownfield sites. But the white buddleia I sniffed today smells of straw bedding, phlox too, only more sugary.

High summer

Everything is browning off – Help! Even the lilies cannot compete with this heat. The earth is cracked but still there is a developing compost scent beneath the roses and lilies. Sweet peas are well looked after and pumping out perfume. Cistus are heavenly, and in their element along with lavender and rosemary and tobacco plants. The phlox come along in quick succession, but they will need masses of watering if they are not to run to mildew. Phlox love water to a surprising degree. They loved that summer when it never stopped raining. No one else did. It made me vow to plant more of them, in spite of the staking they require. But this year there is no rain. And there are people who do not think we humans are changing things like climate and, indeed, smell – the volatiles in the air being bombarded with pollutants and fumes and poisons which blast away the tiny pheromonic signals all invertebrate life survives by understanding, never mind vertebrates. We have no idea what we are doing because we are not even aware of half the wonders of nature around us. We are so arrogant. For now, at least, phlox smell of high summer things, dust on the road, rot lurking, also of brushed cotton.

Lilium African Queen Group

160

Rose and Lily are names, but what about a girl called Phlox? I think she would be a female Flurry Knox (from *The Irish R.M.*), and the actress Honeysuckle Weeks would play her brilliantly. Phlox (they sound plural) are a wonderful addition to the garden absolute, warm, powdery, dusky, with something of gardenia – especially in the case of *Phlox paniculata* 'Discovery'.

PHLOX

Phlox divaricata subsp. *laphamii* 'Chattahoochee' is fundamentally a North American woodlander hailing from neutral to acid, damp, woodland places. It has an Award of Garden Merit, but it can be almost impossible to keep going and we therefore rarely try it in schemes for other people because, when it's work, you can't really muck about with experiments. It is annoying, but it has to be tried and tested. There are two well-known forms: *P.d.* 'Clouds of Perfume' and *P.d.* 'Blue Perfume.' *I cannot* explain the secrets of this difficult but utterly desirable plant. Oddly it is one of those things that Mr B and I just grew when we first started, because we smelled it in the garden centre near Chippenham and we liked it being covered in lavender flowers. We planted it by the back door trailing over the gravel and Mr B put it in a pot because we were short of beds in our first garden at The Ivy, and it worked; having it just seemed like a good idea since it was floppy and smelly.

For home consumption also, because it is always difficult to get other people to grow things from seed, there is the annual *Phlox drummondii*, which is a very different animal. Chiltern's sell one they call *P. drummondii* 'Blushing Bride' (correctly, Blushing Bride Group) as seed, with simple charm: a muddle of cotton white painted over blush. There is also a tall border phlox, *P. paniculata* 'Blushing Bride', which is my favourite, like a nightie or cottage curtain print, white with a small plum eye and smelling of sweetshops.

The border phlox are rather different and rather more accommodating. I love the ones that look and smell like the winceyette nightgowns of my childhood, white with a picotee ink edge, but equally well I enjoy the stained-glass colours, the fuchsine, the mauvine, the ruby red which hold their own in July borders. These phlox are long-lived and showy perennials, flowering for a long period from summer to early or mid-autumn, filling the air with a special very specific and delightful kind of smell which I call powdery. They suffer from powdery mildew and counter-intuitively must therefore be kept damp at all time. They love Cornwall, I discovered when I got here. Mainly originating from North America, where they colonise reliably moist habitats, they prefer a rich soil in full sun or lightly dappled shade. Phlox are thirsty, greedy plants, so apply, thickly, some well-rotted garden compost in spring. Shear off the spent flowers to prevent reseeding.

Favourite blues, violets and magentas. *Phlox paniculata* 'Starfire' has purple stems clothed with deep green foliage that emerges in spring with a red flush, followed by cherry-red fragrant flowers, which open from dark buds at waist height. I suppose it is really quite unusual to have highly scented flowers in the red magenta sector, which is why phlox are really rather special and underrated in my opinion – but then they do love the damp far west, and in East Anglia will be smitten with mildew, which makes gardeners hearts sink and harden. *P.p.* 'Amethyst' is more like shot velvet, the colour of dark buddleia, but medium short. *P.p.* 'Blue and Fragrant' comes from the 1950s and seems no longer to be available – I like that about phlox; they are generally mid-century hybrids born of austerity mixed with a very English aesthetic. *P.p.* 'Blue Evening' is earlier

Lilium African Queen Group and night-scented stocks (*Matthiola longipetala* subsp. *bicornis*)

163

flowering and powdery sweet and looks forget-me-not blue in the evening but definitely *mauve* in the bright daylight. *P.p.* 'Blue Paradise' is the designer's favourite, though it is very much on the mauve side of blue and not really very scented in my experience – but it is a good plant. *P.p.* 'Border Gem', an Edwardian variety introduced by Fairbairn in 1913 has glowing blue purple flowers on sturdy stems from late June. *P.p.* 'Brigadier', bred around 1940, has fuchsia pink with an orange subtext – you are not going to forget these babes – with a striking magenta eye, wearing plenty of perfume right at the end of July. *P.p.* 'Charlotte' has mounded heads like a perm of pale pink.

I love the pale mauves and whites, particularly at night. *Phlox paniculata* 'Rembrandt' is good for brightening areas of light shade; the milky white flowers look luminous at night and also are good indoors. *P.p.* 'David' is an award holder and clump-former, a great booming scented plant, bearing waist-high massive panicles of elegant white blooms. The advice for this is 'a moist sunny border' – keep on hosing it down. I have lots of reliable *P.p.* 'White Admiral', whose flowers have a smidgeon of edging giving the general sensation of single cream, and also *P.p.* 'Mount Fuji', more starry above dark green leaves. Both are late and long flowering, throughout August. Like all phlox they will not tolerate their bed drying out. *P. maculata* can be more mildew proof and I love *P.m.* 'Omega' which is dainty and snowy with a pink eye.

All phlox seem to glow in the dark and I love to take a late night walk through the pullulating stands in the moonlight.

Bean shucking again. Digging up potatoes in dry soil, but that almost-rain hangs in the air and makes the earth smell, roots, minerals, worms, silica, iron and decay. Out in the garden *natura naturans*: leaves, fruit, flowers, rabbits and birds doing their thing, woven together as in a tapestry. The closest one gets to being a child again.

Tobaccos in the night smell with tropical warmth, familiar yet incredible. I am struggling to unpick what it is, but whatever it is, it is that which turns a moth on. The smell of *Nicotiana alata* (syn. *affinis*) and *N. suaveolens* are closely related to those other night emanators the angel's trumpets, *Brugmansia*, and the night-scented stocks. All three are powdery and powerfully narcotic. Research has shown that moths' main tracking device is undoubtedly scent – night scents related to their own pheromones. However, they also distinguish the individual infrared patterns emitted by plants in the dark; while bees and butterflies see further down the cool violet end of the spectrum, moths use thermal imaging.

Nicotiana predictably does have a hint of unlit tobacco leaves. Somewhere in the furriness lies the smell, especially with *N. sylvestris* which is profoundly South American in scent, of guavas and BO thrumming from its sticky leaves and stalks.

TOBACCO

The genus *Nicotiana* is named after Jean Nicot, a French consul in Portugal during the sixteenth century accredited with introducing tobacco to France. In northern climes we use them as summer-flowering annuals rather than the perennials that they truly are. As we are all told incessantly, all parts are poisonous. The plants manufacture nicotine in their roots, from where it is transported to the rest of the plant. Its function is to deter the animals, especially various caterpillars that would otherwise like to eat the rather soft and tasty leaves (sadly, it doesn't seem to work too well against slugs). For scent there are only a few, mostly evening opening, but a very special and useful few to consider.

N. alata 'Grandiflora' has loose heads of chalky green gloriously scented flowers, the most highly scented tobacco plant you can grow and among the most highly scented of all plants, best planted in slight shade. One called 'Lime Green' seems to me to be without scent.

What do they smell of, apart from childhood? They are among the warmest, most powdery smooth- and soothing-smelling things in the garden. Sweet but not sugary, liquid with a spiciness and some cleansing lemon, very fresh fruit, strangely uncloying considering how dense and pervasive a smell it is. It is quite like jasmine and it travels by night, like stocks, so place them where you might sit of an evening; they're good at crossroads, under windows and near doorways. One of the great joys I realised this summer, because we decided to grow more of them than we had recently, is that they work, they do their thing anywhere. You can bung them in pots and they work well, in courtyards and basements and by the back door. The flowers sort of sleep during the day, petals all curled up, but they have to work hard at night pumping out scent. Pale colours open up a luminescence in the gloaming and even the red ones sing out royally as the light dies. They are not really much good for picking: being a bit droopy and sticky they seem to mess up any arrangement, but perhaps that's just me. They can be susceptible to tobacco mosaic virus, which is a great sadness and unconquerable if it chooses to be with you in your garden.

Nicotiana suaveolens is a recherché tobacco, with which we were obsessed for a while on account of the scent. The Australian tobacco, as it is known, is a herb sometimes as tall as myself on our terrace, but only if it makes it to the second year. This, for reasons completely incomprehensible to climate-change deniers, it can, now that winters are wetter and milder. In the South West nowadays, it overwinters as it would in its native Oz. The scent is chemically related to that of the exotic stephanotis and is best enjoyed on autumn evenings. The snag is that it takes a long time to get going in the British Isles; almost like a half-hardy biennial you need to grow it one year, discouraging flower, overwinter the basal rosettes in 9-cm pots in a frost-free corner or glasshouse and plant out the following May. The second year it will grow tall with very long and slender flowers and leaves. It has great daintiness. Patience is required, though, because it starts to really scent the evening air in August. The reward is astonishing, wafts of top-quality absolute for warm autumn nights or through the window.

Nicotiana sylvestris, as tall as me, has flat-topped heads of white tubular flowers in generous pendulous bunches held up on strong stalks above the lyre-shaped leaves, which are rough like the smell. All parts of the plant smell of a sweaty guava fruitiness which does not appeal to everybody. But I find it almost compulsively delicious and strange. On the evening air this smell becomes more diluted and decorous. The plants are easy to grow; statuesque and beautiful; bold enough to add to borders, beds and pots; sturdy with no need for staking; long flowering, glimmering in the dark and liking a bit of shade as their woodland epithet suggests. *N. × sanderae* is very similar and has a hybrid called 'Fragrant Cloud' which is large, strong stemmed and fruity smelling.

N. tabacum is one which I have not grown but Sarah Raven says that 'the strong smell of *Nicotiana tabacum* protects brassicas against the large cabbage white butterfly and prevents them from laying their eggs all over your brassica leaves.'

Which I am quite prepared to believe. The power of smell is so underrated. She is also a big fan of the F1 hybrid 'Whisper Mixed' (correctly, Whisper Series mixed). This is a scented, tall, white-and-pink-flowered version of the unscented but beautiful, dancing, *N. mutabilis*. This last came from Brazil and was first described only in 2002. Its flowers, as the name suggests, gradually change colour, starting creamy white and becoming deep pink, but it's a hummingbird species, so it has little or no scent and will not attract moths, which generally flock to tobaccos as to candles.

Hot scents

I loathe the smell of a brand new hire car. In Spain years ago we filled a rented car with aromatic maquis from the roadside to conquer the nausea of it. I can smell it now: wild cistus, Jerusalem sage and thyme all magnified by the heat of the back windscreen.

The swimming pool is drenched in a scent that was inexplicable at first. I knew it was not the angel's trumpets. Pushing through the undisturbed water freckled with pollen, the scent had sunk to water level, like a bloom just above the meniscus, fruity, rich and waxy. I was afloat on liquid jasmine.

Mr B is obsessed with the scent of his night-scented stocks, which are pluming away making his sleep contented. A hot night, a great night to be a moth flitting and ambling among the stocks and tobaccos, the jasmine blowing by the pool, the almost terrible trumpeting lure of the lilies in the dark and the waving towers of sweet peas.

This morning I was out among the hoverflies and bumblebees, knocking about in the flower jungle, juicy with dew, and cool just after dawn. We were all drawn along by smell. There is a conflict between photographing, looking for the photogenic, which I love and find meditative, and being present in the present, rather than documenting. I should just stop and be here, wherever, in all the interwoven leaf texture, bouncing light, sheerness and spangle, tickling notes and tonics. The bird's song, their lilting flight, how they rustle leaves, and then light upon updrafts and thermals. There is so much to miss out on. Here we are in July already, and midsummer come and gone.

Salvia sclarea var. *turkestaniana* is both stonking and ethereal, though some complain of its scent, which is strong meat, meant to fend from predation, with bittersweet bergamot and shellac. It's definitely distasteful, but it also excites the curiosity and, for my money, is well worth it, especially when it gets going.

BERGAMOT

Monarda – bergamot – without mildew is almost impossible, but *M.* 'Gardenview Scarlet' is a bright red, long-lasting bergamot which may be truly resistant. This new variety has an even more intense flower colour than *M.* 'Cambridge Scarlet', is a vigorous grower and can at least be said to have better resistance to mildew than most. Perfect for adding late colour to a hot border, it will also work well in prairie-style gardens when planted in association with ornamental grasses. The bees and butterflies will flock to it during the flowering period. But monardas can be capricious, and do not like soil that is either too damp or too dry, so it's a dedicated business growing them. You can help by applying a thick mulch.

Nicotiana Eau de Cologne
Series mixed

Poached some plums with orange juice and two big bay leaves. I love the smell of bay leaves. Smell them if ever you are feeling low. Just as good when they are dried. Heartening and rich, the aroma, emitted only when crushed or cooked, beggars description really. There's a background of eucalyptol sweetened by rose and lily but rounded off in an inimitable way with a warm clove spiciness. What did it do to the plums, or what does it do to chicken? Gives depth, frees up pungency, irradiates with its own sun and earthiness. Bay, like fig, is anciently understood, without parallel, and there every day of the year.

Lilium Pink Perfection Group is a late comer, the dirty smoky pink regale lily. A Garbo to the early summer's Ingrid Bergman scented white lilies. Invented in the 1920s by crossing the newly discovered regale lilies from China, it was a pet of Vita Sackville-West's and she ordered vast quantities for Sissinghurst. Vita loved tagetes too. Often overlooked and derided, the French marigold is almost a joke these days, and sold outside the local Spar, to my delight. The most interesting one, *Tagetes patula* 'Cinnabar' can easily be grown from seed collected from the previous year – even we can manage this. It is beautiful as Elizabethan stumpwork and smells, as it should, of the Orient and spice-ship cargo. *T.p.* 'Cinnabar' is good to grow in pots as it goes on and on, right into the late autumn. Pick and put in a jug with the scentless shocking pink *Nerine bowdenii* 'Isabel' in late October.

Edith Sitwell describes the unbelievable heads of regale lilies weighed down with trumpets one sometimes gets: 'We once had a lily here that bore 108 flowers on one stalk: it was photographed naturally for all the gardening papers. The bees came from miles and miles, and there were the most disgraceful Bacchanalian scenes …'

LILIES

Lilies: we have grown quite a few, but for Mr B only the scented ones will do. Let us just deal with the scourge of the lily beetle. We never gave it a thought when we first started gardening but now, especially when specifying for jobs, we must take into account that lilies now require hand grooming if the beetles are to be dealt with without chemicals. That said, we like growing them in pots where we eat outside and so the business is manageable, with the likes of regale lilies, and the African Queens and some later Oriental lilies. Where the beetle is much more of a problem is with the kind of *Liliaceae* that we all like to naturalise, the fritillaries, and the *Lilium martagon*. But it is still possible to do this through luck, and also because it feels like the beetles prefer a juicy hybrid – so perhaps those even draw them away. Timing is another factor: fritillaries being so early suffer much less of their depredations.

Lilium martagon is the Turk's cap lily, so called on account of its completely reflexed petals, the specific epithet 'martagon' being a Turkish word for those pumpkin-shaped turbans you see in miniatures of early Ottoman sultans. They are a true species, but much used in hybridising, and were once naturalised from the meadows of Portugal to the steppes of Mongolia. Stem-rooted, which means plant them as deep as you can to give ample root area for nutrient absorption, they grow waist- to shoulder-height tall bearing up to fifty heads of flower. Typically, a pink-purple with dark spots, but most sought after are the darker near black ones and the ghostly albino ones. The flowers are scented in a strong rustic way, a warm sperm fruity smell of light woodland which some people do not get along with. They seem to like wet feet as I have seen them at my cousin's house in the Thames Valley, where the water table is very high but gravelly, naturalised like crocuses under the shade (which they like) of an ancient plane tree, and they are said to be like that at Spetchley Park in Worcestershire. They flower in June and July.

The Madonna lily is *Lilium candidum*, the form and beauty of which was engraved upon my innocent soul at school shining out from so many of the Renaissance Madonnas adorning my convent walls in reproduction. I remember being fascinated most by the textiles, the Genoese cut velvets and the pink tights, but also by the flora, and those empty desert-like hillscapes dotted with a jewellery of flowers. Thus they entered my consciousness and stuck. John Lloyd, who owned and ran Kelways Nurseries when it was still on the original site, took us round before he sold it all off for housing and pulled some bulbs/corms out of a cooler, like ghostly artichokes, and gave them to me to grow. They never prospered and we have never grown them successfully. Again, they are a plant that, if happy, will thrive and spread. Basal rosettes of leaves form in the winter, everything withering after flowering, which happens in May, which it seems is the time to move or plant or transplant them, and then they throw up new leaves in late summer. Happy Madonnas form big clumps and can flower at shoulder height. They are supposed to like to be planted shallow, in limey soil, heads in the sun and roots in the cool. They often grow well beside water, and hate disturbance – so not for a herbaceous border. The flowers unbud at the beginning of June, somehow magical, mediaeval, white as their Latin epithet, with a thick suede flesh of luminescent pearly-white, bright gilded stamens which shadow the throat with gold; they are almost edible looking and powerfully warmly scented. The smell is not to everyone's taste, but to me they smell as they look, of honey and yogurt. They come from Crete, the Balkans and Asia Minor, flowering severally together on the top of a verdant stem. The whole is irresistible to painters: Walter Crane again and again, Stanley Spencer, Kees van Dongen. They rightly have a long history and cultural importance, particularly associated always with the Madonna in the mediaeval world.

The regal lily and its royal family: *Lilium regale* and *L.r.* 'Album' are pretty familiar to all growers of flowers for pots, picking and smelling. It was an astonishing find from Sichuan Province in south-western China (but long cultivated elsewhere in the East as an ornamental) in 1903 by Ernest Wilson who must have nearly died with excitement and did in fact nearly die in the quest. We grow it in pots within pots, taking them out and storing them after flowering and putting the whole plastic container that they grow in into the middle of a big terracotta pot after the tulips and wallflowers have done. We do this in May when we have tried to keep the lilies back a bit, in the shade, and only about two foot tall, but already loaded with bud. *Lilium* Pink Perfection Group are very similar in build shape and performance but flower a couple of weeks later and are a dusty pink; smart but very slightly unsatisfactory to my way of thinking. However, they are also stinking like regales and very good value. The smell of both is very good, narcotic, romantic, heady and rich. It is a swooning smell and it travels. The next similar one to flower is a big favourite, especially since we have been going glow-orange with the Indian garden round the pool; we use it in tubs and borders and it is called *L.* African Queen Group. It smells more gingery and flowers in late July and early August, magnificent, generous and outrageously glowing golden apricot marmalade. I just love it.

The other scented orange lily – and there are not that many scented orange flowers – is *Lilium henryi*, which has been in British gardens and paintings since the late nineteenth century. You would not expect it to be scented, but it is, and with a good warm lily smell. It is a good border companion: black stems push though other planting either finished, like the peonies, or in fabulous clashing flower, like phlox. It is very easy to grow, establishing and coming back year after year.

Useful in the same way in the late border or a pot are Goliath lilies, a cross between giant Oriental lilies and giant Trumpet lilies and I cannot really believe how big and lovely they are in August and how they grow through everything else with a determined vigour and then create a flower tower of great horns that scent the air. They take a couple of years to settle in but once established they go on forever. Feed them in the growing stage with anything from blood, fish and bone to seaweed extract.

We are all familiar with florist Oriental lilies such as *Lilium* 'Star Gazer' and the once beautiful *L. auratum* which has been bowdlerised by the breeders. *L.* 'Casa Blanca' is a good bet, with that rich amber and sun scent, and unbelievable almost fake starfish flowers. Perhaps if they were not flown in to M&S from Columbia they would have hung on to their magic, but they seem now to be botoxed, having had too much 'work'.

Then there are the lilies that are not lilies, the Jersey and Guernsey (*Amaryllis* and *Nerine*) and the *Schizostylis* (now *Hesperantha*) lilies. The Himalayan or gigantic lily is such a wonder: *Cardiocrinum giganteum*, the largest species of any of the lily plants, growing twice the height of Miss Jekyll. I love planting it for clients because it usually works and is easy but needs patience until it does its thing, years of patience, but then it is an Alice-in-Wonderland plant that knocks everyone for six. It is found in the high Himalayas, China and Myanmar. Normally *C.g.* var. *giganteum* is the one of the only two species for sale. It was introduced into commercial production (as *Lilium giganteum*) in Britain in the 1850s. A bulb grown from seed collected by Major Madden flowered in Edinburgh in July 1852. Cardiocrinum bulbs have a monocarpic life history, which means that they die after flowering. It will normally send up a huge 2- to 3-metre/ 6½- to 10-foot flowering stalk. At the base they produce big yummy-looking fresh and shiny leaves which understandably slugs feast on if you are not careful. Twenty to forty buds will set in its sixth or even seventh season. The cool white flowers open in August, red throated and giving forth an aria of complex lily scent full of Ambre Solaire suntan oil (legendary in the 1970s) and vanilla. Although this flowering stem will die completely, each bulb produces a number of 'offset' bulbs around the base of the old stem which should be dug up and planted alone to flower in five or more years. It sounds like heartbreak but if you planted a bulb or two, not cheap and usually three years old, in a two-litre pot, every year for seven years, you would have a fairy tale of continuous multiplying mystical woodland wonders.

Crinum lilies, not lilies at all but *Crinum × powellii*, grow well in Cornwall and Devon and probably London. They are scented in a lily-ish way and go on flowering into autumn. The white one is particularly pretty and the strap-like leaves are handsome in winter but need grooming.

The pool, though unheated, is melting warm, rain lashed, and smelling opulent. How hot it feels there when the African Queen Group and 'Star Gazer' lilies are out, and fringed with wetted geraniums (all right, pelargoniums, but they smell of Floris Rose Geranium bath oil). The alchemilla is covered in baubles of water held together by unimaginable forces. The spent flowers smell of straw when cut away to promote new flowering. The sweet peas stagger on, pod-laden, short-stemmed, but I would swear they smell sweeter the closer they get to death.

Phlox paniculata 'Blue Evening' and 'Blue Boy'

Mr B picks a pea

Rosa moschata prevails, a little powdery puff, late scented rose which emerges from perfect twisted buds. It has a smell that goes naturally with phlox and powdery mildew.

Lantana is a really compulsively delicious smell to my nostrils. But for inhabitants of the lands where it grows it is nothing but a weed and a nuisance. Here it dies off over winter unless kept in a heated greenhouse. The old thrifty way to do this, as with heliotrope, brugmansias and pelargoniums (a load of half-hardy or tender scented things), was to take cuttings and keep them going over winter for bringing on in the spring and planting out in the summer. Mr B and I are of the generation that never thought we had time for these niceties, and tend to buy them in years when we feel flush or do without. In Cornwall it has been easier to keep salvias, brugmansias and pelargoniums going, but heliotrope require real heat. I yearn for the life where there is enough time to take cuttings and grow everything from seed.

The car was full of melons and smelled liquid, champagne, like the sky this morning when the heavy rain had passed. Water droplets on asparagus, cabbages and lettuces, onions, marigolds and cosmos. The air steamy and opaque, the geometry of the topiary picked out in dewy silver. Had to drag self to computer. At lunchtime, went out and pulled ragwort, which smelled bitter and bruised, a tough green smell, with a meatiness about it. Presumably something about it attracts the waspish swarming caterpillars; perhaps they feel as I do about pickled cucumbers: cornichons are more-ish in much the same way I am sure. Ragwort is host to something like 37 species of insect, yet unfairly reviled by mankind, who are convinced it is a killer of beasts. This is true when it is cut and mixed in with silage or dried and bundled into hay bales, but, though poisonous, grazing livestock will usually avoid eating it.

The bee colonies are now made up of some 45,000 young females of about four to six weeks old. I find this amazing and wonderful.

Magnolia grandiflora

172

Bannerman braziers

Holiday smells

In the garden now in holiday summer, there are new cohorts of scent: dusty and aromatic smells of bergamot, lavender, verbascum, marguerites and milk thistles, which have their own crushed smell. Pink pelargoniums in the pots smell of peppermint and geraniol, balm and balsam. Colossal rain after a dry spell and walking down through the wood to the creek the smell is like music, coming in phrases and cadences. It was easier to see and feel the wood with one's eyes shut; the perception of festering was not there a month ago. The symphony of smell drops into a faecal, feral interlude, sonorous with fungi, a rich broth of leaf and lignum. The walls store warmth; they smell limey, cooled by moss, almost metallic. The hay seed in the open glade kindles a dancing high in the nose. Young kestrels keen above.

Dahlias lush and crimson in a bowl. All pomp and majesty. Picking them moved me sideways with a whoosh of floristry and the smell of genuine serious gardens, not like mine, where serried ranks are properly staked with flower pots to catch the earwigs. Never quite comfortable in my garden, dahlias are supreme inside the house; so grand, smelling sappy and of churches.

July mizzle in Cornwall is curiously cosy. Visibility barely measured in yards, the deliquescence is palpable dew and all enveloping. The droplets draw in the sea and harbour, strange pockets of smell. Holiday smells, coastal smells, hedgerow smells that have dark hearts.

Comparing the smell of certain flowers in June, July and August it seems to me

View to St Stephen's by Saltash

175

that they pump out a more pungent perfume later in the season. Bowles notes this in September. Can it be to do with the pollinators, also those flying and crawling things are now older, lazier, scarcer? And also the climatic conditions, warmer earth and air temperature?

The orchard smells of hay and straw and rank roses and ripening pears. A pungency of mixed herbs steams off the sides of the vertical meadow, the Norman motte, magnified in the hot afternoon: fine wild thyme, oregano, marjoram, fennel, juicy carrot weed and vetches. Each side a different ecosystem, life lived differently by different plants and creatures according to the effect of the sun, wind and rain, and the two holm oaks that – much as I love their broccoli-head magnificence – tower over and entirely alter the workings of the steep hot southern slopes of the motte.

The bay trees at Trematon are big and evergreen too, but they don't do this total holm-oak outfit change; they drop and drip leaves over weeks, new ones coming single and silent. They flower conspicuously with tiny green inflorescences, unscented but then their leaves smell, new or old, not on the air but when crushed. Nigel Slater writes: 'Their work is secret and difficult to define. Their effect on your supper is less obvious than that of rosemary or thyme. Bay is the most discreet of the woody herbs, often overlooked by the inexperienced cook.' I count myself very much among the latter. I have to remind myself of the eerie change a lot of bay leaves will make to a roast chicken. I love rice-pudding with bay leaves in the steep. I often pick them as I pass the several trees round Trematon and suck in the herbaceous aromatic transport of a smell, like very refined cannabis, piquant but balmy, bark and woodland, benign, inducing well-being with a warmth that goes with that rice pudding thing, and the gravy thing too, even though they are so different.

BAY LAUREL

The bay tree, *Laurus nobilis*, is an evergreen tree or shrub with entire, alternate, glabrous leaves often with wavy margins. They are firm, brittle, hard and leathery, and aromatic when crushed. Bay flowers with sexes on different plants, can get tall, and is usually of a dense pyramidical shape. Native of the Mediterranean, but cultivated in Britain since before the sixteenth century, it is the true laurel of the ancients. Its leaves were used to make crowns for heroes and its fruiting sprays to make wreaths for distinguished poets. The term 'bachelor' as applied to those given academic degrees is derived through the French *bachelier* from the Latin *bacca laurea*, laurel berry (and so too obviously the baccalaureate). 'Nowadays,' writes Bean, 'the leaves are put to more prosaic use, flavouring stews and soups.'

What we like most in the world is to sit in summer in the gloaming or wander about the garden like Jane Eyre. 'While such honey-dew fell, such silence reigned, such gloaming gathered, I felt as if I could haunt such a shade forever; but … my step is stayed, not by sound, not by sight, but once more by a warning fragrance. Sweet briar and southernwood, jasmine, pink and rose, have long been yielding their evening sacrifice of incense: this scent is neither a shrub nor a flower: it is – I know it well – it is Mr Rochester's cigar.'

Motte at dusk

Overleaf: Moon over Devonport Docks

176

Shooting Stars

With peach and apricot the garden wall
Was odorous, and the pears began to fall
From off the high tree.

William Morris THE EARTHLY PARADISE

The end of July is when 'nature seems to make a hot pause ...' was how George Eliot characterised it in *Adam Bede*. And William Morris described the garden in August as 'somewhat outworn'. In Cornwall it is holiday time. Headlands like sleeping dragons. Offshore smells, dusty paths and salty curled-up carrot parsley. The gorse nearly cuts your nose off with sharpness of prickles if you bend in to smell it when lucky enough to come across flower this late. It's a pineapple and coconut smell, a treat something like opening jars of boiled sweets, jars that can capture smells, vanilla and rose and violets. The laziest days of August have nights showered with stars. Dawn comes an hour later than a month ago at nearly six, but the evenings still linger, especially if you are on the Atlantic Coast; this is the best place to lie in the dunes and wait for the Perseid meteor shower, so called because the radiant, or origin, of the shower, which accompanies the comet Swift-Tuttle, occurs in the constellation Perseus.

Pears are what grow well in Cornwall, along with some apple varieties, but I have never got an apricot to fruit anywhere, let alone the curly-leaved peach. A high pear tree is a thing of high beauty, much more to me than any fancy arboretum tree.

I almost wept upon finding the first cyclamen hovering about in the recesses of the garden. Already? The sweet smell of summer's end sank through me. I think of them emerging from the earth like pink sugar mice, a phenomenon progressively travelling north and west from the Middle East to spongey old here. Cyclamen are up in the boscos of Italy, along wild boar drives, and in coveys, and light woodland, in garden, under favourite trees, upbeat among the dry shades of late summer, leafless and brave, harbingers of autumn. They do awaken a happy anticipation for the curious pleasures of winter, for sparseness in the landscape, the dry framework of fence and furrow, bleached marshland, yellowed water meadow, black branches and bonfire night.

The garden smells tidy and of hot stone. The vegetable garden smells of contented compost, the hen house has a palpable whiff of ammonia and, in the shade behind the greenhouse, alpine strawberries scent my fingers as I squat under the great belly of the motte before a swim. A sultry day, low with swallows and martins.

Can it be dahlia time again? We bought some from a bucket beside the road. At home I picked armfuls of *Dahlia* 'Bishop of Llandaff'; the smell was sort of drugging. That was after I had been picking the last of the bravely flowering sweet peas, whose stems are already shortened like the days; the 'nose' or smell was long and low with half the sugariness of a month ago. Less sun, less sugar? Bees must remark on it, or song and dance about it. After the delicacy of sweet peas, the

Eucryphia × nymansensis
'Nymansay'

181

clonking woody smell of dahlias was strong medicine. Chrysanthemums are the same; they smell of the end of the holidays, and of being a bridesmaid.

The dahlia border is an analogue of a coarse Turkish carpet, all the colours of aniline dye. Mauveine, or aniline purple, was the first dye to be synthesised, in 1856, by chemistry rather than using animal vegetable or mineral matter, followed by fuchsin, cyanine, safranin and induline. It always seems to me that dahlias were bred after the craze for these new brash colours swept late-nineteenth-century Europe. Since I started gardening, Sarah Raven has created a revolution in understanding how to use these colours. She is the most brilliant editor, and single-handedly brought them back into fashion. I am a sucker for joyous colours any time, and especially all the richly ferruginous colours of the late borders. They make me excited again, only an echo of how I feel in spring, but good none the less; at other times of year, like now, I crave the curious acrid smell of dahlia and chrysanthemum green parts. I would love to get a whiff of the fuzzy felted smells of rudbeckia, agastache and zinnias – which really have no smell at all but have the feel of smell in the nose. Is it a thing that, the later a flower flowers, the more dry and furry it will be? I call them the 'fuzzes' when I am scanning/photographing pelargoniums for instance. The smell of dahlias, because they are generally so double, is more about the sap and particularly easy to recall. Here and now I can conjure the genie from the lamp of my mind and summon up that smell, real as real, almost eerie.

Later flowering borders make the lull of August bearable for Mr B. He has infected me with his loathing of August because it is somehow a slow time. Making the exotic pool and keeping his pots going and the smell levels on 'loud' save him from despondency at the waning of the summer. Some of the finest late herbaceous borders are in Scotland, where a hundred years ago they were conceived to flower only in August when the gentry arrived and needed to spice up the sporting life, their gardens filled with Tyrian purple dahlias, goldenrod, mole-velvet rudbeckias, Landseer-sunset heleniums. The swathes of prairie planting so fashionable a hundred years later come into their own in August too. But asters, rudbeckias, echinaceas, heleniums, whilst they have distinct smells, cannot be described as scented, even by my weird measure. Crocosmias are part of this rainbow season. They are scentless, and I love them especially in the far west where they go rampant and serious gardeners consider them a pest. I cannot help being fond of them, in a vase or to suck the nectar from the narrow end of the flower tube as we did as children (it filled the time). I like the combination of the scentless crocosmia in all its marmalade forms wandering and springing out amongst the tidy bushes of any type of lavender. The colours of high summer and the smell too.

Lavender: what is one to say? The smell is so special but so ubiquitous that it needs to be stripped to mountainsides in Hvar, where it grows undisturbed, timeless, unfashionable or otherwise. It is a smell of heat and health, aromatic, punchy, alcoholic, citrus and saucy.

LAVENDER

A huge genus of short aromatic shrubs, lavender was probably brought to England by Benedictine monks before the sixteenth century, perhaps even before the Normans made the locals build this castle. We think of it rightly as very important in the mediaeval

The Hamoaze from the motte

world for its scent, which permeates the whole plant from roots upwards. The seeds are called nutlets, appearing on a stalked terminal spike; much of the plant sometime, as in *Lavandula stoechas*, is covered in a 'tomentum' or a layer of matted woolly down which invites one to rub it off and release the volatiles of smell. For scenting your drawers or the drawing out of scent for lavender oil one must pick the flowers in bud – which is also the best way of pruning lavender plants to keep them trim. We do neither. August is too lazy for such chores and, besides, time stops on the granite steps of the Indian pool garden if you watch the bees on drone raids over the open flower so abundant with nectar. I cannot face cutting them back, and so the plants become rangy and shorter lived. It is a choice. Of the lavandins, *L. × intermedia*, the Dutch Group contains clones flowering late in the season; they are considered inferior by the producers of lavender oil, but we all grow them – they are often sold as *L.* 'Vera' – because they are hardy, reliable, thigh high and offer that which we find pleasing about lavender: a sagey, a smelly and a tidy bush. The finest oil is said to come from old English lavender, or common lavender, *L. angustifolia*, the smell of which seems most quintessential, most green, flowery and comforting.

The Mediterranean lavenders, the crazy flag-waving spike lavender, *Lavandula latifolia*, and *L. stoechas* – called 'French Lavende' by Gerard – are more fun and feathered; *L. stoechas* has a conspicuous tuft known as the 'coma'. They flower from April but are tender, their oily smell endowed with an aromatic citrus punch to the scent which could only be born of limestone maquis. They need deadheading rather than cutting back. In France, the traditional home of the lavender and its oil production (although now Bulgaria is the biggest producer), historically portable stills were carried to the wild stands at flowering time. I am sure this was true all over the Mediterranean in places like Hvar in Croatia, where the uplands are covered in wild lavender and the oil can be bought from the side of the road along with the scented honey. The *essence d'aspic* from *L. latifolia* is inferior to that of the true lavender (*angustifolia*) and of a different chemical composition; used in perfumery it has the less delectable pungency of camphor. The volatiles responsible for the specific smell of lavender are linalyl acetate and linalool, which are chemicals that are both rapidly absorbed into the bloodstream. Research suggests that inhaling these increases the time you spend in deep, slow wave sleep, and the effects were stronger for women than for men. *L. angustifolia*, we have adopted as the 'English' or 'common' lavender and it comes in many cultivars of differing colour and leaf. For years the pure violet of 'Hidcote' seduced us every time but now I like the idea of mixing the colours so that they play off each other, as Mr B does with honesty. The thing is to grow enough, and the lavender-edged path may be a cliché, but it is a great thing. They love the top of a wall, because they crave dry feet. They are not afraid of droughts or heights, thriving by the sea and inland at even at a couple of thousand metres; they grow exceptionally in the high Cotswolds and inland Britain on limestone.

ROSEMARY

Rosemary is closely related to lavender (and, apparently, sage, as *Rosmarinus officinalis* is now *Salvia rosmarinus*), but I think I like rosemary better. I love the flowers and the smell, and it is a really useful plant. Mr B uses it in borders and gravel, clipped and unclipped, climbing down walls, crawling out of beds and on to gravel, trained into bonsai trees. It is a long-lived, handsome and generous plant that requires very little – even water. It is highly companionable, setting off other plants in an understated way, in the garden, in a vase, in a pot or a vegetable plot, in a house, in the snow or in the rain. There

Nicotiana sylvestris

is a nursery at Bodmin that specialises in growing rosemary and we have tried them all. Despite the fact that Cornwall is not ideal for Mediterranean maquis plants such as rosemary and cistus we perversely chose to make them a big thing in the garden here – with some success. I would warn that prostrate rosemary reverts after a few years and stands up again. The one known as 'Green Ginger' smells only very slightly of ginger and is not particularly good-looking, but all of them are worth pinching as you pass. They do not fill the air; the volatiles are only released with crushing. But then they pour forth as we all know from cooking. The smell oozes from the tomenta on the underside of the needle-like leaves, a keen smell, pine like the leaves, a woody pungency, eucalyptus, and some have more citrus. It is a domestic smell, and a camping smell, making bonfires with aromatics. 'Miss Jessopp's Upright' has good deportment; the flowers do not smell at all. The Corsican narrow-leaved rosemaries, *S.r.* var. *angustissimus*, usually have flowers of a good colour; those of 'Benenden Blue', also scentless, are a singing blue. We have a cutting of a cutting of a cutting from Sue Dickinson, from Pam Schwerdt, from Sissinghurst, *S.r.* 'Sissinhurst Blue'. It grows in an ugly urn like a bonsai tree, spavined but flowering merrily, never watered, and strongly incense and dark churchy smelling. Prostratus Group is trailing – not my favourite habit, but falling over a wall is terrific and what it's best for; it is tender but saved by good drainage, with fresh green foliage, dense and smelling greener than most rosemary. Perhaps less good for cooking. 'Severn Sea' is pretty, arching, but tenderish, being raised in the west at West Porlock by Norman Hadden. More tender still, 'Tuscan Blue' produces wands covered with flower each year above the thickly luminous green leaves – which need to be cut back to help it overwinter. W. Arnold-Forster introduced it, and wrote 'in Tuscany, hedges of this plant are conspicuous from a distance owing to their ceanothus blue'.

Belting out scent just now are the lilies, a hybrid between Trumpet and Oriental lilies concocted by a professor in Chicago that we buy from Parkers Dutch Bulbs, known collectively as Goliath because they are much taller than I am and hugely well-armed with flower. Some are very ugly, and they do not have heroic names. My chosen ones are 'Honeymoon', 'Miss Feya' and 'Anastasia'. With them, phlox feed out their mysterious misty perfume along with the lingering fuchsine raspberry and lime balms of *Rosa* 'De Resht', one of my favourite roses which causes no trouble and flowers incessantly, endowed with rounded perfume.

Night-scented stock is working overtime.

Evening primroses are a sort of fantasy to me. I always felt unsure I was really 'getting' them as a smell, even in vast quantities on waste ground. I think the smell is clinical, of childhood playgroups and nurseries, aniline perhaps, like sticking plaster. It is another of the lost smells that litter old garden literature but are rare now. I love the lemon look though, a rare and iridescent Chinese yellow. It looks wonderful now along with acid-lemon dahlias 'Bishop of York' and with *Patrinia scabiosifolia,* woad (*Isatis tinctoria*) and wild fennel. But they don't do well for me.

EVENING PRIMROSE

Oenothera biennis is described as a 'variable' species of hardy biennials, forming a low rosette the first year and a stem that grows as tall as I am the second season. I find them very variable in quality of smell too. I like the common name, 'sundrops'. The fragile silky Chinese-yellow blooms can smell like crocuses on their only evening of life, or sometimes not. Best in masses on waste ground, they are too short lived to make it into a clever prairie planting but with artifice, at a flower show, they could be used to incredible effect. But I think it would be a bit like taming wild horses. Some forms are grown for their colourful spring foliage, and there is also a new German cultivar of *O. fruticosa* subsp. *glauca* called 'Silberblatt', which has a rosette of leaves edged with white. But generally, oenotheras are not great foliage plants.

After appalling dreams in the heavy night the oppression of the weather subsided. Remembering tea with our dear friend Mrs G under the white horse at Uffington and under a sultry sky. Honeysuckle dripped like molasses through her timber balcony and oozed about the tea terrace. It rained darkly for fifteen minutes. Then the sun battled against plum skies and bell ringers started to practise in the Cathedral of the Vale. Drink and dinner were got from the car and we settled, all in a row, as if at a bus stop, facing out to watch the sun go down over White Horse Hill, the hut with the view, pulsating warmth from the tanalised timbers. Pale in the half-light were three strutting geese and some lazy sheep. Across the field paraded a piebald terrier and a pikey pony called Lily, who smelled my anxiety with horses despite my pleasure in exchanging breaths with her, and she covered my hand with her oily pelt scent. The house smelled of Aga and grass matting, horse tackle, books and magazines and, by the time we left, a good deal of tobacco smoke.

The over-ripe melon attracted fruit flies into the larder, it being a hot day, and so we opened a succulent quarter and ate it, juice running down our chins. Taste and smell a Neapolitan mix of cucumber, sugar, armpits and cumin.

I remember my mother on just this kind of sulking empty August day in London treating us to a melon she had been sniffing and savouring for days, turning it in the sun with her powerful bejewelled hands, like the French peasant she was at heart. It had been expertly chosen from Tatchbrook Street market in Victoria. She was not much of cook, but greedy enough; Elizabeth David was a household god. In the stygian gloom of her London kitchen, the only sash window had crinkled glass, as it gave on to a light well and the sound of fans and blowers which, if you wanted to glamorise your teenage boredom, you might liken to Manhattan. Her 'alcoholic's fridge' was big enough only for butter, wine and ice trays. My father and my teenage self sat next door in the egg-yolk-gloss dining room on the street side, smelling our melon halves and that peculiar dining-room smell of oxidised silver, beneath the aubergine daubs of an Eileen Hogan painting, trying to anticipate whether our little supper together would end in a tirade. This danger point, the combination of drink and hunger, always made the opening movement the most dangerous of any get-together. Night after night the table was perfectly laid: green salad on a Delft charger, huge handsome pistol-handled knives and Mason's Ironstone plates. In the foggy light my mother would ask my father to stop breathing, something he did noisily through his long-ago broken nose, filling the emptiness of the room, irritating her scratchily. He also had to develop a method of hovering on the painted Neapolitan chairs, which were worm-eaten to the point of collapse.

Home was a web of literary, lifeless, urban twilight. Now I feel for my mother and relish the pleasure she found in slicing the single scented melon. She was a

Left: *Phlox paniculata* 'Rembrandt', *Cleome hassleriana* mixed colours

sensualist, and a lazy perfectionist. Ritual demanded that she left the slices scenting the room whilst we all had a gin and tonic upstairs in the drawing room, French windows open, curtains partly closed against August. This resplendent, over-furnished, over-stuffed, ravishing, murky, moth-infested room smelled of horse hair, Ushak rugs, of wool, wool and more stuffy wool. I think you could smell the ink and the writing paper, the print on private view cards, old flower water, magazines, papers, books and the worms eating the tables collapsing under the books. It smelled like a wasp nest. Wafting in through the window came London: taxi fumes, pigeons, dust, pollen, dry leaves and litter.

Mignonette in the greenhouse is just getting going. It is a bizarre and mesmeric smell, very nineteenth century. After several attempts at growing it, I am finally successful and even more at a loss as to why fashion has forgotten it when it was once so revered. The smell of mignonette is concentrated violet cream, marshmallow, sickly, drowsy and edible.

MIGNONETTE

Mignonette, *Reseda odorata*, is a leafy annual, less than knee high. This strange little plant is upright with spikes of flower, like miniature Romanesco broccoli, with a heavy sickly-sweet scent. It is a native of Egypt and the Mediterranean basin. I have found it very difficult to grow, and frequently unscented. One common name is bastard rocket. It is supposed to be a chalk lover, for well-drained soil and seemingly best sown straight into the ground where it is to grow. No luck for me when I did that though, until, finally, I grew some *R. odorata* 'Grandiflora', which Chiltern Seeds promise is the 'quintessential form of the plant now in cultivation'. This suggests that many forms are lost to cultivation, though they may be out there, escapees, and they may have the true powerful scent and robust genes. I grew it in a pot, kept it in the greenhouse, and right at the end of August I found a couple of flowers with a smell that I found compulsive. It brings out the smellaholic yearning, sweet like sweet shops, Parma violets, and violets, and violet creams, custards, rice paper, sugared almonds, puddings and cakes. No wonder the sugar-mad Victorians loved it so.

Right: Wild carrot

Overleaf: Sweet-pea teepees

Eucryphia plumes like holy smoke into the August sky. Unbelievably lovely. At first eucryphia smells of Indian undergrowth, spicy but barely there. A smell can be barely perceptible to stir buried reactions, like subtlety in colour, the timbre of a voice or an indefinable flavour. Along with hoheria, euchryphia is the blossom tree of high summer, but it has the benefit of being scented, densely clotted, more scented than spring fruit blossom, drawing flying things from all around, as attested by the electric storm of susurrating insects about the spire. The flowers are without nectar, so it must be the pollen they are after. The single flowers, taffeta-white and embroidered with silver stamens, are clustered so generously as to totally eclipse the handsome evergreen foliage and dance all over the tree. Mr B saws off branches and buries the ends in stonkingly large glass vases, showing them off and scratching the ceiling. Every room is now in a fever of hay and every surface dusted with pollen smudge.

Buddleia smells to me of circuses and grass inside sunlit tents, the sweet corners of childhood, wands, warm dens, watching butterflies. It almost smells of babies, nappies and talc sometimes, but to Mr B it smells of derelict buildings and sex.

BUDDLEIA

I can only remember how to spell buddleia (with an 'i' for 'Isabel', although Linnaeus spelled it *Buddleja* and we have to, now, when using the Latin name) by summoning a mental vision of the Rev. Adam Buddle, who was honoured by Linnaeus at the request of a young Scottish plant-collecting doctor, William Houstoun. Buddleia is the butterfly tree, the pioneer plant of bombsites and abandoned places. Adam Buddle's life was predictably Trollopian. Born in 1662 near Peterborough, the church, bryophytes, a wife and two children were his life. He was the first authority on liverworts, hornworts and mosses despite living in the driest of counties. Dr Houston collected plants in Jamaica and the Caribbean in 1730, despatching seeds and plants to Philip Miller at the Chelsea Physic Garden. *Buddleja americana,* the most widespread species of the Americas, was one of his finds and he generously suggested Linnaeus name it after the English cleric and botanist, although Adam Buddle was never conscious of the plant, having died in 1715. Unfortunately, the physician Houstoun was unable to heal himself, dying 'of the heat' in Kingston, Jamaica, just seven months after being made a Fellow of the Royal Society in 1733.

Like the bryophytes the tender buddleias thrive in the South West or else under cool glass. *Buddleja asiatica* is a slender graceful shrub with long panicles of white flowers produced in winter and early spring, and bearing a definite Buddle smell but intensely sugary and almost uninteresting. *B. madagascariensis* is a native of Madagascar, with terminal panicles of orange-yellow flowers and violet-coloured berries; it is very tender but is grown on a wall at Trengwainton, near Penzance. *B. auriculata* is an evergreen shrub of lax habit as high on any wall; young shoots are slender, scurfy-downy at first and then glabrous. Flowers are produced and are pongy here in my garden from September to January. A native of South Africa, it grew first against the wall of the Temperate House at Kew and has been as far north as Northumberland. The buddleia that flowers in April is called *B. agathosma*. It has wavy, soft moleskin silver leaves as foil for the palest lilac racemes.

Of the many hardy species and varieties, the lookers and smellers so familiar to us and butterflies are the *Buddleja davidii*. They are deciduous and shrub-like but can sometimes make a small tree with very long, tapered leaves dark green, tomentose at first, soon

Wild carrot

becoming glabrous above while remaining felted beneath; the stalks are very short. The fragrant flowers are densely arranged in short, rounded clusters on slender panicles – the whole effect almost as wagging and cheery as a fluffy dog's tail – from July to October, or later. These are not from the Caribbean but found in the highlands of central and western China and were discovered by the French Lazarist missionary, Père David, who made his name and much botanic history in China. The first garden plants were raised in the Jardin des Plantes, Paris, in 1893 by the nursery firm of Vilmorin, but it is from Wilson's seed, collected in Hubei and Sichuan during the years 1900-08, that the garden varieties of the present day are descended.

Their awkward habit and downy leaves are not naturally elegant, but their flowers have some distinction, with a characteristic smell, and are in possession of magnetic forces for the attracting of butterflies. Some say the smell is like pencil shavings, but it is undeniably sugary. In the UK, it is mostly a group of butterflies known as the vanessids that are attracted to the shrub: the peacock, small tortoiseshell, red admiral and comma. The flowering of *Buddleja davidii* coincides with their main summer emergence. However, the corolla tube of the flowers is too deep for the proboscis of the smaller butterflies such as the blues and skippers, which favour hebe, marjoram and lavender. *B. lindleyana*, its flowers pretty but sparsely given and not very significant, is the best for the hummingbird hawkmoth. The first butterflies tend to emerge in the second week of August, therefore it is best, both for the butterflies and for the late garden, to prune the *davidii* forms of buddleia in April. For late summer, dark is somehow best: papal purples and puce hues come from *B.d.* 'Black Knight' and *B.d.* 'Royal Red'. I like the fat melting flowers of *B.d.* 'Dartmoor', lots of colour and very mauve, reminding me of early summer dripping with lilac. For the blue end of violet, but not truly blue, there is *B.* 'Ellen's Blue' and *B.d.* 'Blue Horizon' with strong orange in the tubes. They remind me of lantana, a plant whose smell I find addictive, as does *B.* × *weyeriana* – a cross between *B. davidii* and *B. globosa* and smartly dismissed by Christopher Lloyd as combining 'the worst features of both parents in a sickly orange, pink and mauve vomit'.

Marvel of Peru – *Mirabilis jalapa* – I have been trying to smell you for what feels like a lifetime. Ever since reading Andrew Marvell as a teenager:

> Another world was searched, through oceans new,
> To find the Marvel of Peru.

Now the runes are right and there you are, a bottle of tropic perfume from an absurdly synthetic looking magenta or yellow flower. I love its artificiality, akin to poinsettia, coupled with a duty-free smell, like water droplets in the rain forest. *Nicotiana suaveolens* has a similar tropical quality. Of smells like this there is never enough.

The *Eucomis* I grew smelled like abandoned trainers.

Yesterday was a sublime day. The world, washed by two days of belting rain, was dancing with insect life. A great day to inhale. The Goliath lily will, given a couple of years in the ground, burst through any amount of border verbiage clamouring for attention. *Lilium* 'Mount Cook' by the pool smells peachy but has a glow beneath the magenta surface that would set a Geiger counter off. On days like this the earth is optimally warm and gives out a rooted, humus-rich smell. Humus is hugely important, contributing to moisture and mineral retention and containing many useful nutrients for healthy soil, nitrogen being the most important of all. It is part of the real scent of life borne through the soil, even though it is dead matter. 'The poetry of earth is never dead' (Keats).

By the evening the air has stilled to breaking point, holding off the wave of weather pressing in from the west, a bow wave coming, relentless, light dimmed, scent stretched.

Lemon verbena gives me stabs of nostalgia. It smells of dark sweet shops that you stepped down into; kitchen cupboards that were kept for baking ingredients, cochineal and essences; school trips, sweetie wrappers in the back of coaches.

LEMON VERBENA

Among all the aromatic herbs that grow along the paths of Provence, there is one whose lemon freshness is utterly reviving, like a sherbet ice: *Aloysia citrodora*. Its distinctive fragrance is said to fill the air around the markets of Provence, but only if you can find it now among the far-eastern-made trash. But this verbena was imported also, by the Spanish, from South America. It can grow to a large shrub but is generally a half-hardy perennial in northern climes. There was once a huge one by the front door here at Trematon, perhaps planted by Sylvia Foot when the Plymouth Liberal Foot family lived here (legend has it the house heaved with books then, also). Lemon verbena is great to have by a door, like myrtle, a scented welcome and an opportunity to pinch an aromatic leaf as you go by. But Sylvia's succumbed to some sudden vicious frost before we took on the lease. Hence, we are wary with ours, keeping some in pots under glass in winter. The outdoor ones look dead at the beginning of the year but spring back, slowly. There is something very heart-warming when, in June, there are enough leaves to make tea again. In July and August leaves abound and can be mixed with lime flowers. Something of a sophisticated continental taste and smell, rich and intense. The active volatiles have been found to be more than a third citral (three times as much as in lemon balm) with nerol (found in hops and lemongrass), which has a sweet rose odour like, but fresher than, geraniol – which is the third, finishing ingredient. The flowers might be called 'insignificant' and are not noticeably scented but have a miniature charm as they look like scaled-down Persian lilac.

VERBENA

Many garden verbenas are treated as annuals as they lack hardiness and will flower the first year when grown from seed. They come from Europe and the Americas north and south. In gardens the showy forms are *Verbena × hybrida* (now *Glandularia × h.*), a complex race of hybrids developed in these isles since 1837. They have a coarseness about them, with toothed leaves and hairy square stems, but some manage to trail and smell, and of these Mr B's favourite, especially for using in pots with pelargoniums, is 'Pink Parfait' because it smells of sweet shops and looks the part, with striking pink and white bicoloured flowers that might be made of brushed cotton.

Myrtus communis leaves. I would have liked these as a child, but it was a long time later that I came across them in the Generalife gardens of the Alhambra, and the 'bosci' of Italian gardens. I did know from chamomile and the yarrows that

Tropaeolum majus
'Fireball'

indefinable, smoky, peaty, forest and fungal nose that is so particular. The rather hard evergreen leaves need crushing to liberate the smell. Myrtle can be clipped like box in hotter countries than ours. The flowers are embroidered between the shiny leaves in rosy round buds with crown-like calyces. They open like shooting stars, a burst of stamens, echoing the Perseids falling for a few days in the August night sky.

Clerodendrons vary. The one here is strongly repellent, smelling of meat and dingy things, for predator repulsion. And yet I have picked the flowers elsewhere and been transfixed by something jasmine hot. It is worth growing – even though it suckers faster than lightning. Clerodendron in Devon brushes you with its scented fingers, smelling of jasmine and straw while the leaves smell of woodland berries. Thinking berries, I think of honeysuckle. Sometimes honeysuckle has berries better than red currants, which bejewel the hedgerows and are the pride of the Cornish lane.

CLERODENDRON

Clerodendron is its old name; other common names include glorybower, bagflower and bleeding-heart. *Clerodendrum* is a large genus of shrubs and climbers of which three species are hardy. Two of these are suckering shrubs, behaving more like perennials, forming a dense thicket of stems over summer but often knocked to the ground in winter. *C. bungei* (formerly its nauseous pong was recognised in the epithet *foetidum* – but no longer), a native of China, introduced by Fortune in 1844, bears wide clusters of flowers between heart-shaped leaves. These flowers, like those of many scented plants such as daphnes, offer a slender-tube opening with a five-part mouth, a tiny trumpet for foraging lepidoptera such as hawkmoths drawn by the tingly fresh scent which is particularly surprising in August. *C. trichotomum* var. *fargesii* flowers in the early days of August and scents the garden with its white flowers, which are shown off so well by their large purple-red calyces. The ensuing pea-sized steel-blue berries sit like jewels in purple-crimson inflated calyces, like an evening coat. Bean says, 'although the flowers are fragrant the leaves when crushed emit a heavy nauseous odour'. Exactly right. It likes an open loamy soil.

Indian pool pavilion

Autumn begins to be inferred

Daily the night falls faster and the smell of decay breathes stronger. Lying out late watching shooting stars, the lawn is loaded with dew, the air still, and the tree shapes crouched down upon themselves. The smell of lawns is still very important in the design of any garden for people. We like them. We like the idea of them. A bit like seats we may never sit on, they offer possibility, a chance to hide under a blanket, smelling the turf, giggling. Horace Walpole was keen on keeping his lawns tempting. The longing to smell mown grass and a lawn 'green enough to disgust a Frenchman' remained with him to the end. Gardening for Walpole, as for myself and Mr B, amounted to hope, promise, anticipation, longing, nostalgia and loss. Lawns were more meadows than the machine-cut patches of today, but about the same time Rousseau wrote in *Julie, or the New Heloise* about the smell of 'lawn' in an orchard, 'the verdant turf, thick, but short and close, was intermixed with wild thyme, balm, sweet marjoram, and other scented herbs'.

We are in the Inner Hebrides. The Rugosa rose 'Blanche Double de Coubert' is later here, so still in its prime. But this may be a less double and a more highly scented clone, as the smell is delicious in bowls indoors, lemony rose with a silky softness that is completely alluring, while mine at home seems to have none of this. It may be the *terroir*: Rugosas hail from Japan, acidic islands not so very different from the Hebrides. Iona smells sweet. Warmly sunlit after a very short but breezy sea crossing. The comfort of its vegetable gardens huddle-walled and bounded with willow, fuchsia, escallonia, came as a shock after the malt-whisky sponge of bracken, heather leather and deep moss of Mull. KKB, my friend from Mull, says the sun always shines on Iona, which is why the monks came here. It seems blessed and the gardens thrive here right on the sea on the protected inner reaches cosseted by Mull. The sea here is another such smell bath; whether it is kippering you in the sun or delivering a sulphurous kelp compress, it still tells of the hardness of life on the margins. The smell and sight of the gardens awoke a desire to husband and grow, purposefully and against the odds.

Back home, and the early mornings in August seemed never more lambent and limpid. The earth is as hot as it will be this year. The shock is the *Cyclamen hederifolium* coming up like shrimpy moths through the dry earth. It is always Mr Observant who notices them first. They are up. They were up on the last day of July. Ants carry away the seeds which bulge behind the desiccated petals, coiled slowly back down to earth in a spring, curled-up until they are ripe and ready for the workers to walk away with.

Chocolate cosmos is like a rush to the brain. The smell isn't exactly floral, it is dry warm cocoa, a complete oddity. 'Gay-Odin' in Naples is the chocolate shop where I first found 99 per cent dark chocolate. Eating it grates your mouth like tarmac but is compellingly delicious.

Feeling chemical this morning. Down by the pool the musty goaty smell somewhere is hexanoic acid – a colourless oily liquid when refined, which has a greedy smell that is fatty, cheesy, waxy, earthy and musty (five of the seven dwarves) – what the wine buffs call 'barnyard'. The mix of plants here is also giving off caprylic acid, found in milk and coconut oil, which produces what one instantly describes as 'rancid' smells. All this rankness is strangely alluring in minute quantities.

Angel's trumpets – once thought of as belonging to *Datura*, but now *Brugmansia* – are flowering. Brugmans was Professor of Botany at Leiden in the late eighteenth century. The name is not catchy, but what of the smell? It flows through you or

Cyclamen hederifolium

you through it, like water. Will-o-the-wisp. It comes when crickets sing, and an August moon picks out the flaring bells, satin, glistening with turn-ups like pagoda roofs. They are, and the smell is, famously narcotic, mysterious and dangerous. It is a smell not just on the air, but it is the air. Especially in the Mediterranean and Morocco where it grows as big as pear trees. It is one of the largest flowering shrubs there is, with the potency of lilies but the lightness of magnolia.

ANGEL'S TRUMPETS

The thing about angel's trumpets is that, even if you do lose them over the winter, cuttings or seedlings will grow astonishingly fast the next year. They don't need much to keep the roots alive in winter, not even light, but they must have protection from frost. It is fun to keep a big plant going because it will get huge over the next summer. But either way the thing is to enjoy the smell of this wondrous weed from South America. It is listed as 'extinct in the wild' because only cultivated clones exist now. Most brugmansia are fragrant in the evenings to attract pollinating moths. One species, the handsome striped red-flowered *Brugmansia sanguinea*, has no scent, and now I understand why: it is designed to be pollinated by long-billed hummingbirds. All parts of brugmansia are potentially poisonous and its hallucinogenic effects were clinically described as 'terrifying rather than pleasurable'.

Brugmansia arborea 'Knightii' is a double hose-in-hose (where one flower appears to be inside another) white-flowered form. Mr B is not a fan of doubles and deems this one a bit like a very high-class dress that the mother of the bride might wear to a wedding – too stiff and silky. But he has had to admit the scent is sublime, and possibly the best of all. He loves best the ochre chamois-leather trumpets of *B. × candida* 'Grand Marnier', which smell almost as good, and whose leaves have wavy margins. The snowy angel's trumpet is *B. suaveolens*; this has tubular, bell-shaped, night-scented flowers in shades of white, yellow or pink from early summer to autumn. The Latin *suaveolens* means 'sweet-smelling' and is one of the few descriptive epithets relating to sweet-smellingness in the entire gamut of the binomial system.

Late summer roses

Rosa 'Madame Isaac Péreire'. She's the top, she's the Colosseum of roses. Roses are the scent of the garden now, and they need to smell. There are a few that I love which don't smell – *R.* 'Complicata', *R. moyesii* and *R. glauca*. But on this morning, everything is heavily dewed, Madame faces east, so she is warmed by the sun but still dewy, bosomy, peerless. There are three blooms, and they smell of woman, not the 'girl' smell of 'Maiden's Blush', but the attar of roses, apples, lemons, plums and peaches. She will be generous with her offerings until Christmas in a lucky year. *Rosa* 'Climbing Devoniensis', a faded lemon colour in a dark corner, catches my eye. It has a purity of hue and complexity of form that astonishes, and it flowers generously from May to October. Its scent is like poking one's head round the door of an apple store, and makes you think of fruit wood burning and the smoke, cider and Devon's lichen-covered orchards.

Roses contain none of the indole found in jasmine, tuberose, lilac, orange blossom and human faeces. This is the element in the smell of orange blossom that lends it a putrid-sweetness that makes it so sultry and intoxicating (to those who like it). On its own, though, indole has no magic. The alchemy of nature is in the complex layering of ingredients, often at infinitesimal levels, the intricacy of which is impossible to imitate, and which is pivotal in the character of the entire complex.

At some point during August, as high-baked summer diminishes, the dew gathers and thickens, rising earlier with the dusk, heavier each night, and hanging on longer in the morning. The moisture releases the captured smells of roses, dahlias, tobaccos, and all those artichokes and eryngiums, milkweeds and field thistles, encrusted with droplets of water. I feel it first in my sinus, the turn: musty, ripe, plummy, pushy moulds and thrusting fungi.

Not only farmers made hay today. It was glorious, victorious, high on harvest. A golden bloom shimmered all the way from Roundway to the White Horse and up to Kelmscott and Kemble and west over Wales. Back home at seven-ish, the paths to the pool at dusk smelled of earth and must. Greenhouse is cool with mignonette; my preciouses are coming along. But please get on with it.

Cleome, the spider flower, is a great annual to push into the border to add zingy pink highlights in August. It has a curious perfume, not to everyone's taste, skunky; but diluted in the dew it smells of pastry in Morocco. I must go out with the camera early now.

SPIDER FLOWER

From tropical America and Africa comes this pungent herbaceous plant, the most common of which we grow as an annual: *Cleome hassleriana* (syn. *C. spinosa*). Hassle it is not. They germinate reliably from April onwards in a propagator because, being from the Pampas, they don't like cold and damp and would hate a Cornish winter more than I do. Wise folk pinch out the seedlings to make them form branching bushy plants as they don't hang about and can grow to be taller than me in a season. This is what makes them fun, along with the strange smell. Seeds come in Queen Series (Cherry, Violet, Rose and White, or all mixed up called Colour Fountain). They should be called daddy-long-legs flowers because this, along with the smell, is their particular characteristic: the spent flowers looking like leggy insects held airily on the upwards-extending stems. They continue to flower for months, dagger-like seed pods emerging above the sticky, bristly, smelly whorls of bright green leaf, and therefore they never look 'over' and are a most useful bedding or companion plant. I love the cannabis smell, obviously aromatic, skunky, animal, almost dangerous. It does not appeal to all but on the up side it is also called beeweed as insects are drawn to this smell, pollinating all around it.

Mint smells to me of being bored as a child and being turfed out like a dog to potter round sniffing and munching on bits of mint and chives, salad burnet, sorrel, maybe a bit of monbretia nectar.

Rosa 'Souvenir du Docteur Jamain' gives a fresh clear rose-water scent in contrast to its amazing richness of petals and stamens. It is reminding me of auriculas. This sort of second flowering is better appreciated, sugar candied and stronger than in the spring flowering. These are the memory smells along with pudding smells of stewed apple and uncooked meringue, doughy white bread mixed with currants and raspberries that make flowers smell so good.

Had to put the light on for the first time since back in spring when I started work today. The room was filled with the scent of myrtle. When brides wore myrtle and mock orange coronets in the past, our flower choice was limited, seasonal, and better for it. Myrtle smell has a strong resemblance to raw smoked bacon, although last night I brought some in and asked Mr B if he too thought it smelled of bacon. He spent a while not smelling it, but shaking and ruffling off the brown spent petals till it looked bright and bushy and then arranged it and sniffed it with almost religious ritual. 'Ridiculous and not in the least' was his rebuff. Chastened I sniffed. Sure enough, it smelled nothing like a Norfolk butcher, but flowery and aromatic. It smells of promise.

Rosa × centifolia 'Shailer's White Moss' still flowering, still reminding me of the sandy paths of my grandmother's Surrey garden and the drone of the planes which, even in the 1970s, flew over every couple of minutes into Gatwick. Dry dusty paths, rusty tricycle and sherbet lemons covered in pocket lint. Musk and moss come on the tails of autumn, dry leaves and dry mildew. *R.* 'Roseraie de l'Haÿ' is still startling sweet, like sugar water, syrup of roses, almost as sickly as 'Magic Tree' air freshener if inhaled too long. Nasturtiums smell to me of pepper, obviously, but strangely of garage pits and mechanics, rubber and Kwik Fit.

August is the time Vita Sackville-West describes as 'too rampant and too lush'; almost all the anticipation is over, and gardeners slacken. And E.A. Bowles writes beautifully of the end of the gardening year when 'the whole air bears a scent of fallen leaves, a rich woodland brand of scent, most noticeable on damp mornings and towards evening, while calm sunny hours at midday before the advent of sharp frosts, are full of balm and spices from Asters … Tea-Roses, and Heliotrope, and there always seems to me a richer bouquet in their incense on these days than earlier in the season.'

CHERRY PIE

The glowing scent of cherry pie – heliotrope – drugs high summer. They are native to Peru, where they are subshrubs and the smell must be knockout. The word heliotrope means sun-follower, but was first recorded as a descriptive adjective for the deep purple colour in 1882. The smell is not so much a scent as a comely syrup of voluptuous vanilla and chocolate; rounded, rich and joyous. The cocoa perfume is enriched with caramelised plum and that curious 'cherry' smell of the common name. Their tiny tubular flowers are borne in bunches of saturated violet to palest lilac, cushioned on a chartreuse quilt. *Heliotropium arborescens* 'Marine' is the most strikingly 'cherry-pie' flavoured, better is 'Midnight Sky', but preferable in smell and form to me are the laxer ladies 'Mrs J.W. Lowther', 'White Lady', 'Princess Marina' and the pale 'Chatsworth'. In 1883 William Robinson named some tantalising lost varieties 'Florine', 'Marguerite' and the incredible sounding 'Roi des Noirs'. Tender plants, all of which may be grown from seed if you believe the catalogues, but which are most successfully reproduced asexually, grown from late softwood cuttings which like to spend the winter in a warm greenhouse. They look gawky, need pinching out and mothering into tender trophies with feed and gossip. By June when these debutantes 'come out' after the luxury of the greenhouse bench, fed and cosseted, they are rounded and abundant bushes that break into flower in late July and go on performing until put to bed again in October.

Early morning and the paths are wet from hosing. Steamy earth like bread. The heliotrope reeks round the pool. A Sicilian day, with hot air blowing in like a hair dryer through the landing windows. A storm brews up in the afternoon and the scents intensify, particularly the moss rose smell. There is incense in the stillness and gathering gloom, crickets stop play. At 3.30 p.m. the storm cracks and down by the cistus it smells like the deepest, darkest, most gold-encrusted Spanish church on Good Friday. I love labdanum, that which oozes from or makes a tacky coating to the leaves of rock roses – particularly *Cistus ladanifer*. The gum resins, some of which are the origin of amber, can be found in plants all over the world and mankind has found innumberable uses for them. The cistus smell is broken by the sudden breeze and back-breaking thunder. How I love a storm.

Box bushes and other digressions

Leaving just as the garden opened to the public, I found a woman standing before the wicket gate tense with breathing, like a pointer on the prowl. When I bid her 'good day', she said that she was just drinking in the smell of box, so we fell into conversation. That box is a magnet for dogs wishing to cock a leg; that cats love to roll and cavort in it; that neither Queen Anne nor Louis XIV could abide the smell so dominant in their complicated parterre gardens. It is said to smell of cat litter, horse pee, elderberries. I once saw a *Lonicera nitida* hedge thigh high and an elbow's width across, so beautifully trimmed that it was better than box – and no disease. Mr B is very rude about *L. nitida*, but, equally, John Gerard, not given to the mincing of words, found box 'Loathsome and Evil'. In America they call *Buxus* 'boxwood' or 'boxtrees' rather than plain old 'box'. This was one of many transatlantic differences or rather puzzles of translation I found when working on the British 9/11 memorial garden we designed in New York. In meetings it could be mystifying talking about comfort zones, and letters of comfort, and comfort stations. Many of these curious differences between our languages are archaisms, hangovers or linguistic survivals.

I learned many such linguistic and other particulars from a wonderful eccentric uncle, after whom I am called Sinclair. He was a philologist, studied phonetics and linguistics, and was a big advocate of reforming English spelling so that it reflected pronunciation and stopped being so obtuse. He lived at the very top of a house in Chelsea which he crammed with lodgers, books, curiosities; a Prospero's cell. He smelled very foxy, perhaps on account of taking snuff and wearing a lot of unwashed corduroy. Snuff was deeply fascinating to us children: intensely perfumed and very disgusting. He let us all try it, giggling uncontrollably at our expressions of horror. He had appalling teeth and black Eric Morecombe spectacles which made his eyes huge, but he was fabulously funny and wheezed and snortled when he laughed at his own jokes. He treated children as absolute equals and explained many magical and memorable things about vitamins and minerals, biology and philology to tiny me, youngest of all his nephews and nieces. When an East Coast American family took over a house down the road in our village, he explained to me that many of the curiosities in their pronunciation were probably a relic of seventeenth-century English, as spoken on the Mayflower, which had survived by being cut off from the swirling changes in language back home. His theory was that if you wanted to know how Louis XIV spoke, listen to Québécois.

Box wood is indeed remarkable stuff. In Gerona, Spain, we bought maybe thirty slotted spoons and long-handled utensils, peppered with drainage holes but strong as steel, made from box wood growing in the foothills of the Pyrenees; beautiful leopard-splotched yellow wood, of immense durability.

Overleaf: Dew, fennel, *Thalictrum* Splendide White

203

Through Leaves

It is yellow in colour, as if it wore a daffodil
tunic, and it smells like musk, a penetrating smell.

It has the perfume of a loved woman and the same
hardness of heart, but it has the colour of the
impassioned and scrawny lover.

Its pallor is borrowed from my pallor; its smell
is my sweetheart's breath.

When it stood fragrant on the bough and the leaves
had woven for it a covering of brocade,

I gently put up my hand to pluck it and to set it
like a censer in the middle of my room.

It had a cloak of ash-coloured down hovering over
its smooth golden body,

and when it lay naked in my hand, with nothing more than
its daffodil-coloured shift,

it made me think of her I cannot mention, and I feared
the ardour of my breath would shrivel it in my fingers.

Shafer ben Utman al-Mushafi

Quince is queen, is the dream, is *Cydonia oblonga* or vranja (a name that could be straight out of *Vathek* by William Beckford). Felted, fulvous, fat fruit swell on the mildewed tree. Sometimes these little trees have no leaves by August. But it does them no harm. The quince is perhaps the most truly fragrant and sensuous of tree-borne fruit. Prized from Asia Minor to the Atlantic seaboard of Portugal, they do not fester like the greengage but, picked perfect, then can be kept indoors to scent the room snoozing in a big Spanish dish. The variety *C.o.* 'Vranja' was found growing in Serbia (although there is some confusion as to whether this, and other examples, might be the variety 'Bereczki'), and the fruit is breast shaped, of a clear shining chrome yellow, and exceptionally fragrant. Jane Grigson in her *Fruit Book* likens the Chania quinces of Crete to the marble breasts of Michelangelo's sleeping 'Night'. For the Greeks and Romans, quinces were the golden apples of the Hesperides; they were the golden apples Aphrodite used to prevent Atalanta from winning the race against her suitor Hippomenes; and, notoriously, they were the apple that Paris, in his Judgement, awarded to Aphrodite. Hence they became the fruit of love, marriage and fertility. Jane Grigson writes that it is very much the scent of the beginnings of love: 'In spring on a warm day, if you sit in the lee of flowering quinces, you become quietly aware of a narcissus scent on the puffs of breeze. The furling

Cydonia oblonga 'Vranja'

twist of the bud, pink and white, opens into a globe of pale pink, ruffed with leaves – its mildness goes unnoticed if you walk by without stopping.'

The scent of the woolly-coated fruit is good to sniff, and good to leave on a plate, like a Dutch still life, to fill a room with indefinable ether. The fruits are harsh and astringent, gritty, if eaten raw, though left to overwinter they become softly edible in spring. But cooked they not only deliver their remarkable perfume to a pie or tart of apples or pears, when the mysterious line between 'perfume' and flavour is crossed, but the flesh changes colour as if stained by an earthy red ochre. But what is the smell like? It is like nothing else, fruity but perfumed, animal as well as vegetable, artless and yet with supreme artifice. The whole is matchless; only an Arab poet from tenth-century Cordoba could express it.

Through the mist, the smell of undergrowth and then September sunshine. The sun rises through water vapour at six thirty on September 1st. Often at this time the Hamoaze is a milky invisibility below us. I realise the point where the sun rises has swung back violently, now to the right of the Gatehouse. The setting of the sun is behind the curtain wall, stealing the light well before the eight o'clock of true sunset. If only Benjamin Tucker had torn down a bit of wall to the west and let the late sun flood into the front of the house as he did on the east side. But he was a naval man, and practical. Why would you want to expose yourself to the prevailing westerly winds? Woolly-minded nonsense to sailors and gardeners both. But not to evening idlers.

Above the undergrowth hang more 'Souvenir de la Malmaison' roses, *Magnolia grandiflora*, fantastically warm heliotrope and a belfry of brugmansias outpouring in a still corner. This year Mr B has put late-grown cornflowers in with the heliotrope, a pick-and-mix of azure fireworks on a violet sky. The pots are having their moment, the *Salvia involucrata* 'Hadspen', acrid and currant-leaf smelling. They are very brittle branched, rather ruffled by any gutsy gusts, completely broken by December; it is not frost which gets them but the gales. 'Pink Parfait', the verbena for sniffing at pot height, is great for picking too. All the nicotiana are in top condition; the *Nicotiana mutabilis* in pots are good and airy because Mr B is religious about stripping out the big fat basal leaves, which otherwise would be overweening. Weeding desperately calls. I will do my best but by October the weeds will again be overweening. Come friendly frosts and fell them there.

3rd September
Heliotrope is in its prime. The one they all rave about is 'White Lady'. It smells great and it looks great, but like all white versions of purple things, you notice the browning off and feel a bit browned off about it. It is my dad's birthday today. Of course, one remembers these things, but from a very young age I remember trying to imagine what it was like to listen to Mr Chamberlain on the radio announcing that Britain was at war, on your birthday, a callow fifteen-year-old on September 3rd, 1939. He didn't talk about the war enough, or much at all, but occasionally you could get him going on long car journeys on the daily life of infantrymen, cooking up bully beef with tinned tomatoes, how lucky they were to have an armoured car like a tortoise shell for a home; and once, in a blizzard, he explained that shrapnel was like the snowflakes that were coming

towards us, in that the one in the middle that didn't seem to be moving at all was the one coming right for you.

The species *Rosa moschata* is a pretty fine thing to find flowering now. We bought the named hybrid *R.* 'Princesse de Nassau', a princessly later-flowering beauty whose pearly buds open sequentially, teasing out a long flowering, and smelling like sunny pillows of down, warm musk and vanilla.

Rosa 'De Resht' is generous still, though intermittently, while 'Madame Pierre Oger' and 'Madame Isaac Péreire' are coming to the boil again with a few big fat buds and, after a vicious pruning, *R.* 'New Dawn' is flowering again. I had forgotten to think of it as deliciously scented.

Marigolds, nasturtiums and tomatoes – a salad, in the nose or the bowl, of scent and flavour. Tomatoes smell sort of sweaty like armpits … but delicious ones. Rosemary and cistus very sticky and stinky. Maybe this is the most scented month, a wonderful balance of coming and going, earth and nectar.

Cyclamen have a way of coming up through the earth behind you, friendly yet steely. It is such a small thing, a constellation of cyclamen and such a small smell, like violets at the other end of the year. Naked, pink, fragile, in patches of bare brown earth on a blustery September day. It is a smell of freshly opened pharmaceuticals. Mushrooms too: suddenly they're behind you when you only turned your back for a moment. A friend of mine took mushrooms and some while later he noticed an over-sized mushroom with a fearsome personality propped up in the corner of the room. He turned away in fear, but, unable to resist another glance, he turned back to the mushroom and it said, 'Oy! you! you ate my fuckin' friend.'

'Presently, we were aware of an odour gradually coming towards us, something musky, fiery, savoury, mysterious, – a hot drowsy smell, that lulls the senses, and yet enflames them, – the truffles were coming,' writes Thackeray. The smell of cèpes on Exmoor, beech mast everywhere. Exmoor, Hartland Point, Westward Ho! – each has a distinct smell. But do we still have the capacity to recognise the terrain – Dartmoor or Dovedale – by its scent only?

At six this morning, walking round with the pug, I am shocked how dark and silent it is, smelling of herbs and spices for a bad curry, as if we had planted santolina and wormwood. Yet turning the corner to the sea side the scent changes to a green leafy smell and something floral, perhaps from the late flush of *Rosa* 'Blanche Double de Coubert', and also a freshness from the west indicated only by a high ripple bank of cloud moving in silently and fast from deepest Cornwall.

Before it expresses its deepest notes, autumn comes on a calm morning after stormy Tamar-tossed days. A woeful wind complained all day yesterday. Was completely hushed at dawn. A slither of moon fell into the river mist and vanished as the sun came up over the singing pink nerines. Caryopteris sings out too, aromatherapeutic, clinical turpentine at ten metres. The cistus suffuses the air less insistently. It's the same sort of smell but less chemical and more Mediterranean.

Spectacular September morning with rolling smoky clouds on the Hamoaze. I could hear a big ship's engine chugging and glimpsed suddenly a small frigate floating between mercury and gaseous vapours. And then it vanished, but I could still hear it and the tugboats calling to one another. The garden was a blanket of dew. There is plenty of flower: tithonia, dahlia, *Rosa* 'Cécile Brünner' having a second coming, and cow-parsley-white blobs of silene taking over among the fennel and late phlox, and Robert Bridges's 'few lingering scents/Of streaked pea, and gillyflower, and stocks/Of courtly purple, and aromatic phlox.' But in truth there is little scent, only the smell of autumn and compost heaps.

Went out to try to photograph the perfect still Mediterranean evening. The Hamoaze was glassy like enamel set in pewter, the sky bearing this golden orb and the air surprisingly suffused with spicy *Elaeagnus × submacrophylla* (syn. *E. × ebbingei*). Smelled it this afternoon as well and it is reassuring to be reminded that it really does float on the air.

I was painting the roof with sonorous smelling aluminium and bitumen light-reflective paint. The vents on the conservatory roof were open in the considerable heat and a sweet mistral of air was forced out through them by convection. I stood by and sniffed, being a human gas spectrometer, separating vegetal, vine and brugmansia smells from the air oozing out.

I must speak of bonfires. I lit one made of grass strimmings, and the thick clotted smoke was like chowder, delicious but bringing on a sadness. Smell of an autumn evening wet with dew and dusty with harvesting. There is smoke, usually, somewhere and midges; mellowing, diminishing light and a big moon rising. So different from the smell of a late winter afternoon when the sun has gained enough strength to warm up a few snowdrops. Girls on ponies clop by in the lane leaving a trail of natural and unnatural fragrance. Cornwall is all in a mizzle, the creek, the river, the tidal sucking, seaweed, sweet chestnuts, slate and bracken.

Mr B picked *Magnolia grandiflora* and some *Gladiolus murielae* and put them in round flat vases. The following morning, coming into the dark kitchen at about six, I might have been in Costa Rica such was the pong of passion fruit and frangipane pulsating across the room. Gladioli are from the iris family and these Abyssinian gladioli are a treat. They look as extravagant as tulips, and are as scented as a white narcissus, giving it out now at the other end of the year. Their scent is pale, light and laundered in the Indies.

BUGBANE

Bugbanes used to be *Cimicifuga* but have now merged with the genus *Actaea*. There is a bugbane we saw in John Massey the nurseryman's garden, a big white one, and it completely took me by surprise that it smells so terrific. They are spectacular plants for the back of a shady border, providing masses of flower in late summer and autumn – sometimes into November. Tall wands of fragrant, creamy to pinkish-white bottlebrush flowers are held high above pale green, lacy foliage. They prefer cool, moist, rich soil, and are happy in shade, needing protection from hot sun. They generally don't need staking, and are pest-resistant, as their common name suggests; the original genus name, *Cimicifuga*, derives from the Latin *cimex* – bug – and *fugere* – to flee. Native Americans use *Actaea* (syn. *Cimicifuga*) *racemosa*, black snakeroot or black cohosh, as an herb and early American settlers stuffed mattresses with it as a bed-bug repellent; *A. cimicifuga* (syn. *C. foetida*) is used in Siberia as an insect repellent.

The last latent heat of a September morning. Perhaps the last week for swimming in the pool. Peeling away the bubble cover, the volatiles hang for a moment in the rising mist, wafting pods of cardamom and juniper berries from the oak-leaf geraniums (pelargoniums). At the water level the absolute lies above the unbroken surface, mingling brugmansia toxins with the scent of ginger plants. A finely tuned fragrance in which no human has had a hand.

The extinction of smell in flowers has come largely through breeding and mass production, particularly in the cut-flower industry. Absence of smell and development of a 'norm' that is smell-less is what is happening. Just as a world without butterflies or flies or wild flowers or elephants is simply becoming the 'norm'. How can we miss what we never knew?

Quinces again. I picked a bowl of them and put it in the sitting room, and yesterday and this morning I can smell them in the hall. I go to admire the bowl of odd-shaped ugly fruit, flocked with a slightly mangy pelt. The smell is apples and pears and hay, tingled with spiced jasmine. They glow in the slanting low light that spells September. The apple store smells sweetly of cider and old fruitwood. I have always been hopeless at storing things. Wrapped in newspaper, set apart from each other, ventilated, yet still everything rots in a heap of disappointment.

The vernal equinox

My feeling for autumn is very much in tune with that of Alexander Pushkin, who loved it 'for its quietly glowing beauty' and who knew 'The Russian cold is good for my well-being.' The lack of a true dry bright winter in the West Country has always tempted me and Mr B east, Norfolk skies and soil. Right now, we are between that crystal clarity of winter, which comes rarely down here, and the stewed surge of summer. The sun rises and sets on two days at right angles east and west along the parallel latitude: 50° 44'N; those days are a couple of minutes longer than twelve hours, starting at just after seven in the morning and closing at just after seven in the evening. I think this may have something to do with the source of my diurnal happiness in September and in March. This equilibrium is calming, it makes sense. In the smell zone, September is the kindest month. The earth is at its warmest, and the seas and rivers too, best month for swimming.

Daylight has tipped, all is autumn. The morning comes diamond dewed and the pug is reluctant to get his paws wet on the grass. The *Gladiolus murielae* are still spring perfect amid the tired hydrangeas and shameless dahlias. More tomatoes ripening.

Motes, flotes, sedges and bulrushes.

Have you ever smelled bulrushes? Do it. The time is late summer through autumn. We moved in to our last house in late August and I brought my newborn Bertie back to three weeks of long-lit September days full of motes and flotes, flying insects, harvest dust and big moons. The house and garden were derelict and not in a particularly pleasing way. A minefield for small boys and a newborn baby. But we settled happily each day in a neglected summer house in the monks' carp garden, which still has a bent-over mulberry, perfect for miniature mountaineers, and plenty of frogs and bulrushes. Crazy paving provided a metropolis of ants and inside the summer house Mr B had ripped up the middle concrete paviours in a fit of detective work, and so 'Jurassic Park' could be fashioned from the nice dry sand beneath. All those hard-plastic dinosaurs were transported from the house; fronds and palms for trees; a Lego 'visitor centre'; trucks churned through the dunes. My mother came to stay and 'opened' Jurassic Park with tears of delight. The ponds outside were choked with bulrushes thronged with frogs, toads and newts. The delight in destroying the cigar-scented, spicy, velvety, moleskin perfection of a bulrush does not diminish with age, and together with the two- and four-year olds we all scrabbled to open up and puff the dandelion fluff inside, exponentially expanding like cooking honeycomb. Sweetly scented, smoky, a lapsang tea of dry sedge, and redolent for me of the finest malt whisky with that incomparable boggy sweetness.

SWEET FLAG

Acorus calamus, as a friend of the Fenland, needs to grow near running water. The flowers are foul smelling and form a sinister if magnificent spadix or green erection from tall stems, which Roy Genders describes as 'having a sombre beauty' like a brown church spire. The stems and leaves of the sweet flag, however, are fabled for their fragrance when crushed, releasing a delicious fruity scent, likened to tangerines by some and to ripe apples with cinnamon and lemon by others. This festive flavour, attested in one common name, sweet cinnamon, made them hugely in demand for strewing about mediaeval homes and churches, covering the floors of Ely and Norwich Cathedrals. In dry southern England flags had to be imported at great expense from the estuaries of Europe. One of the notable extravagancies of Cardinal Wolsey before his fall was flashing sweet flag about in huge quantity at Hampton Court.

It was also imported from the New World and then from India where it grows in the Naga Hills. In the eighteenth century this stronger-smelling rush from hotter climes could be sold for as much as £40 per acre on the London market. Like the orris root of Tuscany, the distillation of the rhizome has a long history of use in perfume making and aromatic vinegars, and it was also used in the clarification of our national drink, beer. When dried and powdered it was used in talcs and snuffs. The taste is bitter, the smell has something of camphor oil, and from the root the apothecary Faust extracted the bitter principle acorin. Ranging across northern Europe to Asia Minor, the plant and its essential oil were integral to the ancient world and appear in the book of Exodus. Thomas Tusser's *Five Hundred Pointes of Good Husbandrie* (1573) – a book full of useful smelly recipes and uses for roots, leaves and flowers along with country and farming lore, written in rhyming couplets – mentions plants that are good for strewing, including sweet flag, melissa, hops and many labiates.

Autumn soup

Stopped the car – a bemusing flurry of flashings and peepings having alerted us to the large book bought in a charity shop and left on the roof – and I was assailed by the smell of nettles bashed by the car door. It's a great smell, warmly aromatic, meaty. Above it floated the smell of autumn soup; the air, particularly warm this weekend, rich with the nutty, fruitful, verdant, herbage of acorns crushed in tarmac and a million leaves descending. It's a good smell, somehow confidently elegiac. I think of it with mint, which is much more soothing to

Brugmansia × cubensis 'Charantais'

the head and in all early herbals and as far back as Pliny to the stomach. Pliny lists sixty remedies derived from mint and pennyroyal, yet only seventeen from violet, 'as for the garden mint, the very smell of it alone recovers and refreshes our spirits'. It is interesting that since Hippocrates we have classed perfumes with medicines and particularly prescribed them for nervous diseases.

Were it not for the underlying scent of atrophy, September would be my favourite scented month, full of subtle charms such as the sweet olive *Osmanthus*. I am a bit short on patience for these handsome evergreens because they're such slow growers.

OSMANTHUS

Osmanthus has spring- and September-flowering species. *Osmanthus delavayi* and *O. × burkwoodii* have poor-man's jasmine-scented flowers in spring. But *O. × fortunei* and *O. fragrans* – the sweet olive, a slightly more tender osmanthus – have small, insignificant, but by far the most scented white or greenish flowers, which give out warm vanilla pie smells from September to November. Then there is one, *O. yunnanensis*, which is the least good-looking but flowers in December and January. To my mind scent travels on the air best in autumn, because the earth and air and sea are warm. And these osmanthus do like to be beside the seaside. All are slow growers, which I find frustrating, but eventually they can make big shrubs or small trees. Whilst the spring ones have grey-green holly-like leaves (different in that they are alternate not opposite as in holly), the autumn flowerers have green shiny leaves, and both can add useful 'body' to a border or scheme and are clippable and densely leaved, if slightly boring. However, flowering is seriously interrupted by vigorous pruning. In China the flowers are often used as a tisane and flavouring.

Walked out into the perfect evening, dusk at seven, cyclamen sky. The dell is darker and scented with decay, slightly dangerous; below, the creek is full, dark water straining at high tide. All this makes you feel like an ingénue, little as Red Riding Hood. Out in the meadow though, among the crickets, the light is still caught in the grass stalks as they thicken with dew.

The sun rises at 7 a.m., milky and hot, and on my border tour I found roses still flowering – 'Albéric Barbier', 'Souvenir de la Malmaison', 'Climbing Etoile de Hollande', 'Sander's White Rambler', and 'Princesse de Nassau' (syn. *Rosa moschata* 'Autumnalis'). They all smell thicker, more molasses, more fruity and more edible. The long border is richly musty, musky, foxy, rusty (further companions of the seven dwarves). Chrysanthemums and Michaelmas daisies are a bit of a mystery to me, but my friend MK's favourite, hardy and dainty white, is called *Chrysanthemum* 'E.H. Wilson'. It has the quality of another plant she introduced us to, *Erigeron annuus*, the annual fleabane, a late simple white daisy – why have I not planted some for ages? We gardeners are so fickle, so forgetful. Order some seed right away.

The pool garden left me standing in awe, everything held in resin. Thyme and fig fugue by the pool, with roses – 'Souvenir de la Malmaison' especially – fennel and pineapple sage. Caryopteris and cistus smell like boiled sweets left in a furry pocket, falsely blackcurrant. *Nicotiana suaveolens* is, at last, a concentrate of

Humulus lupulus

tobacco plants lifted on the evening air. They are so slow to get going. There are some smells that I love but I don't want all year round. This is true though of other things, like the flavour of broad beans; it means a lot more because it may only be around for a few weeks.

BLUEBEARD

I never knew until recently that *Caryopteris* was called bluebeard. I had never heard it so called, and *Caryopteris* is a rather pretty name as it is. It is a lover of sunshine from eastern Asia, and we know it as a sub-shrub which we cut back in March, so it never gets bigger than a metre round. *C.* × *clandonensis* is dainty with silvery down on the lanceolate leaves; it has a Mediterranean aromatic flavour, reminiscent of lavender, much more when crushed than on the air, and pretty if rather insignificant blue flowers arranged round the stems like the tiers of a wedding cake in September. There are good named varieties such as 'Heavenly Blue' and 'Kew Blue'.

CISTUS

The yellow-centred pink and white single flowers of rock roses, *Cistus*, are a joy in early summer. But they have no scent. It is for the gummy aromatic smelling stems and leaves that I grow them, and the smell really emanates in late summer, in August and the smelly month of September. The rocky Mediterranean smell is best in *Cistus ladanifer* var. *albiflorus*, a form with plum blotches near the stamens of a papery white flower. Sadly, for me, it hates Cornwall and quickly goes black and fungus-y although I persist by planting it again because at Hanham Court, where the garden was built up and wildly free draining, they scented the air far and wide. Bean describes them as 'branches clammy with a shining resin'. Leaves, clasping the stems in pairs, are linear-lanceolate and glutinous. It has been grown in these isles since 1629.

One of the best forms for the non-specialist to try is *Cistus* × *cyprius*. This hardy hybrid of *C. ladanifer* and *C. laurifolius* is an excellent garden plant. *C. laurifolius* is taller, more open, one of the hardiest and best rock roses, making bold mounds of evergreen, its flowers – white, frail as butterflies – come later in the summer. It also has glutinous aromatic leaves, a rather dull green, and peely bark. The leaves are glabrous on top with a close down beneath, mildly gummy on both surfaces. Native of south-western Europe and introduced to these islands in 1731, it brings us on hot days a billow of Provençal maquis, incense and amber. There is a form called *C.* × *dansereaui* (syn. *C.* × *lusitanicus*) 'Decumbens', which lazes about on the gravel paths very prettily.

At my Pilates class we lie on our backs under Brunel's Royal Albert Bridge and watch the light bouncing off the water on the ceiling. Tugboats chug and the swans with seven cygnets hang about, knowing there will be sandwiches. But the best thing about my class is that it brings me regularly to the seashore and the smell of flotsam and kelp, the ozone-scented tinkled throbbing world of harbour and sailor. The whole point of Cornwall is that it is interwoven with the sea and the possibility of lands beyond the horizon, the ancient links with Brittany, Wales and Ireland. It is washed with the smells that birds may use to navigate, that communicate so much and we don't even notice.

Rudbeckia hirta 'Cherry Brandy' and *R.h.* 'Cherokee Sunset'

216

Mr B watering a banana
tree

Cardiocrinum lilies flower in June and July, but now their seed cases are
Palaeolithic jaws designed to open, filled and quickly spouting paper seeds,
leaved in hundreds like a book. The orchard is fermenting with apples and
wasps, feasting jackdaws squabble on the ground, and bees work hurriedly.

Greengages are always best stolen from someone else's sunny orchard;
just as borrowed clothes are much better than one's own. Greengages taste
of September sun yellowing to honey, hot and jammy, with apricot kernel
nuttiness, a compote of the orchard from primroses to the noble rot.

Late random flowers of such as the roses 'Souvenir du Docteur Jamain' and
'Prince Charles' are not as good looking as earlier in the year, but their smell
has incredible late luxuriance and depth. They look and smell magnificent in a
bunch with heliotrope.

I know you cannot smell nasturtiums unless you pick or pull one to stop it
strangulating something, but the smell, once released, is as evocative as a cloud
of butterflies. Squishy with sap and water-laden in these dry days, it carries with
it the back of old cupboards and forgotten drawers. It draws out memories of
snuff, pepper and boot polish from the dark recesses of my mind. I recollected
manly places as I sniffed it, potting sheds, gardener's dens, warmed in a flicker
of methylated spirits and grass clippings. Monet's cataracts dimmed his colour
vision in a way which we can actually witness in his late paintings, strong
oranges and blues becoming muddy because the cataracts create a yellowy film
on the cornea, turning everything to gravy, and thus he sought ever brighter
nasturtiums to shine through the fog.

Late summer leaves

Elaeagnus × submacrophylla (syn. *E. × ebbingei*) is a plant which is verging on the very tedious whilst being very useful as a fast-growing evergreen barrier. It resembles holm oak, is dead hardy, and its inconspicuous flowers smell of bay laurel, one of the great smells and flavours. Bean makes much of its 'scales' – the platelets that make it look almost silvery. A pervasive scent in a quiet, misty way. *E. angustifolia* is useful because it is similar but flowers in late May and smells of hay. But if you clip it as a hedge or a dome you reduce the production of its utterly subtle flowers. September is short on scent but *E. × submacrophylla* might unexpectedly cuff your nose with a great bluff of hay smell with cardamom, and cinnamon. Mr B and I first experienced this molestation at Mount Edgcumbe by Plymouth and had to track down its source. By the sea, loose among many holm oaks, it feels at home.

I was in Somerset, among the commercial and happily multiplying orchards, and I could smell the wasp-eaten apples that litter the sward. It is the polar opposite of the spring smell of bliss. Here we rarely have frosty mornings but today was our equivalent, heavily watered with dew drops. Here water trembles in the air, clings to everything with a kind of cool desperation, glittering, smothering, still and comprehensively covering, and plants smell of something dark and loamy.

Yesterday was brilliant, but cooler, and the elaeagnus ponged in the sheltered dip of the drive by the smelly path. Today opened steaming wet and then the afternoon was broken up by stormy gusts in which the jackdaws dared each other in wall-of-death flights round the battlements, chatting, almost hysterical, in the whipping ash boughs before taking flight again together like forty fast black bombers.

ELAEAGNUS

Elaeagnus angustifolia is usually seen as a large shrub, quick growing and often clipped into an informal hedge – the variety 'Quicksilver' is the most used, but it gives the plant a bad name, being much more coarse and less scented than the species; it can grow to be quite a large tree. They have willow-like leaves that are a pale sagey colour on top with silver undersides. Both *E. angustifolia* and *E. × submacrophylla* look shimmery because of the scales that cover almost every part, the scales reacting to light like a very simplified version of the scales on butterfly wings, refracting and bouncing the light waves. Even the almost insignificant flowers are scaly and hence a grey chamois-leather colour and texture which has its own beauty. When I photographed the flowers very close up, they became like jewellery (not like Swarovski jewellery, but like pieces by the jeweller Romilly Saumarez Smith) – iridescent oxidised silver jangles, as though they were made of Roman glass and buried for a thousand years. In late spring the shrub gives out a wind-carried scent of dewy hay. I have a prejudice against its many variegated cousins.

Best by far, certainly from the smell point of view, is the September-flowering *Elaeagnus × submacrophylla* (syn. *E. × ebbingei*). The flowers are unearthly and very fragrant. The scent, which travels on the air, reminds me of bay leaves. The great thing about being a September-scented plant is that not much else is flowering, and, more important, scent is more easily emanated and enjoyed when the earth is warm and the air damp.

From the troubles of the world I turn to reading about basil in the Chiltern Seeds catalogue. Reading a good catalogue such as this, or that of Orchard Dene Nurseries – now sadly giving up – is a literary pleasure.

Gerald Brenan tells us, in his *South from Granada*, that sweet basil was brought by the Arabs from India, where it is sacred to Krishna, to Spain where it is known as *albahaca* (from the Arabic for basil). The great seventeenth-century botanist John Parkinson, in his *Paradisi in Sole Paradisus Terrestris*, 1629, wrote of basil that 'Gently handled it gives a pleasant smell but being hardly wrung and bruised it will breed scorpions,' – a fine example of fiery Jacobean English usage. (Incidentally, is it not tickling that the apothecary to James I and Royal Botanist to Charles I chose to make a joke on his own name in Latin, 'Park-in-Sun', for the title of his magnum opus?)

BASIL

If you plant seedlings of basil, *Ocimum basilicum*, outside in the garden, pick a warm, sunny place because basil needs strong light, eight hours a day. This explains how it just fades off in September and pretty much might never get going in a wet low-lit West Country summer such as those we encountered when we first moved to Cornwall. It likes well-drained soil, and perlite is a good idea to lighten up the compost or soil. For very sweet fragrance and distinctive, mellow, rich flavour and a luxuriance of rounded, light green, deeply crinkled leaves, I would choose the variety most commonly grown in the Naples region called 'Napoletano'. 'Genovese' basil is grown in the north of Italy and combines well with garlic. Basil 'Aroma 2' from Chiltern is supposedly the best scent and flavour ever. I like ordinary sweet basil very much, and not any purple variety – I cannot abide a purple plant, let alone eat one. And I cannot see the point of basil that tastes of something else, like liquorice or lime or cloves. I like bush or Greek basil, *O. minimum*, for its looks, but perversely it is said to come from Chile.

Scented geraniums, basil and tagetes grow in pots by the tomatoes. A greenhouse might smell of the cedar wood of which it is constructed, or the cool-glass white paint sploshed over in summer, but now it also has these rather insecticidal smells, all a bit sticky along with the blackcurrant gum of *Salvia discolor*, a silver salvia overlaid with the cogent aroma of cassis. A fruit cage smells in spring of rhubarb and the citrus of narcissus; in summer, a pudding of strawberry and currant leaves and fruit, the coming-along raspberries, currants (black, red and white) plus the cabbage-flower smell of bolted purple-sprouting broccoli and *cavolo nero*.

Root scents and secretions have powerful properties. For instance, emanations from the roots of potatoes are what make the eelworm hatch. All these underground scents are a huge mystery; there are, for example, odours that induce specific and complex reactions in creatures such as moths. We know moths are sensitive to scent, but not just how sensitive, and so it is with things that dwell in the earth or even the sea. Moths can detect each other by smell at distances of many hundreds of metres and some can track possible partners several kilometres away. Some marigolds and tagetes will kill eelworms up to a metre away from their roots and can discourage the growth, though not eliminate it, sadly, of expansive weeds such as bindweed and ground elder.

Overleaf: Mr B watering *Pelargonium* 'Sweet Mimosa'

How immense, complex and how little understood is the network of chemical activity which goes on underground, and much of it scent-based, unwittingly disturbed by our reckless use of synthetic pesticides and fertilisers.

FLEABANE

Some fleabanes, like *Erigeron karvinskianus*, the Mexican fleabane, and *E. annuus*, the annual fleabane, are delectable white daisies. But the common fleabane, *Pulicaria dysenterica*, is a yellow-flowered, furry, fleshy-leaved weed. It looks like a pot marigold and if you crush its leaves you catch that strange essence of cats and carbolic and chrysanthemums. That chrysanthemum odour is an insecticidal smell to us because pyrethrum obtained from chrysanthemums (particularly *Tanacetum cinerariifolium*) is the most famous plant insecticide.

Grown from seed sown in spring, *Tagetes patula* 'Cinnabar' is performing its last blooming. Felty velvet rosettes in a ferruginous cigar colour, the flowers are like appliqué on an Elizabethan gauntlet, while the leaves emanate a musty curry smell, jungle undergrowth, which I find appealing. Tagetes have a smell that is strong, almost edible like coriander and cumin, yet deplorable and defensive. It is a deterrent to whitefly and carrot root fly. At the end of the month, the odd smell of calendula rises, and they flower again.

Smell is the jam in the millefeuille of life. I smelled a white cashmere cable jumper in a shop, which made me remember that I used to love the smell of shops and hotels, of uptown New York and, yes, of airports. I still do sometimes.

Feeding the garden with slow-release fertiliser for the winter, and smelling hoof and horn, a weird smell like filing one's nails, something I try never to do.

Today I peeled garden carrots which were truly, sweetly, earthy with a delicate tang that filled the kitchen and that crops up again and again in the carrot family and in all parts of umbellifers, the leaves stalks and roots too.

Of all the seasons autumn most provokes meditation, philosophising … a drift from description into redolence, to seeing through things as the leaves leave, a shift to elegy. Rilke wrote letters about the coming of autumn in 1907 to Clara, his wife, who was in north Germany when he was in Paris. He describes the 'strong and serious smell which is really the scent of autumn earth. But how glorious is this scent. At no other time it seems to me, does the earth let itself be inhaled in one smell, the ripe earth.'

I like the romance of the smell of hops and, besides, they are beautiful vines, their fruit architectural as artichokes, pineapples or pine cones, yet they're flimsy, wafery, papery lanterns. The smell is human, yeoman, pungent as sweat, yet not unpleasant – on the seamy side perhaps, almost tending towards those smells that come from alliums of various kinds like nectaroscordum. It is summer encased in spicy dry green pockets. Is it the smell of fathers? Doris Lessing describes being repulsed by the smell of her father, who came home a soldier and a stranger, when he pressed her tiny face into his woolly serge uniform. I liked my father's distinctive smell, and shortly after he died my son grew to be exactly the height of my nose and his scalp smelled of my father when I cuddled him standing and buried my face in his hair.

Grand pots of
pelargoniums

HOPS

Native across Europe and the Americas above the equator, *Humulus lupulus* is a climbing vine of scrubby damp waste places, with square stems that can reach great length and deeply lobed leaves. It has cone-like female flowers, which mature in the early autumn and are highly aromatic. If you open one of these cones you will see the source of the bitter and sedative oils. Each lobe is studded with bright yellow glands which contain the mixture of oils and resins known as lupulin. This is readily released: an aroma with touches of the pungency of garlic and the fruitiness of autumn apples, but with a freshness, warmth and body that is unique to the hop. Along with such scented herbs as lavender and marjoram, it has historically been the obvious choice for pillows. Continental hops remain celibate, small and only mildly scented, whereas in these isles we grow promiscuous and full-bodied smelly varieties.

We are moving the scented geraniums – pelargoniums as gardeners call them – to winter quarters. Being tender subshrubs, we are trying to save them through winter, and should take cuttings and keep pots of them on windowsills and so on. Time to consider the astonishing velvet leaves of the peppermint-exuding *Pelargonium tomentosum,* like pulling an eiderdown up under one's chin and thinking of caramelized mint humbugs. It takes me back to the sewing room at school, which was a haven and an extraordinary luxury. I suppose the nuns in their wisdom still thought that sewing was very important for young women in the late 1960s when they built this chapel of Singer sewing machines. And they were right: it should be a skill learned at school by boys and girls, and not left to small children in Bangladesh to perform so cheaply that we can throw the results away when we tire of them. We made summer dresses out of old curtains and looked ultra-cool in army surplus. The sewing chamber at St Mary's Convent Shaftesbury was like a Huguenot weaving loft. It had high windows all along the east side, and on the sills Sister John kept scented pelargoniums, hirsute, scraggy, slightly neglected. School, like hospital, is a sensory desert, but if by accident you brushed by the geraniums on opening a window you found there a secret world of mental escape. It took you out into a woodland understorey, aromatic, wormwood strong for warding off insect infestations.

Leaf smells are generally bitter, potent, pithy, but the scented-leaved geraniums have been bred specially to delight with an admixture of compost and orange or rose. Rose geranium is the most familiar, a memory of rose wrapped in an aromatic parcel, quite peculiar, but a genius bath oil. Mr B loves the smell of pelargoniums, musty and sunny as they are.

PELARGONIUMS

About 280 species of rather tender perennials and subshrubs which are part of the geranium family, mostly hailing from South Africa. They usually get to the size of a small shrub, or whatever size suits your pot. There are two semi-tender night-scented pelargoniums from South Africa, *Pelargonium gibbosum* with small green flowers and *P. triste* with brownish flowers both stongly scented, but I have never grown them.

Gladiolus murielae pots in porch

They dislike cold, wet and stagnant air, as who does not. They are generally grown in pots and moved outdoors in summer and placed in porches and on window sills. With the possible exception of what some perceive as the smell of 'baby-sick' emitted by *P. denticulatum* 'Filicifolium', they are all interesting to the smellaholic. There are so many scented pelargoniums that there are books devoted to them, but here are a few of my favourite pellies:

P. 'Queen of the Lemons' has big, single pink flowers with good deeper pink guidelines. Guess the smell.

P. 'Mabel Grey' and *P.* 'Citronella' both have a sharper lemon smell in the leaves, and clusters of mauve flowers.

P. tomentosum, the peppermint geranium, is a robust clambering very fuzzy and delicious plant with sprays of dainty single white flowers like moths in full sun. It is less floriferous but extremely tolerant and luxuriant when grown in shade. The leaves make a pleasant, mint-flavoured tisane. Invaluable.

P. 'Graveolens', the rose geranium, commonly grown for its essential oil. Palest pink single flowers and easy to grow.

P. 'Sweet Mimosa' is a robust cross which has pungently balsamic-lemon- and rose-flavoured leaves and endless fresh cottagey single pink darker splattered flowers which make it a favourite for pots.

P. quercifolium, the village oak or village hill oak geranium has oak-shaped leaves, deeply lobed and softly hairy with showy tight bunches of flowers all summer, but not a great smell to my mind.

P. 'Lady Plymouth' has cream-grey variegated leaves, rose-peppermint scented with clusters of small pink flowers on a small bush. The variegation is off-putting to Mr B.

P. 'Attar of Roses' is the rose-scented pelargonium cultivated commercially for its essential oil. Good for flavouring sugar to taste of roses.

P. odoratissimum has small, pale green leaves, soft and pleasant to touch, releasing a fresh apple scent. They flower prolifically, producing a constant abundance of dainty white flowers on semi-trailing stems.

P. 'American Prince of Orange' has dark green leaves that are glossy and crinkled, with a much stronger orange scent than that of its near namesake *P.* 'Prince of Orange'. Strong, long flowering with pink blooms, and easy to grow. In cooking, the leaves provide an orange flavour without the acidity of citrus fruit.

P. 'Clorinda' has possibly the prettiest gaudiest shocking pink flowers; descriptions of its perfume range from eucalyptus to cedar, although it is agreed that the scent is woodsy – like walking through an avenue of resinous trees. 'Clorinda' forms a large plant and can be trained as a standard; with all this generosity it can be more temperamental than other pelargoniums.

P. 'Deerwood Lavender Lad' has lavender-scented, dark, grey-green leaves, accompanied by small, dark pink flowers on semi-trailing stems.

P. grossularioides 'Coconut' has rounded leaves with a tropical, coconut-like scent. While the plant won't survive winter outdoors, it seeds itself freely and you can often find seedlings sprouting nearby. It will grow in damp conditions, a blessing to the Cornish gardener, and is useful as ground cover.

P. 'Ardwick Cinnamon' has grey-green leaves with an unusual cinnamon fragrance. It is relatively fast-growing and compact, with pretty pale flowers. The leaves can be thinned to encourage good air circulation and then used to add a lovely cinnamon flavour to cakes and biscuits.

The air was balmy with the glow of voluptuous violet heliotrope, a syrup of vanilla with chocolate, possibly white. Gerard talks about the 'breath of flowers' and here it is, faultless and complete. So too the marvel of Peru, *Mirabilis jalapa*, comely, intense of colour like those alpaca jumpers we all had in the 1970s, and so too the intensity of the smell. Ours are in pots near the pool to take advantage of warm nights and high humidity. The pool evaporation acts like a still, condensing a bath of scent.

'Madame Isaac Péreire' produces more roses, more gorgeous and more perfect still.

In Ireland

In mid-October myrtles have a foxy red-bark smell in Ireland, their late and pollen-generous flowers covered in bees, and here there are nettles covered with peacock butterflies. Even in October the magnolia buds are showing two fur coats, softly furry as hunched gerbils.

The garden we are working on is slightly acid; the water springs up pure and delicious. It is the house where 'All things bright and beautiful' was conceived and so would make a great bottled water, as we discussed with our charming and delightful Irish hosts. Much of the planting is of exactly the date of the hymn, first published in 1848 in Mrs Cecil Alexander's *Hymns for Little Children*. I never liked that droning tune by Henry Monk, to which is it most commonly sung, even as a child. But the lyrics interest me now for their poetry taken from Psalm 104 and Coleridge's *Ancient Mariner*; for its world vision with God as divine watchmaker, ordering the estate of the rich man in his castle, the poor man at his gate – a work of divine social engineering. In some small way it unwittingly encapsulates much about nineteenth-century attitudinising.

Planting in a place like this often tells of a complex history, if you take time to read it. Newly imported firs and conifers nurtured from tiny seedlings with excitement and optimism. Kalmia from the Adirondacks, all the plethora of acid-loving exotica from the Antipodes and the Far East found their way into every such garden and altered the landscape forever. And not only visually, but they changed the olfactory landscape also and contribute to the acid-loving plant smell of a county Wicklow garden, especially noticeable after a desiccating early morning Ryanair flight and a mad dash to make the most of the daylight before we go back.

My father had some 'little aunts' (as they were known) who lived together in a Grecian pavilion on the river Dargle, looking out over Dublin Bay, in county Wicklow. This paragon of a bungalow was called 'Knockmore' and it is for sale, as I write, on Rightmove. He took us there once as children on an eventful camping holiday in the Austin Maxi, an odyssey which culminated in his giving away the remaining smidgeon of Irish property that he had inherited in the Bog of Allan. Perpetually pained as he was by the Anglo-Irish ancestry which had, in the late eighteenth century, provided his lowland Scottish forebears with a fortune made canalising Ireland, he sensibly gave the lock keeper's house back to the community, and our last night of the holiday was an unforgettable peat-smoked ceilidh by the lock. It was the best night and a great ending. He went as a child to Knockmore in the summer holidays and loved the place and the aunts, who slept throughout the summer out on the veranda for the improvement of their health. Together they nurtured the nineteenth-century-made garden there, at the top of the valley through which burbles the Dargle river and the tulgey rhododendron wood, east towards the Irish Sea. The story of the garden and its history was told in *A Year in an Irish Garden*, Ruth Isabel Ross's prize-winning book published in 1999. It was good to find we are working just down the road and with a similar, if vestigial, palette of plants. It was the smell of pine that stayed with me from this fir-scented place.

Back home, today the garden smelled warmly felted in a Halloween way. It is brewing, shedding seed and leaf. Mr B cutting the grass was a sad smell, summer lost and darkness at six. It has been sunny all day and the gypsy caravan smelled of paint and blankets. *Rosa* 'De Resht' had two perfect buds and a small open flower which is slightly scented and still a good deep saturated colour.

Working in Sussex and wandering slightly we found ourselves by Didling parish church, at the end of a track beyond which sheep were safely grazing in a glacial amphitheatre, fringed with trees clinging to the rearing downland with its flotsam of oak and ash. To the right a solid shadowy yew and a wooden gate. The church was small as a tea caddy, almost entirely invisible, girdled as it was with hazel and field maple. All this loveliness drew me into the chicken-wired porch and standing within a swelling euphoria overtook me – parish notices, hinges, lime wash, it was none of these. It was a smell. The smell was of an apple store. The door within gave way to my urgent shove. What revealed itself was a cool, creamy, woody, chiaroscuro larder. A fine intimate place of worship from the Plantagenets to last Sunday's Harvest Festival. This extraordinary, dignified and timeless place, walls washed with mealy lime, slab dry pews, gnawed by the centuries, curved belly of a roof, cool condensation, clammy floor, three tiny lattice-leaded windows behind the altar and nothing of the twentieth century whatsoever. Harvesters had left their marrows, pumpkins, berries, brambles and wheatsheaf bread for the field mice and for me to enjoy. Old man's beard, hips and haws, posies of prized late stunted roses on the altar. Mr B padded in behind me, and, once outside again, I asked him what he had noticed before he got inside. 'The scent of apples.'

It reminded of a description by James Joyce of just such a moment outside a church. 'There was a cold night smell in the chapel … That was a smell of air and rain and turf and corduroy. Just outside the porch the church smell reached me. It was less a smell with identifiable layers than a sensation …'

Walked through a field of recently topped and regrown knee-high nettles. They were lustrous and edible in the wet warm October soil and they exhaled a nettlesome perfume, a feisty bitter sweetness that was deliciously disturbing. Nettle leaves and walnut leaves: through leaves we walk in autumn and we notice their smell. Ash leaves have a smell that puts off ants and walnut leaves smell of turpentine – that might put off ants too. Some leaves smell of sugar in autumn and the sugar is responsible for the colour.

WALNUT

Walnuts, *Juglans regia*, are deciduous trees, with pinnate leaves that are deeply aromatically scented although few people notice. The smell is somewhat acrid when the leaves are rubbed. The flowers are unisexual, the male a slender pendulous catkin, and the few female flowers, which have no colour or beauty, grow in a short terminal spike. They are fertilised by wind, and from the inferior ovary the fruit, a

Tithonia rotundifolia 'Torch', *Canna* lilies Cannova Red Shades

Salvia involucrata
'Hadspen' with *Gladiolus murielae*

hard-shelled, variously sculptured and delicious if bitter-flavoured nut, develops. The dense and highly figured bole is valuable timber, used for furniture and the stock of shotguns. They should always if possible be grown from seeds, unless grafted, as they resent transplanting.

21st October

Trafalgar Day – this is the sort of useless fact you pick up from a lifetime listening to Radio Four. Cercidiphyllum is known as the katsura tree after a story about a wayward woodcutter. But it is better for me to think of it as the caramel tree because it smells of that on warm autumn days. Not all decomposition smells foul; it's the carbon chemistry playing around with sugars.

CERCIDIPHYLLUM

Cercidiphyllum, the katsura tree, has a burnt sugar smell that fills the air around it on warm autumn days. The leaves are also very pretty, emerging pink or bronze, becoming lettuce-green come summer, and yellow, orange, pink or purple in autumn. As they fall, they also smell of candyfloss. Candyfloss, too, describes the pink flowers that crowd the bare branches in early spring like jacarandas or Judas trees. There are only two species, *C. japonicum* and *C. magnificum.* In its native habitat in Japan and China it is a great big long-lived tree, one of the largest deciduous trees in Asia.

Salvia involucrata
'Hadspen'

233

Something reminded me of the smell of *Exchange & Mart* magazine. All magazines smell of printing ink and the shiny ones of china clay from St Austell in Cornwell, which is shipped out to glaze paper. *Exchange & Mart* had a cheap smell and the strength of my memory may be connected to the very long time it took to read about all the weird and wonderful things that could be bought for nothing. In the smell of hot cars, hot leather is so much better than hot plastic. My mother, in one of the brash extravagant modes which made my father paler than his dead Irish ancestors within the Pale, went out and bought a new car. She must have bought and sold a piece of furniture very well, forgetting – as my father would try to explain – that the difference was not all profit, there were things called 'overheads' when you ran a shop. The car had a marque we had never heard of. It was called an Audi. It was milk-chocolate brown outside, with a chrome trim like a Courrèges dress, and the inside was not leather but 'taupe-' or perhaps 'ecru'-coloured velour. The whole combination was like a Malteser, but smelling very synthetic, of polymers, an alien smell which I could never learn to live with as it made my car sickness much worse. That sick-making smell made my mouth water like a miserable dog. Instinctively I have always flinched from the smell of polymers and plastics, and when my brother went to be a salesman for Courtaulds selling plastic packaging, poor lamb, he told me never again to eat anything, not so much as a sandwich, wrapped in plastic. This might have been possible then, but how inconceivably impossible is it now?

Planting bulbs in the afternoon sun. It is later than the clock says, because the clock has been turned back for some fiercely annoying reason. It feels like late evening in summer, but the sun will not get to the bit where I need to weed. Happier then to plant bulbs in the sun and think of it as starting a small avalanche. Over future years the incremental doubling up of bulbs is like dominos knocking out more dominos ad infinitum. I know the snowdrops at Hanham are still multiplying annually; like a golden investment, they should be there and be increasing for at least a hundred years. Fritillaries, titchy nuggets that we are chucking and tucking in now, should, with luck, settle and then run into their hundreds, seeding as they have also done at Hanham. Like trees spreading unfathomably underground in mycorrhizal canopies, so too one sets something going in perpetual motion when one plants some things, lily of the valley or self-seeders such as honesty and hesperis. Sometimes the fire fizzles, other times you have lit the green fuse.

Sitting in the warm tea-time sun taking out rank courgettes, chucking the frighteningly gnawed marrows, the pod-seeded rocket, the faint blue final chicory flowers, I nibbled some shot, burning hot mustard leaves.

The temple bell dies away
The scent of flowers in the evening
Is still tolling the bell.

Matsuo Bashō
English version by R.H. Blyth

Pine, moss, mushrooms, lichen

234

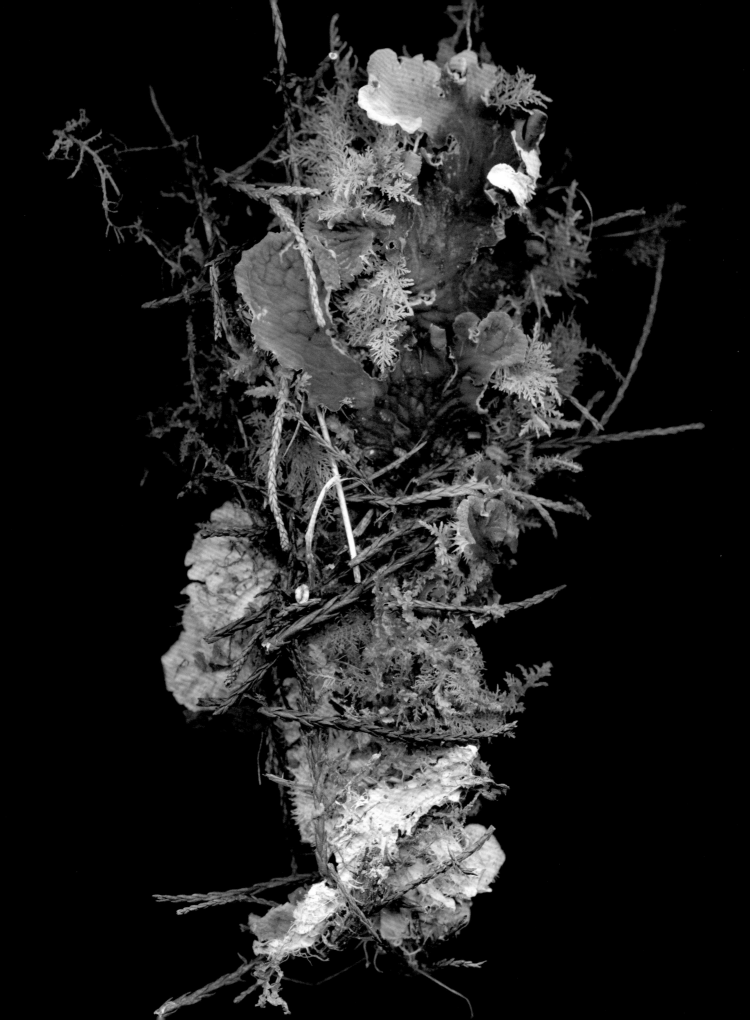

Smoke, Honey, Pine and Clementine

Today I think
Only with scents – scents dead leaves yield,
And bracken, and wild carrot's seed,
And the square mustard field;

Odours that rise
When the spade wounds the root of the tree,
Rose, currant, raspberry, or goutweed,
Rhubarb or celery;

The smoke's smell too,
Flowing from where the bonfire burns
The dead, the waste, the dangerous
And all to sweetness turns.

Edward Thomas DIGGING

In November Margery Fish dusted herself down and wrote, 'By this time the less devoted gardeners have hung up their tools and retired indoors to continue gardening by the fire.' She was a humble gardener and it seems that for her, like me, a bright frosty day or torrential rain was a huge relief. I sometimes declare a work-to-rule, but more often than not I find the weeds are still growing in Cornwall on account of the perpetual mid-teens temperatures and in spite of the low light levels that make me feel low. With no sign of frost before Christmas I am obliged, very reluctantly, to don the chaps (which keep my knees and thighs dry but not my bottom) and get out there with Mr B, who is undaunted by any weather and has always made me feel like a closet townie and a fake. But I would rather be gardening by the fire. I particularly love the smell of hazel burning; it would be my kindling of choice. Richard Mabey, while saying that lilac wood is the most aromatic, quotes Honor Goodhart's 'Logs to Burn':

Pear logs and apple logs,
They will scent your room;
Cherry logs across the dogs
Smell like flowers in bloom.

And in *The Shining Levels*, his memoir of being a forester on Cartmell Fell, John Wyatt, a connoisseur of woodsmoke, wrote that 'there is little to match juniper … Holly and birch have a clean tang. Ash, particularly green ash, smells like washing day. Old oak has an honest lusty smell.'

The pulse of growth is slowing to a standstill. November's first full moon, in the new early evening gloom, under a shroud of cloud. The Rubicon known as the end

Magnolia 'Atlas' bud

of British Summer Time has been crossed a while now. It upsets me for at least ten days, well into November. I wish I could shake it off lightly. But it spells doom to me. There I was gently acclimatising and then bang: it's dark before you have even got going. I should just adjust and smell the rotting with infinite pleasure. It means we can stop gardening – once the bulbs are planted. Everything relinquishing, shrinking, diminishing into dormancy or death.

But, of course, there are exceptions: *Camellia sasanqua*, for instance. This is a camellia I really like. It has similar qualities to those turn-petal roses *Rosa glauca* and *R. × odorata* 'Mutabilis'. Mine is outside the kitchen window near the bonkers rustic bird table – this is a perfectly ordinary one made 'rustic' by my son BB and he kindly re-dresses it with lichen-furred twigs every year for my birthday because the birds not only feed on the seed but steal the twigs. Mr B has the best view of the quarrelsome goldfinches alighting from his giant pots of pink pokers, *Salvia involucrata* 'Hadspen'. Utterly different from the fuchsine pink of the salvia bracts, more a pink like shells or ears, are the poised buds and shaggy flowers of the *C. sasanqua* near the bird table. They have a smell as fine as a petal, light as orange flower water, barely there, an almost imagined jasmine. At any other time of year this camellia would not really rate as scented flower, but in November it is a delight to eye and nose. I do not know the name of mine: it might be 'Jean May', but it is hardy here, and happy even though here is not acid. The warning would have to be with sasanquas – and this is perhaps why they are not more widely grown – that some are half-hardy and, in principle, they like an acid soil.

CAMELLIAS

Native of the acid lands of Japan, like the common *Camellia japonica*, *C. sasanqua* is perhaps the most popular of all camellias in its native land. It was not introduced into Europe until 1896, where it flowers in late autumn. Of the several Japanese garden varieties you can find in nurseries, one of the best is 'Narumigata', along with 'Paradise Blush' and 'Rainbow', all of which have large, white, pinkly edged, single flowers which can open in October. Even earlier to flower is a white called 'Fukuzutsumi', which grows very well with N.G. Hadden at Porlock, Somerset, but there is something odd about camellias in flower when the leaves are still on the trees.

Camellia sasanqua 'Hugh Evans' is shocking pink, reminding me of *Rosa* 'Complicata' though the flowers are not so big. So single are they that the petals do not touch each other – an ideal tattoo subject. I often think that camellias are winter's roses, especially when I am trying to like the big bossy bold ones. I tell myself 'think of them as roses'… but then they don't smell. I love and have planted *C.* 'Cornish Snow', which is everywhere down here, and quite rightly as it makes a great big bush covered in small white bells with golden stamens in March. No scent though. A better discovery for the late winter garden is *C. transnokoensis*, a loose evergreen, postbox-sized shrub, from the island of Taiwan, dotted with single, scented – but lightly I have to admit – white flowers from pink-splashed buds in February. The look is full of charm, blossom-like with embossed with gilded stamens, and the flowers smell a little like a sasanqua, but borne with greater abundance and a certain insouciance, making quite a good loose hedge. Mr B calls it the winter philadelphus; the pink staining on the petal backs making it not unlike an inside-out *Philadelphus* 'Belle Etoile', and ordered as many as he could, which wasn't many. It can be got from Trehane, the great camellia nursery. It has the fairy-tale quality

238

of winter flowerers such as *Prunus × subhirtella*, only more confident. Of the sasanquas the white double called 'Paradise Pearl' and a peony-like deep rose double called 'Winter's Joy' have a similar insouciance. Some make quite large shrubs, but camellias love being clipped and groomed as they are tea plants, and are surprisingly fast growing, down here at least.

Since moving here, we have decorated our Christmas table with camellias in festive colours, red, pink and white. It looks fabulous, full of cheer in candlelight. Many Japonicas are out and happily we can afford to cut whole boughs and stuff them behind the pictures and around the looking glass. For the Christmas table there is *Camellia × vernalis* 'Yuletide', which has scented flowers, singletons with lobed and separate petals, a sumptuous cherry-red cushion for a diadem of golden anthers.

Smells abounding, joy resounding. Out there is a light show in smell: cidery, nutty, asphalt, all sweet, uplifting. I love Halloween smells; so nostalgically exciting, with all the childish happiness of half term. The prospect of dark evenings is still something I'd look forward to wholeheartedly, were it not for the enforced hurtling of the time change. At school it meant no longer spending Saturday afternoons in our dens tangled among the rhododendrons and sweet chestnuts – the woods were somehow best in high October and the earth was warm like the sea. I still love October and November for the light, the smell, the sadness and the sense of excitement at the coming of cold.

Indoor days and rootling around in cupboards one realises they are lumbered with smells – imbued with Mr Sheen, Antiquax, yellow dusters, things we don't use any more like shoe polish and Silvo. Bathroom cupboards with toothpaste and talc, cupboards under the stairs and sink stink of superheroes – Flash, Vim, Ajax – who live in the dark with dank cloths, sponges, scrubbers and rubber gloves. Art-room and theatre-wardrobe smells are uplifting. School was an odyssey of strange smells – light years from home smells. Chapel; stationery; dining hall smell; the smoky, biscuit gas of the staff room; 'toe-gas' in the locker room; that wooden varnished music-practice-rooms smell on hot evenings missing chapel. Then there are farm smells; dog smells; airport smells and train smells; van smells and hired cars; hotel smells; drains and canal smells; taxis and bazaars; fish markets; seaside fish-and-chip smells; pub smells; mowing and haymaking; flailing the hedgerows; rats, cats and frowsty front door mats; old people and baby smells; Play-Doh and plastics; air-conditioned bank smells; and morning in the pub smells.

Tidying out of doors is much more pleasurable than hoovering. This sunny morning, we attacked the greenhouse, dusting, washing down, scrubbing. The smell of thinly bleached water and clouds of dust as we swept out flotsam was heartening.

Frost
A rare frosty morning before Christmas in Cornwall. Unable to stay asleep I shuffled out with Popeye the pug at about five-twenty this morning. The morning half-moon was so strong in the south shining through the glasshouse that I thought a light was on. Popeye tore out into the bright night, like me invigorated by the diamond chill. Crunchy frozen gravel. So sudden after all those balmy months we've had. Shocking the memory. Tasteless, empty, dry air. Like a couple of bees

on a mountain top, pug and I meandered, stopping for a poke, a peer at a dahlia colourless in moonlight. Together we looked up in silence, pug seeing nothing from his poppy eyes, at 'the old star-eaten blanket of the sky'. I love this line by T.E. Hulme written about the Embankment on a winter's night. I collaborated once with a blacksmith to make a polypody fern leaf in iron and gold leaf, and I thought his black T-shirts and jumpers were indeed star-eaten, eaten by a thousand racing sparks, just like this time before dawn.

We were all taken aback, rather shaken by the frost. But walking up the side of the motte to the chickens, mid-morning, the sun on the eastern slope had produced a fermenting warmth, yeasty, like bread with wild herbs. In the weeks that followed this rare frost, Cornwall discovered an Appalachian 'Fall'. Thinking about it, the leaves don't generally colour much down here. They usually remain green, like London planes in London parks, until a week before Christmas. But this year everything is aflame and the sunshine with it.

There's a rich tawny-ness about trees in spring, with oak, walnut, poplar, all glossy and festooned with flowery tassels, but in autumn there's a dry tawny-ness, a colour David Vicary called 'the muds of England'; clay colours, like Gainsborough or Reynolds leafage, that ochre brushwork, papery and bleached, the woods stacked up like the side screens of early theatre.

Brightest and boldest of mornings. Last night there was frost again. We were off to Avebury along black tracks, through curvy downland glittering in a fine frock of diamanté frost, the land rising like dough. The stones stood cold but full of welcome, conversing with their shadows. Hunger drove us to Calne and breakfast by a car park full of mahonia in full flush. Though ice-frizzled, the mahonia still smelled, and we picked some and vowed to plant it for the picking, though the plant is an ugly sod. E.A. Bowles in *My Garden in Spring* sums up just the sort of dump where mahonia somehow ends up. 'In the days of my early youth a vast clump … of evergreens occupied the space which now forms my home for demented plants. It was the sort of planting one sees at one end of a London square. Portugal Laurels there were, and the still more objectionable Common Laurel; Lauristinus bushes, which in showery weather exhale an odour of dirty dog-kennel and an even dirtier dog …'

MAHONIA

A hardy evergreen shrub, almost certainly originating in China but long grown in Japan, and in Europe since the nineteenth century, with a stiff habit and generally holly-like. Flowers in long drooping spikes of a greenish- livid- sometimes primrose-yellow bells, looking spriggy and smelling a little like lily of the valley, full of charm, ideal for a buttonhole, which is why they are worth growing for picking. It smells of spring in winter. In a jug you would not know that it comes with a gawky hopeless prickly bush that always feels plonked, like it doesn't belong. They happily grow in the dingiest corners, and on account of their very adaptable manners they have long been consigned to back places and council car-park planting. I was almost knocked sideways stepping out the back door of a house the other day by the scent from a huge and rather handsome bush of *Mahonia* × *media* 'Charity'. *M.* × *media* varieties are the first to flower from late autumn. *M.* × *m.* 'Buckland' is perhaps the most handsome one, with desirably long stems covered in flower. It was bred along with *M.* × *m.* 'Lionel Fortescue' (as big as a shed, which means it could be used for hiding things) up the road at The Garden House. I like the fact that garden birds love mahonia's black berries. I am determined to see how to use them to greater effect and make them more glamorous.

Today we 'groomed' the pelargoniums in the greenhouse. Like quick-fingered monkeys we picked and turned the leaves and branches, combing over each plant, flicking out bits of yellowed leaf with focused concentration. Shaking and blowing in an atmosphere plangent with warmly spiced neroli, the smell of orange spangles and rose geranium, the unmistakeable tang of geraniol, which seems to bring a warmth and comfort associated with dust motes in sunlight. The most velveteen scented geranium is *Pelargonium tomentosum* and, when you crush a leaf between your fingers by your nose, you might be opening up huge jars of mint and humbugs. The leaf, soft and rumpled like the pug's ears, hangs on the end of elbowed limbs which are easily snapped. Outside we have got it to over-winter and were amazed to find that in spring it was haloed in a storm of moth-like flowers. Tidying all these plants for winter, potting and chopping, is a joyous chore, a chance to mind travel.

Recently I was introduced to an Australian plant that I had never heard of: *Philotheca myoporoides*, previously known as *Eriostemon*. This long-leaf wax flower belongs to the larger family of plants called *Rutaceae*, which also includes citrus fruits like orange, grapefruit, key lime and lemon. Hence the pleasure it gives when the small blisters on the back of the bullate leaves (botanical for blistered or puckered I discover) are rubbed and popped releasing an essential oil which smells of oranges, but oranges out in the wild accompanied by a smell of scrub, aromatic and woody – almost the wood of pews in church and orange-scented Christmas trees. It has white waxen flowers as pretty as citrus blossom but the smell is of citrus with undergrowth-cum-shed.

Visited a possible garden to do in a fold of deep woodland. By a crashing brook echoing to the cough of pheasants, it smelled of trapped low-lying wood smoke and water droplets, which you felt would remain until March. Couldn't resist taking a tiny grape from the wall, creating a sucking explosion of concentrated autumn in the mouth, blackcurranty, raisins, leaves and limestone encapsulated in a bitter skin. I then combed the vine for every grapey mouthful I could get. We walked around the wet garden in the gloom and it smelled of fennel and box and juniper, spicy like superior aftershave. I came back jewelled with tiny droplets.

Fungi everywhere. Photographing them makes the office reek. Waxcaps, jewels of the fungi world, emerge in glistening emerald, ruby, topaz, and smell of wood violets. Violet is a smell type that crops up again and again; now, here, it is coming from an edible gilled mushroom, a wood blewit, *Clitocybe nuda*, but it is a smell that hangs in a rose, a leaf, and in the root of irises.

Planting tulip bulbs I bathe in the smell of quietly composting leaves and earth. This connection to the earth seems to me fundamental to feeling right. It is natural as a child to dig in the deep smelling soil, break nettles, turpentine twigs, watch woodlice crawling under bark with a mixture of terror and irrepressible curiosity. To deny oneself this is madness and desiccating. Fishing, pot-holing, mountain biking, dirt biking, den building, duck shooting, hunting, allotment tending, wine tasting, sailing, rambling, orienteering, all take you back into the wet-dog world

Lemon and dead bird

of smells from nearer the ground. Bulb planting, digging, potting, planting, these things magnify again the often-edited completeness of being part of the entire living earth.

The question of the smell of tulips is a bit vexed. I have tried to grow the scented tulips such as 'Ballerina' and 'Verona', and I cannot really count them among the great scented plants. Among the species tulips, the bronze orange *Tulipa whittallii* (correctly *T. orphanidea* Whittallii Group) have a refined, spicy scent. *T. sylvestris* has star-like flowers with long pointed pale yellow petals that are shaded green on the outside and offer a deeply soft scent somehow redolent of their favoured habitats: chalk pits and calcareous meadows, woodlands and orchards of Somerset, Gloucestershire and the South East. We found them naturalised under beech trees outside Burford and were so ignorant of them that we were nearly knocked sideways with delight. One of the most enchanted moments of a gardening life. The scent must be stronger at night – but I have not yet had the pleasure – for it is moth pollinated.

Today I picked a bit of sweet rocket and made a bunch with lingering *Geranium* 'Ann Folkard', *Verbena* 'Pink Parfait', *Pelargonium* 'Pink Capitatum' – both these smelly pinks so smelly and so pink – finished with a good purple wallflower which certainly smelled of grannie's bathroom and warm sweetshops on rainy days. I picked half-a-dozen roses, among them 'Madame Isaac Péreire', 'De Resht', old blush China (*Rosa* × *odorata* 'Pallida') and 'Princesse de Nassau'. They were all in their autumn flavour, which is different from summer.

Saw a goldfinch in the bare fig and crushed a last leaf for the smell. Fossils of sterile figs dating from 9400 BC have been found in a Neolithic settlement in Jordan, which means they were being cultivated before wheat or barley. Their juicy sack bags smell rich and sticky when ripe, but so do their fragrant and handsome lobed leaves.

On this day, November 27th, Gilbert White wrote in his *Natural History of Selborne* of 'fierce frost. Rime hangs all day on the hanger. The hares, press'd by hunger, haunt the gardens and devour the pinks, cabbages, parsley etc.' We did a garden once where pheasants, put down in their thousands I should imagine, did this; they grazed the pinks all winter and I have never seen better, tighter, more shimmery hassocks come the summer.

Ivy fruit and fern

244

So low is the ebb of the year. The sun rises about 8-ish and hangs around in the extreme low south and sets at about 4 in the afternoon. It barely penetrates below the box hedges. Paths are greening with moss. Even the dank smells are leeching away and what Mr B calls 'the rotten scent of England' is much less perceptible than a few weeks ago. I picked antirrhinums, white hydrangea and dark purple wallflowers from which I could hardly conjure a whiff; altogether they looked fresh, but rather ugly.

The garden is silent of smell. December brings rain that chills, but November has been the most astonishing stasis. The crowned heads of oak are still weighed down with tawny turbans. Then Mr B brought in a wintersweet flower, the earliest in recollection, and thus belied what I've just said. The garden is never absolutely silent of smell.

December 1st
Picking nasturtiums on the first day of December is not bad, but is it weird? Anyway, as I pick the strands of nasturtium out of the wheelbarrow they smell hot and peppery, packed with summer peas and watercress beds; I tip the rest of the barrow on to the hazel-reeking bonfire. We don't have much pine to burn but I think of it burning deliciously resinous in California (in a fabulous hotel rather than the ravaged burning of whole hillsides) or in Spain in winter.

Volatiles above a pine forest, emitted from a trillion needles, give the air a quality which is in part visible to the naked eye and hence the origin of names such as Blue Ridge or Great Smoky Mountains. *Dictamnus* or burning bush is a clear example of visible volatiles; although I have been quite unable to grow it, I have seen the haze about it, seen it lit by a match and above all smelled the terpene smell of the entire plant and its seed pods, which I would love to be able to grow and keep in a bowl indoors where they would be better and very much cheaper than Santa Maria Novella pot pourri. Terpenes are sought by moths.

Helen Keller wrote an account of a visit to Mark Twain. Showing Keller – the first deaf-blind person (let alone woman) to get a Bachelor of Arts degree in the United States – the view from his window Twain said, 'it is a delight this wild, free, fir-scented place'. Helen observes that 'over dinner his talk is fragrant with tobacco and flamboyant with profanity'. Pine pollen is obviously a much bigger deal in the States. The American novelist Denis Johnson writes in *Train Dreams*, 'a mustard-tinted fog of pine pollen drifted through the valley'. Perhaps the same pollen that Darwin noted on the southern seaboard of Alabama which he guessed had drifted four or five hundred miles from the pine forests of the north. My experience of this mustard gas is confined to yew pollen, which sometimes, on a dry March day, will drift in exactly the way described, and with a powder-dry, pollen smell – no resin or terpene in it.

I love, too, the wood smell of builder's merchants, hardware stores – even the smell of B&Q gives me a sense of purpose – and the smell of powdered retsina definitely adds to thrill of the mission. Nurseries and garden centres have their smell fix too.

The wintersweet moment may be short, but it is so enjoyable to shut your eyes and breathe in the scent on a cold winter's day and inhale the life force therein. Even on a lifeless dim day box too has its morbidly attractive smell. Ferns smell delicious, trickling water smells, and the grass has been cut this week releasing a

Echium skeleton and
Nicotiana sylvestris

faint green ghost of a smell. Mr B bought a pot of rosemary at the garden centre and suddenly the car smelled like Crete.

Paperwhites came out in a flush of sweet orangey scent. Above the orange blossom was a bluebell smell producing a sense of comfort and bright rightness, an echo of spring in the sitting room on these dark December days. So glad that we bothered to pot them along with the burgeoning hyacinths in the airing cupboard; a store of friendly feeling. They are the best salve or balm for Christmas or whenever. If they are late, or ridiculously early like now, it doesn't really matter because you probably need the comfort of their smell any time. You can't quite buy the same feeling – well, you can buy hyacinths much better potted and going strong for almost nothing from the market, but our own paperwhites are childishly touching, even as they fall over and fold their Bambi-leg stems. Kept somewhere a bit cooler, in an unheated place (the porch is best), they stay fresh and plump and scented for weeks. Hyacinths too are better for being cooler; that initial liquid juice scent, if it lingers, turns rancid in a hot house. But outdoors they will grow wilder and prettier under some hedge and be good for picking next year and after.

Snow
Snow suppresses all scent, it is silent, shiny, slightly ersatz. The sky a brittle blue, a Magritte. The most living thing I found outside was the shape of the place where a hare had stopped a while, as in Yeats's poem 'Memory':

> Because the mountain grass
> Cannot but keep the form
> Where the mountain hare has lain …

The shape of the bottom of the hare or rabbit was like a jelly mould and the grass so green in the snow that I reached down to see if it was still warm, but the hare had long gone. The memory of my mother is like that. Impressed upon me forever, but long gone, and the days before she died were dry and scattered with snow, the cracked time, December days like this one. As Wallace Stevens says, it was the time of year of 'nothing that is not there and nothing that is'. I remember driving to pick up the children, through Bitton in bright terrifying light with the threat of snow and knowing it was coming, bitter bits of hail pricking the windscreen and my eyes.

By the ends of our lives our heads are full of extinct smell, the extinct smells of childhood. A rotting wooden fence long ago treated with creosote, smelling of tar and decayed earthy mushroom smell. The invigorating resin and citrus smell of the thuja hedge at Burrows hill, within which we children hung and clung like lemurs, quietly drinking in a chapel of scent, that invigorating smell that is turpentine and lemon rind, and nearby the meaty green leather smell of elder bushes. Hawthorn smelling of honey and fish-paste, fig leaves in the sun smelling of cellulose and an ellipsis of something fruity to do with prunes. Smell memories are different from other memories and the emotions that go with them are different from those that go with other senses. Proust famously makes a case for taste and smell as the memory-evoking human senses. 'When from long-distant past nothing subsists, after the people are dead, after the things are broken and scattered, taste and smell alone, more fragile but more enduring, more immaterial, more persistent, more faithful, remain poised a long time, like souls …'

248

Talking of tar, the white viburnum still has green leaves; the flowers are little white sails or flags, scented with almond and coal tar, as it smells in the graveyard in Chagford where Julian's heavenly sister Susan is buried. Pink *Viburnum farreri* has an immensely awkward habit; the leaves are gone now, the buds have a pinkness that is fleshy and always a browned-off bit somewhere. Coal tar smells of childhood illness, says Mr B. I think my childhood illnesses smelled of Lucozade more than anything. But he thinks that smell of *V. farreri* is just a horrible smutty, nutty, almond skins, old soapiness, astringent, unguent, ointment smell.

But smells are hostages to circumstance. Ivy smells of deserted gardens, combined with nettles, brambles, stings and scratches but also of Christmas, of dragging pagan branches into the house in dim late December. Filling the house with the iron smell of the woods. Fragrant palimpsest of the year laid down, year upon year like wine. We go and collect a gigantic ball of mistletoe from SS, who has orchards on the Somerset levels. Sarcoccoca, the Christmas box, is cut and coming inside the house, along with all sorts of bits of trees, firs and conifers, and there is the smell of cleft oak. Sawdust spewed and dusted down on the floor is generally a good smell. The smell of pine is bright and clean, the smell of Christmas, a smell of renewal. As Laurie Lee sees it, the Christmas tree lets out 'the lonely smell of a long-stored fertility'.

Tangerines and clementines everywhere about the house in the run-up to Christmas. As a child the exoticness of tangerine or orange boxes was thrilling. The smell of the cheap, splintering deal of those boxes was a positive smell, the miracle of fruit *with leaves* was too exciting. Of all the oranges and lemon smells that have the comfort of marmalade, clementines and tangerines have the mildest nose-tingling sparkle, like bubbles and tree baubles tinkling in the dark in a draft.

ORANGES AND LEMONS

A semi-hardy and tender group of evergreen trees and large shrubs with lustrous green leaves, smooth like card, which need cleaning when growing indoors. The star-like flowers are waxy-white, borne singly or in clusters; those of lemons have purple tinged undersides. Citrus are thought to have originated in China and Vietnam, but have been cultivated in the Mediterranean for over five hundred years. It feels like I have been trying to grow citrus for five hundred very unsuccessful years: the effort rarely succeeds. I yearn for the addictive smell of the blossom, and I buy anything that claims to smell of it. There is something intangibly romantic and head-molesting about a real hit of that smell. But for the hopelessly addicted like me I suggest the lemon *Citrus* × *limon* 'Garey's Eureka' (syn. 'Menton') and the orange *C.* × *aurantium* (Sweet Orange Group) 'Valencia', since both can be kept in a pot as a small tree in some kind of frost-free glasshouse. Kumquats, *C. japonica,* are naturally very bushy and can tolerate winter temperatures down to 7C, being among the hardiest of all citrus, most of which like it to be 10C at least. All citrus seem to resent sudden changes in temperature or their watering regime. They should be stood in a water saucer to keep up the humidity but should not be overwatered especially in winter. Think of where they come from: what they really want is rain-soaking intermittently. They need repotting every March and the best compost should be equal parts loam and leaf mould with some charcoal. Washing the leaves with soapy water or spirits helps to stop scale insects from infesting. But I have always found it tricky to keep citrus going, and not for lack of love, but perhaps because of it.

249

Winter Solstice

The sun rises long after eight as far south and east as it goes, just over Rame Head on the sea and sets – having made a small journey round to a point as west-south-west as it will go – at a quarter past four; only most days it will have been dark for some time already, or so it feels. The potential – if it's not cloudy – daylight hours are eight and barely a minute, the fewest of the year. From the winter solstice on, the sun sets moments later each afternoon. But what is strange to note, having become obsessed by these daylight tables, is that the sun rises two minutes later here at Devonport *after* the Solstice, over Christmas, and the pendulum does not start to swing back with the sun rising earlier until Epiphany on the 5th of January. Thereafter the length of the day increases, by about five seconds a day to begin with, and later this increase grows incrementally with each day of the new year.

We brought the Christmas trees in today. Mr B stuck three together because he couldn't get a decent one. One year he got one so big he chopped off the top and stood it up and decorated it in the boys' room on the floor above, as if it went through the ceiling.

Those 'amulets of pine' Emily Dickinson observed are the gums and resins which smell so divine. Being conifers, all parts of a Christmas tree contain resin, which consists of two main elements: a volatile oil (turpentine) and a solid (rosin) known to fiddle players. Conifers have more fractious branches than hardwoods and rosin or resin not only forms a hard scab once the volatiles have evaporated, and hence an unassailable seal on any wounds, but also has antibiotic and anti-fungal properties protecting the plant. Bees know this and collect it to make propolis, and honey from pine forests is deliciously retsina impregnated because I suppose it has great quantities of coniferous pollen.

A forest has stepped into the hall; I am sure it shuffles silently nearer the fire when we are not looking. In my imagination, it smells of cedars and the mountains of the Lebanon in the silent snow. Bottled, the smell would be electric green. I am half expecting to find ceps, *Boletus edulis*, sprouting from the skirting. Moss, warmed bark and, somewhere, cinnamon permeate the ground floor. After all the hollering, and needle sweeping, fetching and carrying, the precious boxes reveal their glittering cargo. The weekend becomes contemplative with the cowbell clink-clonk of meeting glass baubles, shock shatterings, sibilant swear words, the snap clicking of wire snippers, creak of ladders. The scent seeps out as the branches settle and relax, fingered and tied-to, almost gaseous but benign. Tomorrow morning the whole house will resonate with a resinous air, like a violinist preparing a bow, drawing music from the glitter, febrile and reflective. Christmas can be torment and too much hype, but bringing the forest into the parlour is a good thing. To surrender to the end of another year of woody green growth in a celebration of berries and burning logs reawakens a series of beacons in the brain. The teenagers feel it, as do the dogs, and the delivery men. I think of Ezra Pound's 'The Garret'.

> Dawn enters with little feet
> like a gilded Pavlova,
> And I am near my desire.
> Nor has life in it aught better
> Than this hour of clear coolness,
> the hour of waking together.

Trematon winter dawn

250

Index of plants